SCHOOL OF ADVANCED STUDY UNIVERSITY OF LONDON
Institute of Modern Languages Research

Christian Felix Weiße the Translator

Cultural Transfer and Literary Entrepreneurship in the Enlightenment

imlr books

Established by the Institute of Modern Languages Research, this series (formerly known as igrs books) aims to bring to the public monographs and collections of essays in the field of modern foreign languages. Proposals for publication are selected by the Institute's editorial board, which is advised by a peer review committee of some fifty senior academics in the field. To make titles as accessible as possible to an English-speaking and multi-lingual readership, volumes are written in English and quotations given in English translation.

For further details on the annual competition, visit:
https://modernlanguages.sas.ac.uk/publications/imlr-books/

Editorial Board

imlr books **Volume 15**

Volume Editor
Dr Anne Simon

Christian Felix Weiße the Translator
Cultural Transfer and Literary Entrepreneurship in the Enlightenment

Tom Zille

SCHOOL OF ADVANCED STUDY UNIVERSITY OF LONDON

Institute of Modern Languages Research

2021

Published by the

Institute of Modern Languages Research
School of Advanced Study, University of London
Senate House, Malet Street, London WC1E 7HU
https://modernlanguages.sas.ac.uk

The Institute of Modern Languages Research is an imprint of
University of London Press

Cover image
Anton Graff, Portrait of Christian Felix Weiße (1769)
Art Collection of Leipzig University; photograph by
Marion Wenzel © Kustodie der Universität Leipzig

First published 2021

ISBN 978-0-85457-2731
ISSN 2632–9573 (Print)

Meinem Vater
Oliver Zille
zugeeignet.

Extra Lipsiam vivere est miserrime vivere.
[To live outside Leipzig is to lead a miserable life.]
Benedict Carpzov the Younger

Contents

Acknowledgements

The author's work on this book was supported by the *Elmar-Tophoven-Mobilitätsfonds für die Erforschung von Übersetzernachlässen* (German Translators' Fund / Robert Bosch Foundation); by St Edmund's College, Cambridge; and The Bibliographical Society.

Illustrations

Abbreviations and Textual Notes

Throughout this book all translations, unless otherwise attributed, are my own and reference is given to the original text. In quotations from eighteenth-century German manuscripts and printed matter, italics mark words that are written in Antiqua in the original. In the transcriptions of period manuscripts, only the most obvious spelling errors have been silently rectified. Christian Felix Weiße is generally shortened to C. F. Weiße. In a number of cases the name of the author in question did not appear on the title page of the original edition. However, where a work is generally known and accepted as being by that author, the use of square brackets, although strictly correct, has been dispensed with.

The following abbreviated titles are used for sources cited in this study:

BSWFK	Bibliothek der schönen Wissenschaften und der freyen Künste
GSA	Goethe- und Schiller-Archiv, Weimar
NBSWFK	Neue Bibliothek der schönen Wissenschaften und der freyen Künste
UBL	Universitätsbibliothek Leipzig

Introduction: A Forgotten Translator

Christian Felix Weiße (1726–1804) was a busy man. While a somewhat obscure figure compared to his contemporaries who have entered the literary canon, he is still known to specialists as one of the most popular German dramatists of the eighteenth century, specifically as the librettist behind some of the period's most successful (though now forgotten) musical comedies; as a poet of some renown; and one of the founding figures of German children's literature. While especially the latter part of his oeuvre has never ceased to attract attention, in more recent years his significance as a major figure in the German (sometimes: the Saxon) Enlightenment has also come into focus, particularly with regard to his editorship of the journal *Bibliothek der schönen Wissenschaften und der freyen Künste* over many years.[1] Considering the variety of Weiße's literary exploits, it comes as no surprise that some parts of his body of work have been explored more thoroughly than others. Nevertheless, it seems remarkable that one of his most extensive activities has so far gone almost unnoticed: his work as a literary translator.[2]

1 For an overview of Weiße's place in German Studies, cf. Jürgen Krätzer, 'Christian Felix Weiße in der deutschen Germanistik. Ein Forschungsbericht', in *Sächsische Aufklärung*, ed. by Anneliese Klingenberg and others, Leipziger Studien zur Erforschung von regionenbezogenen Identifikationsprozessen, 7 (Leipzig: Leipziger Universitätsverlag, 2001), pp. 147–60. The other contributions in this volume, as well as in the collection *Christian Felix Weiße und die Leipziger Aufklärung*, ed. by Katrin Löffler and Ludwig Stockinger (Hildesheim: Olms, 2006) represent the variety of recent interest in Weiße's multifaceted work. The most recent biographical work is Anne-Kristin Mai's *Christian Felix Weiße, 1726–1804. Leipziger Literat zwischen Amtshaus, Bühne und Stötteritzer Idyll* (Beucha: Sax, 2003).

2 The only critical survey of Weiße's translations so far consists of the brief second chapter of Richard Francis Wilkie's unpublished doctoral thesis, 'Christian Felix Weisze and his Relation to French and English Literature' (University of California, Berkeley, 1953). The author is grateful to Elena Lichtenthaler (Berkeley) for providing access to this study.

In a career that began in the mid-eighteenth century and spanned over fifty years, Weiße became the most prolific German translator of English literature in his time and a highly productive translator of French literature and works in the classical languages. The bibliography of his translations which forms the backbone of the present study lists ninety titles, over two-thirds of which are translations from the English. With eighteen titles, French occupies the second place; and the remainder are German renderings of Latin, Greek and, in one case, Italian works. Weiße's translations include works by some of the most popular writers of his age and range across many genres – from children's and didactic writing by Anna Laetitia Barbauld, Hester Chapone and Madame de Genlis to novels by Fanny Burney, Louis-Sébastian Mercier and Charlotte Smith to the poetry of Thomas Gray, Ossian and Alexander Pope.

With the bibliography as its basis, this book provides the first comprehensive study of Weiße's career and output as a translator and their significance within the broader context of his own writing and the literary and economic environments in which the latter took shape. Thus, the study is primarily intended as a contribution to the history of the book and the social history of German literature. The literary-historical significance of Weiße's translation work will, of course, also be considered. However, unlike most of the 'canonical' translators of his time – such as Johann Joachim Christoph Bode, Johann Arnold Ebert, Luise Adelgunde Victorie Gottsched,[3] Johann Gottfried Herder and Christoph Martin Wieland – Weiße's significance in the history of translation is not so much of a literary kind: what makes him a singular figure (aside from the sheer extent of his work) is his role in the emergence of the professional translator, a process which was part of the broader evolution of the eighteenth-century literary industry. One of the main points of interest of the present study will, therefore, be Weiße's networks, which were perhaps the widest-ranging of any translator in his period. Be it through his co-operation with Philipp Erasmus Reich, the Leipzig-based publisher-bookseller who revolutionized the business (Chapter 4), his work as an 'entrepreneur' of translations for a variety of German publishers (Chapter 7), or the way he used his post as editor of the *Bibliothek* to publish, review and promote translations from numerous languages (Chapter 8) – Weiße's position at the heart of a European

3 The title of this book is inspired by Hilary Brown's study, *Luise Gottsched the Translator* (Rochester, NY: Camden House, 2012).

network of publishers, writers and translators allowed him to shape the German reception of foreign literature of the Enlightenment period in a unique way.

Like most of his contemporaries, Weiße himself held translating in what nowadays seems rather low regard and his work as a translator receives little mention in his autobiography and letters; like most of his colleagues, he also never formulated anything approximating a theory of translation. Always shy of conflict, Weiße even avoided publicly taking sides in the eighteenth-century debates surrounding certain contentious issues in the theory and practice of translation. For all these reasons, his views on these matters can often only be inferred from his own practice and the critical judgement he passed on the work of others. To this end, this study surveys Weiße's published translations, with special attention given to the translator's prefaces and the notes he added to many of them, as well as his extensive correspondence with colleagues. It is Weiße's letters which also provide the best insight into his vast networks; and the correspondence chosen for closer analysis in this book – the letters Weiße exchanged with the writer, publisher and translator Friedrich Justin Bertuch; the philosopher and translator Christian Garve; the civil servant and art critic Christian Ludwig von Hagedorn; and the poet Karl Wilhelm Ramler – can be regarded as exemplary and two chapters have been devoted to the survey of networks alone. The analysis of all these sources, with the addition of the auction catalogue of Weiße's library, will also provide an answer to the question of how Weiße achieved his singular productivity in the first place. A final minor, but by no means insignificant, concern of the present study is the process whereby this whole section of Weiße's oeuvre was all but forgotten, even amidst periodic revivals of interest in his work.

Weiße's translating in many ways intersects with his other literary activities, most notably his ground-breaking writing for children (Chapter 9), but also his dramatic production (cf. Chapter 2). The current investigation focuses on the translations themselves, but it occasionally proves necessary to discuss the influence which the translations and original literary work had on each other. Likewise (as discussed below), in the eighteenth century the line between translation and adaptation is still much less clearly defined than today; the bibliography therefore includes several plays and poems which are free renderings rather than translations in the narrow sense of the word. At the same time, those of Weiße's original works which used French or English models merely as inspiration have been systematically excluded, not least because this part of his oeuvre is among the best documented and researched.[4]

As far as the languages from which Weiße translated are concerned, it seemed reasonable to make his translations of English-language literature the main subject of this study. This is not simply because they account for more than two-thirds of his overall output. Unlike with his French translations, the way Weiße introduced British literature to a German audience, and the manifold genres and even media in which he did it, are significant enough within the overall context of the German reception of foreign literatures in the period to make this part of his activities stand out. Like few others, Weiße not only shared in the wave of Anglophilia that swept Germany in the second half of the eighteenth century, but also helped to create and sustain it. This is reflected not least in the genres he translated: while more than half the French works Weiße translated were plays of a very traditional kind, his output of translations from the English is characterized by innovative forms of long prose which only a century previously had not existed in this form – most notably, the popular novel. One of the major exponents of the genre, Fanny Burney, was introduced to a German readership by Weiße; and his translation of *Evelina* is discussed as an exemplary case in Chapter 6.

In terms of its approach to the material, this study takes a positivist outlook and, in keeping with its primarily historical approach, in its survey of eighteenth-century literary culture pays closer attention to contemporary than to latter-day theories and critical evaluations. Nevertheless, one relatively recent approach shall be mentioned here because it augments this positivist outlook. Through all his various exploits in translating, and in brokering and promoting the translations of others, Weiße can be seen as an exemplary agent of what has come to be conceptualized as 'cultural transfer'. Matthias Middell succinctly defines cultural transfer as:

> ein aktiv durch verschiedene Mittlergruppen betriebener Aneignungsprozess, der von den Bedürfnissen der Aufnahmekultur gesteuert wird. In diesem Sinne kann es auch nicht zu einem Missverstehen einer fremden Kultur kommen, sondern zu deren notwendigerweise selektiven Wahrnehmung entlang einer Idee von

4 Cf. Wilkie, 'Christian Felix Weisze', as well as Walter Hüttemann, *Christian Felix Weisse und seine Zeit in ihrem Verhältnis zu Shakespeare* (Duisburg: Buschmann, 1912; also doctoral thesis, University of Bonn, 1912); and Jakob Minor, *Christian Felix Weiße und seine Beziehungen zur Deutschen Literatur des achtzehnten Jahrhunderts* (Innsbruck: Wagner, 1880). See Chapter 2 for an extended discussion.

> der eigenen Kultur oder Gesellschaft, für die nach Anregungen zur Reform diagnostizierter Mängel gesucht wird.[5]
>
> [a process of appropriation actively driven by various groups of intermediaries, which is determined by the needs of the receiving culture. In this view, foreign cultures cannot be misunderstood; instead, the necessarily selective perception of them is governed by an understanding of one's own culture or society, suggestions for the reform of whose perceived shortcomings are sought.]

Due to their origin in French and German academia, early Cultural Transfer Studies focused almost exclusively on French-German interaction.[6] More recently, however, the focus has broadened to include other regions, as well as more explicitly acknowledging the intersection with Translation Studies.[7] The virtue of the view which cultural transfer theory takes of intercultural engagements is that it breaks up the traditional binary of influence and reception between one monolithic culture and another. Instead, it takes into account the multifarious ways in which the agent of this transfer shapes its product and the forces which, in turn, shape the agent's work. This involves paying closer attention than more traditional comparative approaches to the interests and intentions that motivate the act of cultural transfer and the demands and preconceptions of the receiving culture which shape the process. Aside from initial interpretations and appropriations of foreign cultural objects, this can involve significant reinterpretations and recontextualizations, an aspect which is particularly relevant in the realm of literary

5 Matthias Middell, 'Kulturtransfer, Transferts Culturels', *Docupedia-Zeitgeschichte*, 28 January 2016 <http://dx.doi.org/10.14765/zzf.dok.2.702.v1> unpag. [accessed 26 October 2020].

6 Some of the seminal texts in this respect, and especially with regard to the subject of the present study, are *Von der Elbe bis an die Seine. Kulturtransfer zwischen Sachsen und Frankreich im 18. und 19. Jahrhundert*, ed. by Michel Espagne and Matthias Middell (Leipzig: Leipziger Universitätsverlag, 1993); *Frankreichfreunde. Mittler des Französisch-Deutschen Kulturtransfers (1750–1850)*, ed. by Michel Espagne and Werner Greiling (Leipzig: Leipziger Universitätsverlag, 1996); and Michel Espagne, *Les transferts culturels franco-allemands* (Paris: Presses Universitaires de France, 1999).

7 E.g., Susanne Göpferich, 'Translation Studies and Transfer Studies', in *Doubts and Directions in Translation Studies: Selected Contributions from the EST Congress, Lisbon 2004*, ed. by Yves Gambier, Miriam Shlesinger and Radegundis Stolze (Amsterdam: Benjamins, 2007), pp. 27–39; and *Cultural Transfer through Translation: The Circulation of Enlightened Thought in Europe by Means of Translation*, ed. by Stefanie Stockhorst (Amsterdam/New York: Rodopi, 2010).

translation, of course, and especially so in the context of eighteenth-century German Anglophilia.[8] To name but one more strength of this approach vis-à-vis more traditional ideas of cultural exchange and reception, cultural transfer theory allows a greater focus on regional cultural specificities rather than explicitly national frameworks, another feature which makes it particularly suited to the study of an oeuvre which, though in some ways of international significance, could only be conceived in one particular place.

To be clear, this study does not attempt to read Weiße's work as a translator exclusively as an instance of cultural transfer; nor does cultural transfer theory provide its methodological basis. For the reasons outlined above, however, the concept of cultural transfer informs the interpretation of Weiße's work as a translator and especially as a broker of translations. A whole section (Chapter 8) is dedicated to his role in the German engagement with literature in languages from which he himself did not translate; perhaps better than any other aspect of his work, it illustrates the great variety of the activities of the 'typical' agent of cultural transfer, which Weiße combined in a singular way.

The structure of this study distinguishes between two kinds of sections. The longer chapters are more purely historical in outlook and survey Weiße's translations from a certain bibliographical distance, focusing on their publishing environment and the biographical, economic and intellectual context in which they were produced. These sections are interspersed with slightly shorter interchapters (Chapters 3, 6 and 9) which act as case studies of certain genres of translation particularly characteristic of Weiße's activities. These involve closer textual analysis than the longer chapters and, where appropriate, comparative critical evaluation. Given their nature, they are less rigidly bound by the overall chronological structure of the study than are the regular chapters. Throughout the main text reference is made to the bibliography of Weiße's translations at the end of this volume; for the sake of brevity, in the chapters themselves bibliographical information often appears in condensed form only. The number under which the entry for the work under discussion can be found in the bibliography of translations is given in [square brackets].

8 See the summary in Matthias Middell, 'Kulturtransfer und historische Komparatistik – Thesen zu ihrem Verhältnis', *Comparativ*, 10 (2000), 7–41 (p. 18).

1. Anglophilia and the Background of Eighteenth-Century Translation

The eighteenth century witnesses the rise of commercialism and of the novel, expanding cultural and commercial exchange especially between the central and western European nations and a spreading knowledge of modern foreign languages among the newly self-confident, educated middle classes. The Continental Enlightenment is characterized by Anglophilia and the repulsion of French models bound up in its wake. All these processes contribute to the emergence of the professional translator and the modern book trade and to the accelerating evolution of the German literary idiom. It is also the century in which Leipzig, the city in which Weiße lived and worked, rose to become a commercial and intellectual centre of European dimensions and the printing and bookselling capital of Germany. Since the apex of Weiße's literary career coincides with that of many of these developments, and since the peculiarity of his achievement can only be understood against their background, an overview of the intellectual and historical conditions in which his oeuvre took shape is necessary.

Anglophilia and the Knowledge of Literatures and Languages

'England bringt die grössten Seelen hervor, weil daselbst dem Denken nichts im Wege steht' [England produces the greatest souls because nothing impedes the intellect there], wrote the influential Saxon politician and public administrator, Thomas von Fritsch, in an essay on governance, law and the economy in 1761.[1] This essay, as well

1 Thomas von Fritsch, *Zufällige Betrachtungen in der Einsamkeit,* 2nd edn (Leipzig: n. pub., 1762). Thomas (von) Fritsch (1700–1775), born into a family of publisher-booksellers, initially combined a moderately successful political career at the court in Dresden with the continuation of the family business; towards the

as its sequel, contained reflections on the superiority of the English commercial spirit and legal system and on how the Germans might learn from them.[2] Fritsch's book, in the publication of which Christian Felix Weiße had been instrumental, was entirely characteristic of the contemporary German fascination with British concepts of statehood, culture and society as they were understood by German interpreters. Bernhard Fabian goes so far as to call the eighteenth century 'the English one' in German cultural and intellectual history; and indeed there is no area of German culture and society that was not deeply affected by the widespread Anglophilia.[3]

The emergence of German national cultural consciousness and public discourses was closely linked to the cultural transfer of British ideas. As Fabian writes:

> The impact of England on Germany was the impact of an established culture on an emerging national culture. From the Germans' point of view, theirs was a massive attempt to assimilate a foreign culture in all its manifestations and to use it as a stimulus in their efforts to modernize the country.[4]

---

end of the Seven Years' War the Saxonian Elector Frederick Augustus II made Fritsch head of his Restoration Commission, a move which put him at the helm of the bourgeois pro-Enlightenment reform movement in Saxonian politics at the time. His economic and fiscal reforms were instrumental in the country's recovery after the war (Gerhard Schmidt, 'Fritsch, Thomas', in *Neue deutsche Biographie,* ed. by Historische Kommission bei der Bayerischen Akademie der Wissenschaften, 28 vols (Berlin: Duncker & Humblot, 1953–2020), v (1961), 624–25; Klaus Rek, 'Englandrezeption und Aufklärungskonzeption in der "Neuen Bibliothek der schönen Wissenschaften und der freyen Künste"', in *Sächsische Aufklärung,* ed. by Klingenberg and others, pp. 197–210.

2 The sequel is Thomas von Fritsch, *Zufällige Betrachtungen in der Einsamkeit. Zwote Sammlung* (Leipzig: n. pub., 1762). See, e.g., pp. 33 and 81.

3 Bernhard Fabian, 'Englisch-Deutsche Kulturbeziehungen im achtzehnten Jahrhundert', in *Europäischer Kulturtransfer im 18. Jahrhundert. Literaturen in Europa – Europäische Literatur?,* ed. by Barbara Schmidt-Haberkamp, Uwe Steiner and Brunhilde Wehinger (Berlin: Berliner Wissenschafts-Verlag, 2003), pp. 13–30 (p. 13). The studies cited here usually focus on German Anglophilia; for a wider perspective, see, for instance, Ian Buruma, *Voltaire's Coconuts; or, Anglomania in Europe* (London: Weidenfeld & Nicolson, 1999).

4 Bernhard Fabian, *The English Book in Eighteenth-Century Germany,* The Panizzi Lectures, 1991 (London: British Library, 1992), p. 4. It should be noted here that the terminological confusion between England and Britain which we find in Fabian's statement, as well as in Fritsch's observations cited above, is entirely characteristic of the period. For the most part the two entities were treated as synonymous by German writers (cf. Michael Maurer, *Aufklärung und Anglophilie in Deutschland,* Veröffentlichungen des Deutschen Historischen Instituts London, 19 (Göttingen/Zurich: Vandenhoeck & Ruprecht, 1987), p. 18).

In this way, the German appropriation of everything British encompassed not just intellectual and political concepts, but extended to the areas of religion, science and technology, commerce, fashion and what might be termed 'popular culture'.[5] The key concept in German Anglophilia was that of Britain as a 'free' nation which formed a natural counterpart to Absolutist France and allowed German writers to criticize, more or less covertly, the political set-up of their own states, which often imitated the French model.[6] German Anglophiles of the Enlightenment therefore:

> sahen England als ein blühendes Land, die englische Nation als Ideal einer germanischen vor sich, als ein besseres Deutschland: was Deutschland, abgeschnitten von den fluktuierenden Einflüssen auf dem Kontinent, ohne seine dominierenden Fürsten, mit einem starken Bürgertum, hätte werden können. Die Zeitumstände brachten es mit sich, daß diese Selbstfindung der Deutschen in Abgrenzung gegen die Franzosen geschehen mußte: nicht so sehr gegen die Franzosen als Aufklärer, als vielmehr gegen die Franzosen unter den Deutschen, gegen die französische Hof- und Adelskultur in Deutschland.[7]
>
> [viewed England as a flourishing country and the English nation as the ideal of a Germanic one, a better Germany: what Germany could have become if cut off from the fluctuating influences on the Continent, without its dominant princes and with a strong bourgeoisie. Under the circumstances prevailing at the time, this German self-discovery had to take place in opposition to the French: not so much the French as Enlightenment thinkers, but the French among the Germans, the French culture of the nobility and courts in Germany.]

Early German Anglophilia had been prompted by French thinkers of the Enlightenment, especially Voltaire and Montesquieu, in the 1730s and 1740s and thus the dualism between France and Great Britain that characterized the contributions of those intellectuals became an integral part of the movement in Germany as well.[8] Beyond the purely political realm, this meant 'breaking away from the cultural

5 Cf. Jennifer Willenberg, *Distribution und Übersetzung englischen Schrifttums im Deutschland des 18. Jahrhunderts*, Archiv für Geschichte des Buchwesens – Studien, 6 (München: Saur, 2008), pp. 19–94.

6 Cf. Willenberg, *Distribution und Übersetzung*, pp. 46–59; Maurer, *Aufklärung und Anglophilie*, pp. 60–70.

7 Maurer, *Aufklärung und Anglophilie*, p. 409.

8 Willenberg, *Distribution und Übersetzung*, p. 20. For France as a Continental mediator of Anglophilia, see also Maurer, *Aufklärung und Anglophilie*, pp. 26–39.

supremacy of France'.[9] We shall see the implications this had for German writers at the time.

The way Anglophilia spread through the German-speaking states was determined largely by geography and religious affiliation. The four main centres of this cultural transfer were the staunchly Protestant cities of Hamburg, Zurich, Göttingen and, eventually, Leipzig as well.[10] What unites them from the beginning are religious affinities with Britain. Through its trade relations Hamburg also had long-standing commercial connections to the British Isles.[11] Göttingen's affiliations in this period, on the other hand, are bound up with politics. The Hanoverian succession in 1714 led to the establishment of close bonds between Hanover and Britain; and when the Elector Georg Ludwig acceded to the British throne as George I, he created a 'Regentschaftsrat' [governing council] to govern his German state – which, therefore, unlike many of the others, never adopted the Absolutism of the French model.[12] During a visit by his successor to Hanover in 1732 the foundation of a university at Göttingen was decided; it would become the most influential public institution in the cultural transfer between Britain and Germany in the period. From the outset, students at Göttingen could learn English there and the university library quickly amassed a large collection of English books.[13]

Leipzig, something of a late-comer among the German centres of Anglophilia, earned its place by becoming the capital of the import, trade and translation of English books in Germany. The undisputed centre of the German book trade since the mid-eighteenth century, Leipzig was the home of numerous highly productive publisher-booksellers whose combined output was almost equal to the sum total

9 Fabian, *The English Book*, p. 5.

10 Horst Oppel, *Englisch-Deutsche Literaturbeziehungen*, 2 vols, Grundlagen der Anglistik und Amerikanistik, 1 and 2 (Berlin: Erich Schmidt, 1971), I, *Von den Anfängen bis zum Ausgang des 18. Jahrhunderts*, 56.

11 Maurer, *Aufklärung und Anglophilie*, pp. 41–44. Hamburg was also the site of the first English bookshop in Germany, founded in 1788 by William Remnant (Bernhard Fabian, 'Die erste englische Buchhandlung auf dem Kontinent', in Bernhard Fabian, *Selecta Anglicana. Buchgeschichtliche Studien zur Aufnahme der englischen Literatur in Deutschland im achtzehnten Jahrhundert*, Schriften und Zeugnisse zur Buchgeschichte, 6 (Wiesbaden: Harrassowitz, 1994), pp. 216–38).

12 Maurer, *Aufklärung und Anglophilie*, p. 44.

13 Willenberg, *Distribution und Übersetzung*, p. 26; Bernhard Fabian, 'An Eighteenth-Century Research Collection: English Books at Göttingen University Library', in Fabian, *Selecta Anglicana*, pp. 177–94.

of books published in all other German cities.[14] The two important trade fairs – at Easter and Michaelmas – set the publishing rhythm for the whole industry. The leading importer of English books and publisher of translations from the English was Weidmanns Erben und Reich, with its managing director Philipp Erasmus Reich as the driving force behind it.[15] Weiße's collaboration with this publisher, who shaped the modern German book trade like few others, is the subject of a separate chapter. Suffice it to say at this point that in the second half of the eighteenth century Leipzig was the ideal place for anyone interested in the introduction of English literature to Germany.[16]

As Jennifer Willenberg notes, the importance of imports and reprints of English books remained smaller than that of translations, which emerged as the preferred medium of exploring England.[17] As Latin was gradually replaced by modern languages in scholarly communication, the earliest genres to be translated were devotional and medical works.[18] Literary works only began to take centre stage mid-century, but from this point onwards, as Bernhard Fabian observes, 'the development of German literature is inconceivable without a constant reference to English literature'.[19] The height of German Anglophilia in the 1770s and 1780s coincided with an explosive growth in the market for translations. Another factor which enabled this singular cultural transfer was the new market for literary journals, a medium that quickly came to revolutionize national and international information and communication.[20] The first German literary journal, *Acta Eruditorum* (published in Leipzig in 1682), had been modelled on the French *Journal des Sçavans*, but as early as 1713 a moral weekly published in Hamburg, Johann Mattheson's *Der Vernünfftler*, was based on the precept of the English *Spectator*

14 Willenberg, *Distribution und Übersetzung*, p. 107.

15 Another publisher based in Leipzig with whom Weiße worked, Engelhard Benjamin Schwickert (1741–1825), became the third-largest importer of English books at the Leipzig fairs in the last third of the century (Willenberg, *Distribution und Übersetzung*, p. 114).

16 Cf. also Bernhard Fabian, 'Die Meßkataloge und der Import englischer Bücher nach Deutschland im achtzehnten Jahrhundert', in Fabian, *Selecta Anglicana*, pp. 141–53.

17 Willenberg, *Distribution und Übersetzung*, p. 7; cf. also pp. 119–31.

18 Fabian, *The English Book*, p. 6.

19 Fabian, *The English Book*, p. 17.

20 Cf. Willenberg, *Distribution und Übersetzung*, p. 132.

and *Tatler*.[21] In the second half of the century Leipzig had become the place of publication of most periodicals of this kind.[22]

Soon, explicitly Anglophile journals began to be published, the first being the *Brittische Bibliothek* (1756–67) edited by Weiße's friend, Carl Wilhelm Müller, who went on to serve several terms of office as Mayor of Leipzig. Starting in 1775, there was J. F. C. Schulz's *Englische allgemeine Bibliothek*, which contained reviews from the *Monthly Review* and *Critical Review* (journals which themselves enjoyed an increasing German readership in the last third of the century);[23] and two years later Johann Joachim Eschenburg began his *Brittisches Museum für die Deutschen* (1777–80).[24] Not explicitly focused on English-language reviews, but an important journal in this respect nonetheless, was the long-running *Göttingische Anzeigen von gelehrten Sachen*, published under this title since 1753. The reviews of new English publications in these journals were instrumental in popularizing English literature in Germany and often preceded translation of these works.

One of the reasons why German translations and reviews remained so crucial in the cultural transfer between Britain and Germany was that, unlike French, English for a long time remained a language spoken by only a few isolated intellectuals in the above-mentioned centres of German Anglophilia. Early evidence of its being taught in German secondary schools can be found in the seventeenth century and English was part of the curriculum of several *Gymnasien* [grammar schools] in central and northern Germany in the early eighteenth century; nevertheless, as a regular component of the school curriculum it remained an exception until much later.[25] Many translators had taught themselves English from books. Jennifer Willenberg cites several examples, among them the Königsberg professor Christian Jakob Kraus, who learnt a whole

21 Eric A. Blackall, *The Emergence of German as a Literary Language, 1700–1775* (Cambridge: Cambridge University Press, 1959), pp. 51, 60. Especially for the early German imitations of these journals, see Fritz Rau, *Zur Verbreitung und Nachahmung des Tatler und Spectator*, Anglistische Forschungen, 145 (Heidelberg: Winter, 1980).

22 Lawrence Marsden Price, *English Literature in Germany*, University of California Publications in Modern Philology, 37 (Berkeley, CA and Los Angeles, CA: University of California Press, 1953), p. 53.

23 Willenberg, *Distribution und Übersetzung*, p. 155.

24 Cf. Maurer, *Aufklärung und Anglophilie*, pp. 312–17.

25 Willenberg, *Distribution und Übersetzung*, pp. 72–74.

dictionary by heart; and Johann Jakob Bodmer, who learnt English by reading Milton's *Paradise Lost* with the aid of a Latin-English dictionary.[26] Aside from self-education and the universities that taught English (more than half the German universities did so by 1789), private tutors were a third option, but their availability varied greatly between regions.[27] Unlike French tutors, these were often native speakers of German, as were many of the authors of English textbooks and grammars.[28] With beginnings such as these, it is no wonder that, in surveying eighteenth-century German translations of English literary works, one is often struck by the less-than-perfect command of the English language which so obviously constricted the translator's work.[29] Unlike French, English also never advanced to the status of a language used in social discourse among the educated.[30]

All this notwithstanding, the English language and literature gradually began to usurp the place previously held by their French equivalents.[31] More so than the latter, they provided impulses for the evolution of a German national literature: '[T]ranslating helped to develop the language both of the individual writer or speaker and of the language community as a whole'.[32] As with other aspects of British culture, many German intellectuals felt that a kinship existed between English and German. As another of Weiße's friends, the philosopher and translator Christian Garve, put it in 1767, in a review of Herder's *Fragmente* in which Herder had recommended that German enrich itself by emulating the English language:

> Die englische Sprache kömmt unsrer alten Sprache näher [als die französische]; und was Wunder, da sie mit ihr eine Mutter gehabt? In ihr finden wir viele Constructionen wieder, die uns gehörten [...] und endlich, wenn nun durchaus nachgeahmt werden sollte, so wäre

26 Willenberg, *Distribution und Übersetzung*, p. 76.

27 Willenberg, *Distribution und Übersetzung*, pp. 78, 88.

28 Willenberg, *Distribution und Übersetzung*, p. 81.

29 Marce Blassneck cites the example of Locke's *Some Thoughts Concerning Education*, the first German translation of which (1708) was apparently so bad that some German readers still preferred the French translation (Marce Blassneck, *Frankreich als Vermittler englisch>deutscher Einflüsse im 17. und 18. Jahrhundert*, Kölner anglistische Arbeiten, 20 (Leipzig: Tauchnitz, 1934), p. 28).

30 Fabian, *The English Book*, p. 77.

31 Marsden Price, *English Literature in Germany*, pp. 35–50.

32 Fabian, *The English Book*, p. 55.

> es immer für uns besser, wir ahmten die Engländer nach. Die guten Übersetzungen aus dieser Sprache haben also wirklich die unsere bereichert.[33]
>
> [The English language is closer to our old language [than the French is]; and is that surprising, since they had the same mother? We find many structures in it that used to be ours [...] and, ultimately, if there shall indeed be imitation, it would always be better if we imitated the English. Good translations from this language have really enriched ours.]

Indeed, the German lexicon at the time incorporated an extraordinary variety of Anglicisms and expressions based on English models.[34] This was by no means uncontroversial: as the discussion of Weiße's translations in the following chapters shows, the way translations from the English (and, to a lesser extent, French) shaped the German literary language was among the most contentious issues discussed in the literary world. Beyond the purely linguistic kinship, a literary one was asserted by Anglophile German writers with equal conviction – and with the confident assumption that German literature could use English writers as models for its own perfection. As another Leipzig-educated poet, Justus Friedrich Wilhelm Zachariae (1726–1777), put it in his poem *Die Tageszeiten* (first published in 1755):

> Patriotische Freude färbet mit Feuer die Wange,
> Daß auch die deutsche Dichtkunst sich ihrem Mittage nähert.
> Manches große Genie erhebet den rauschenden Flügel,
> Und steiget über den niedern Haufen prosaischer Sänger
> Weit in die Wolken hinaus; umsonst versuchet die Dummheit
> Ihm die Stärke der Flügel, die kühnen Metaphern zu nehmen,
> Kühne, doch wahre Metaphern, die Britten so mächtig erheben.
> Und warum ists falscher Geschmack, dem Britten zu folgen?
> Ist er nicht näher mit uns verwandt, als Galliens Sklaven,
> Denen Gebrauch und Grammatik die stärksten Flügel beschneidet?
> Deutsches sächsisches Blut schlägt in Britanniens Barden.[35]
>
> [The cheek is flushed with patriotic joy
> Now that German poetry approaches its midday.

33 Cited in Rek, 'Englandrezeption und Aufklärungskonzeption', p. 201. For Herder, cf. Michael Maurer, 'Herder als Theoretiker der interkulturellen Beziehungen', in *Übersetzen bei Johann Gottfried Herder. Theorie und Praxis*, ed. by Clémence Couturier-Heinrich (Heidelberg: Synchron, 2012), pp. 29–44.

34 Cf. Peter F. Ganz, *Der Einfluss des Englischen auf den deutschen Wortschatz 1640–1815* (Berlin: Erich Schmidt, 1957).

35 [Justus] Friedrich Wilhelm Zachariae, *Die Tageszeiten. Ein Gedicht in vier Büchern* (Rostock and Leipzig: Koppe, 1756), p. 62.

Many a great genius raises their whirring wing
To soar over the lowly heap of poetasters
Far up into the clouds; in vain does foolishness attempt
To take away their wings' strength, the bold metaphors,
Bold, yet true metaphors, which lift the Britons so mightily.
And why is it the wrong taste to follow the Briton?
Is he not closer kinship to us than the slaves of Gall,
Whose usage and grammar clip the strongest wings?
German Saxon blood pulses through the veins of Britain's bards.]

In terms of popularity, the English writers most eagerly received in the middle of the century were poets and dramatists: Alexander Pope, James Thomson, Edward Young and George Lillo; the influence of Joseph Addison and Richard Steele's moral weeklies has already been mentioned.[36] Milton had been 'discovered' earlier than Shakespeare, but in the second half of the century German drama was profoundly influenced by the increasingly broad reception and appropriation of the Bard, which were put onto a firm foundation with Wieland's translation of the plays (1762–67).[37] From the mid-1760s onwards the German reception of Ossian, the mythical Celtic poet whose works had been partly invented by the Scottish writer James Macpherson, became one of the most complex processes of cultural transfer in the period; Weiße's extensive contributions to this are discussed in a separate chapter.[38] Simultaneously, Thomas Percy's *Reliques of Ancient English Poetry* (1765) created an enduring German interest in traditional English poetry.

At the height of German Anglophilia in the 1770s, the production of German publishers was characterized by translations of English novels, chief among them those of Henry Fielding, Samuel Richardson and Laurence Sterne. Lawrence Marsden Price is probably right when he asserts that 'no really important English novel of these years escaped the attention of the translators, and no important English

36 Cf. Maurer, *Aufklärung und Anglophilie*, pp. 76–80; and Oppel, *Englisch-Deutsche Literaturbeziehungen*, pp. 61–65.

37 Bernhard Fabian, 'Englisch-Deutsche Kulturbeziehungen', p. 22. For an overview of the German reception of Shakespeare, see Roger Paulin, *The Critical Reception of Shakespeare in Germany 1682–1914: Native Literature and Foreign Genius* (Hildesheim/Zurich/New York: Olms, 2003).

38 For an overview of the German reception of Ossian, see Wolf Gerhard Schmidt, *'Homer des Nordens' und 'Mutter der Romantik'. James Macphersons Ossian und seine Rezeption in der deutschsprachigen Literatur*, 4 vols (Berlin: de Gruyter, 2003–04).

novelist'.[39] The fact that after 1780 the number of translations of English novels began to decline actually marks the success of the cultural transfer: inspired by foreign models, the 'native' German novel was beginning to come into its own.

After reaching its high point in the 1770s and 1780s, Anglophilia in Germany was on the wane. While its political strand had been challenged by the American War of Independence, during which Britain was overtaken by America as, ostensibly, the progressive home of freedom, the ideal of England as a 'free' nation had survived it.[40] Even in the mid-1780s Johann Wilhelm von Archenholtz's extremely successful travel account, *England und Italien* (published in Leipzig in 1785), further popularized the image of England as a country of enlightenment, culture, tolerance, reason and prosperity.[41] The conservative British reaction to the French Revolution, however, created the first major dint in the armour of this concept.[42] Nevertheless, while the years after 1780 were increasingly characterized by a focus on native traditions and developments, the model of England had helped to drive the evolution of German politics and culture, with long-lasting effects.[43] Especially German literary production in the second half of the eighteenth century cannot be properly assessed without considering this background of Anglophilia.

Theories of Translation

As the importance of translation grew, not just in literary circles but in the German book market as well, so did the output of literature on the complexities of translating itself. To be sure, the majority of literary translations in the eighteenth century, especially of the popular literature that forms such a large part of Weiße's production as a translator, were rarely directly inspired by theory. As Thomas Huber observes, the disparity between the theory and practice of translation

39 See his preface to Mary Bell Price and Lawrence Marsden Price, *The Publication of English Literature in Germany in the Eighteenth Century*, University of California Publications in Modern Philology, 17 (Berkeley, CA: University of California Press, 1934), p. 16; see also Carl Heine, *Der Roman in Deutschland von 1774 bis 1778* (Halle: Niemeyer, 1892).

40 Willenberg, *Distribution und Übersetzung*, pp. 59–62 (p. 61).

41 Maurer, *Aufklärung und Anglophilie*, pp. 185–97.

42 Willenberg, *Distribution und Übersetzung*, pp. 62–68.

43 Willenberg, *Distribution und Übersetzung*, p. 319.

is characteristic of the Enlightenment; and while translation theory occasionally prompted critical debates, commercial translation was mostly independent of these.[44] Nonetheless, beyond that, contemporary translation theory engaged with many of the same problems and challenges commercial translators faced. Aside from the fact that a translator such as Weiße, who primarily saw himself as an original writer, would certainly have been aware of the treatises on the subject, which were often part of larger poetics, the theory of translation also formed a cornerstone of literary discourses around the emerging German literary idiom. For these reasons, a brief summary of the most important developments in the theory of translation, most of which took place in the generation immediately before Weiße's, is necessary, not least to illuminate the critical background against which a translator's practical decisions were critically judged. At the same time, the discussion will largely be limited to native (i.e., German language) discourses that had a direct impact on the kind of literary translation practised by Weiße.

Like previous periods in German literature, the Enlightenment did not produce a comprehensive theory of translation. Beyond their place in manuals of rhetoric, comments on individual problems and issues were usually published in 'small forms' such as essays or reviews.[45] The concept of translation itself was still rather loosely defined, especially as far as its demarcation against various forms of adaptation and imitation was concerned.[46] Only during the Romantic period were the latter beginning to be regularly excluded

44 Thomas Huber, *Studien zur Theorie des Übersetzens im Zeitalter der Deutschen Aufklärung 1730–1770*, Deutsche Studien, 7 (Meisenheim am Glan: Hain, 1968), p. 7.

45 Anneliese Senger, *Deutsche Übersetzungstheorie im 18. Jahrhundert (1734–1746)*, Abhandlungen zur Kunst-, Musik- und Literaturwissenschaft, 97 (Bonn: Bouvier, 1971), p. 1.

46 Precisely because eighteenth-century notions of the distinction between translation and adaptation are so hazy, the distinction made by the present study is based on a far more recent understanding – though it should be noted that, even today, definitions of translation and adaptation respectively are often by no means mutually exclusive. The *Routledge Encyclopedia of Translation Studies* defines adaptation as 'a set of translative interventions which result in a text that is not generally accepted as a translation but is nevertheless recognized as representing a source text. As such, the term may embrace numerous other notions such as appropriation, domestication, imitation and rewriting' (Georges L. Bastin, 'Adaptation', in *Routledge Encyclopedia of Translation Studies*, ed. by Mona Baker and Gabriela Saldanha, 3rd edn (Abingdon/New York: Routledge, 2020), pp. 10–14 (p. 10)). Thus, even modern-day definitions admit a 'tenuous borderline' between translation and adaptation (p. 13).

from definitions of translation.[47] Part of the reason why the theory of translation in the period appears underdeveloped is that, compared to other arts and sciences, there were fewer classical precepts to which eighteenth-century *Kunstrichter* [critics] could have recourse.[48] One of the few exceptions to this rule was Cicero, who in his prescriptive treatise *De optimo genere oratorum* had outlined the principles according to which he translated the speeches of the Attic orators, Aeschines and Demosthenes:

> nec converti ut interpres, sed ut orator, sententiis isdem et earum formis tamquam figuris, verbis ad nostram consuetudinem aptis. In quibus non verbum pro verbo necesse habui reddere, sed genus omne verborum vimque servavi. Non enim ea me adnumerare lectori putavi oportere, sed tamquam appendere.
>
> [And I did not translate them as an interpreter, but as an orator, keeping the same ideas and the forms, or as one might say, the 'figures' of thought, but in language which conforms to our usage. And in so doing, I did not hold it necessary to render word for word, but I preserved the general style and force of the language. For I did not think I ought to count them out to the reader like coins, but to pay them by weight, as it were.][49]

Reappropriated in many an eighteenth-century preface and rhetorical treatise, this became an oft-quoted summary of what ostensibly characterized a good translation.[50] As such, it also appears in *Ausführliche Redekunst* (1736), the manual by Johann Christoph Gottsched, the Leipzig professor and *de facto* head of the literary establishment of the city at the time. With respect to his own translations of the classics, Gottsched declares that:

47 Alexander Nebrig and Daniele Vecchiato, 'Einleitung: Translatorische Kreativität um 1800', in *Kreative Praktiken des literarischen Übersetzens um 1800. Übersetzungshistorische und literaturwissenschaftliche Studien*, ed. by Alexander Nebrig and Daniele Vecchiato, Untersuchungen zur deutschen Literaturgeschichte, 152 (Berlin/Boston, MA: de Gruyter, 2019), pp. 1–16 (pp. 1–2).

48 T. R. Steiner, *English Translation Theory 1650–1800*, Approaches to Translation Studies, 2 (Assen: Van Gorcum, 1975), p. 27.

49 Marcus Tullius Cicero, *De inventione; De optimo genere oratorum; Topica*, with an English translation by H. M. Hubbell, Loeb Classical Library, 386 (Cambridge, MA: Harvard University Press, 2014), pp. 364–65.

50 However, as if to exemplify the above, the very same passage has been cited as an example of a definition of the concept of adaptation (Bastin, 'Adaptation', p. 10).

> Ich muß aber von meinen Bemühungen, ebenfalls mit dem Cicero gestehen, daß ich sie nicht, als ein ängstlicher Dollmetscher, sondern als ein Redner übersetzt habe; indem ich nicht sowohl jedes Wort, sondern vielmehr den Nachdruck ganzer Sätze auszudrücken bemüht gewesen bin.
>
> [Regarding my endeavours, I have to confess that, in the words of Cicero, I did not translate them as a timid interpreter, but as an orator, inasmuch as I was striving to express not every word, but the impression of whole sentences.][51]

While by no means the only approach to translation in the period, this one was certainly as prevalent as it was, by and large, uncontroversial. A purist in matters of the German literary idiom, Gottsched was among the most vocal proponents of a translation that remained faithful to the original form while conforming to the stylistic and grammatical conventions of the German language as he understood it:

> Man bemühet sich aber, nicht so wohl alle Worte, als vielmehr den rechten Sinn eines jeden Satzes mit solchen Redensarten auszudrücken, die seiner Sprache eigenthümlich sind. Endlich muß man, so viel möglich ist, alle Figuren, verblümte Redensarten, auch die Abtheilung der Perioden, aus dem Originale beybehalten.[52]
>
> [Rather than all the individual words, one endeavours to express the proper purport of each sentence in such a phrasing as is appropriate to one's language. Wherever possible, one must, furthermore, retain all figures of speech, allusive phrases, even the structure of the sentences in the original.]

Like most literary theorists of his time, Gottsched and his circle subscribed to a rationalist philosophy of language in which words were interpreted as signifiers for abstract concepts which in many ways transcended the cultural specificity and historicity of any

51 Johann Christoph Gottsched, *Fortsetzung der critischen Dichtkunst, Ausführliche Redekunst,* 5th edn (Leipzig: Breitkopf, 1759 [1728]), p. 459. This is a German rendering which, incidentally, exemplifies the very principle it describes, given its rather loose paraphrase of Cicero.

52 Johann Christoph Gottsched, *Handlexicon oder kurzgefaßtes Wörterbuch der schönen Wissenschaften und freyen Künste* (Leipzig: Fritsch, 1760), col. 1585. It should be added that in Gottsched's view this rule applied primarily to prose translation. In his *Versuch einer critischen Dichtkunst vor die Deutschen* he admits that translations of poetry must necessarily be granted greater licence in questions of formal equivalency (Johann Christoph Gottsched, *Versuch einer critischen Dichtkunst vor die Deutschen* (Leipzig: Breitkopf, 1730), pp. 6–7).

one language. The earliest precedents for this understanding of signification can be found in Aristotle, but eighteenth-century philosophers of language such as Christian Wolff (1679–1754) made more frequent reference to immediate theoretical precursors in this vein, most prominently John Locke (1632–1704) and Gottfried Wilhelm Leibniz (1646–1716).[53] The degree of artistic licence which any given theorist of translation would allow therefore was directly dependent on the theorist's position on this interpretation of language. Gottsched's main opponents in questions of literary aesthetics, including the theory of translation, were the Swiss 'camp' of theorists around Johann Jakob Bodmer (1698–1783) and Johann Jakob Breitinger (1701–1776).[54] Their difference was not over the rationalist language philosophy, which they shared, but over the poetic imagination's licence to transcend it.[55] It was their very respect for the autonomy of literary language that led the Swiss to stress the criterion of formal equivalency to an even greater degree than did Gottsched; in a section headed, 'Von der Kunst der Uebersetzung' [On the Art of Translation] in his *Fortsetzung der critischen Dichtkunst* (1740), Breitinger writes:

> Von einem Uebersetzer wird erfodert, daß er eben dieselben Begriffe und Gedancken, die er in einem trefflichen Muster vor sich findet, in eben solcher Ordnung, Verbindung, Zusammenhange, und mit gleich so starckem Nachdrucke, mit andern gleichgültigen bey einem Volck angenommenen, gebräuchlichen und bekannten Zeichen ausdrücke, so daß die Vorstellung der Gedancken unter beyderley

53 Zoltan Gendler Szabo, 'Language, Early Modern Philosophy of', in *Routledge Encyclopedia of Philosophy*, ed. by Tim Crane (London and New York: Routledge, 2001) <https://www.rep.routledge.com> [accessed 22 September 2020]; E. J. Ashworth, 'Language, Renaissance Philosophy of', in *Routledge Encyclopedia of Philosophy* <https://www.rep.routledge.com> [accessed 22 September 2020]. See also Senger, *Deutsche Übersetzungstheorie*, pp. 35–36; and Helmut Knufmann, 'Das deutsche Übersetzungswesen des 18. Jahrhunderts im Spiegel von Übersetzer- und Herausgebervorreden', *Börsenblatt für den deutschen Buchhandel*, 91 (1967), 2676–2716 (pp. 2692–93).

54 For an overview of the protracted conflict between Gottsched and the Swiss, see Detlef Döring, 'Der Literaturstreit zwischen Leipzig und Zürich in der Mitte des 18. Jahrhunderts. Neue Untersuchungen zu einem alten Thema', in *Bodmer und Breitinger im Netzwerk der Europäischen Aufklärung*, ed. by Anett Lütteken and Barbara Mahlmann-Bauer (Göttingen: Wallstein, 2009), pp. 60–104.

55 For a review of the aesthetic matter under dispute, see also Frederick C. Beiser, *Diotima's Children: German Aesthetic Rationalism from Leibniz to Lessing* (Oxford: Oxford University Press, 2009), pp. 101–17.

Zeichen einen gleichen Eindruck auf das Gemüthe des Lesers mache. Die Uebersetzung ist ein Conterfey, das desto mehr Lob verdienet, je ähnlicher es ist.[56]

[A translator is required to express exactly those terms and notions which he finds in his model in exactly that order, combination, context, and with the same force, using other, similarly valid, common and established signs accepted among a nation, so that the evocation of the notions from both kinds of sign leaves the same impression on the mind of its reader. The translation is a likeness that deserves the more praise the more similar it is.]

Beyond the mere rationalist equivalency of signs, this already anticipates the 'equivalency of effect' that dominates the theory of translation today. While this is still largely uncontroversial, it is the question of inter-language influences that drives a wedge between Gottsched and the Swiss faction. Bodmer and Breitinger believe that in terms of style and idiomatic variety, languages may well enrich one another:[57]

Sollten [...] die Sprachekündiger, alles, was eine Sprache vor der andren eignes und schönes an sich hat, auch den andern, denen dieser oder jener besondre Ausdrucke diese oder jene kräftige Redensart manglet, beyzulegen, und sie damit auszuschmüken, / sich angelegen zu seyn lassen, so würde dieser unbekannte Schatz bald einem jeden Volcke gemein, und jede Sprache dahero nicht nur merklich bereichert werden, sondern fast zu einer niemahls verhofften Vollkommenheit gelangen.[58]

[Should the linguists [...] make it their mission to add all which is peculiar to and beautiful in one language to those which lack this particular expression or that strong idiom, and to adorn them with these, then this unknown treasure would soon be shared by all nations, and every language would not only be enriched considerably through it, but would almost attain an unhoped-for perfection.]

56 Johann Jakob Breitinger, *Fortsetzung der critischen Dichtkunst*, intro. by J. J. Bodemer (Zürich: Orell; Leipzig: Gleditsch, 1740), p. 139. Cf. Huber, *Studien zur Theorie des Übersetzens*, pp. 33–45; and Winfried Sdun, *Probleme und Theorien des Übersetzens in Deutschland vom 18. bis zum 20. Jahrhundert* (Munich: Hueber, 1967), p. 23.

57 Cf. also Franziska Münzberg, *Die Darstellungsfunktion der Übersetzung. Zur Rekonstruktion von Übersetzungsmodellen aus dem 18. Jahrhundert* (Frankfurt am Main: Lang, 2003), pp. 199–200.

58 Johann Jakob Bodmer and Johann Jakob Breitinger, *Der Mahler der Sitten*, 2 vols (Zürich: Orell, 1746), II, 512–13.

This idea of a 'naturalization' of foreign idioms and expressions, as it were, met with flat-out rejection from Gottsched and his followers, who saw it as their aim to preserve the purity of the German language.[59] Gottsched himself responded by saying: 'Unsere Sprache ist an sich selbst reich genug. [...] Diese unzeitige Begierde aber, unsre Mundart zu bereichern, macht manchen oft unverständlich und rauh; oftmals auch gar lächerlich' [Our language is rich enough in itself. [...] But this undue desire to enrich our idiom makes some incomprehensible and crude; often even completely ludicrous].[60] It was only natural, then, that Gottsched should rail against 'die schweizerischen [Sp]rachverderber' [the Swiss corrupters of language].[61] Perhaps the most entertaining product of this increasingly polemical debate was Christoph Otto von Schönaich's *Neologisches Wörterbuch* (1754), which, from the perspective of the purists, collected the worst of the linguistic 'misdeeds' of the age.[62] It should be noted that while Bodmer and Breitinger's suggestion that the language could be enriched through the addition of loanwords and borrowed expressions was innovative, the insistence of Gottsched and like-minded critics on the 'purity' of the German used in translation was the product of a tradition (fully acknowledged by Gottsched) that reached back to Martin Luther's *Sendbrief vom Dolmetschen*, first published in 1530 – yet where Luther had suggested that the touchstone for the comprehensibility of a translation should be the idiom spoken by 'common' people, Gottsched and his retinue had an altogether more select audience in mind.[63]

59 While significantly less influential in the period than Gottsched himself, Georg Venzky's treatise *Das Bild eines geschickten Übersetzers* (1734) was the most systematic and comprehensive attempt at a theory of translation produced by a follower of Gottsched's.

60 Johann Christoph Gottsched, *Versuch einer critischen Dichtkunst*, 4th edn (Leipzig: Breitkopf, 1751 [1730]), p. 240.

61 Gottsched, *Versuch einer critischen Dichtkunst* (1751), p. 241. See also Senger, *Deutsche Übersetzungstheorie*, pp. 45ff.

62 Christoph Otto von Schönaich, *Die ganze Aesthetik in einer Nuß, oder Neologisches Wörterbuch* ([Breslau: Hebold], 1754). The collection is characterized by a mixture of aggressive ridicule and often rather lame attempts at satire. Typical examples include 'aetherisch' [ethereal] – 'Aber was ist nun ätherisch? Etwas, das man gern beschreiben will und nicht kann' [But what, then, is ethereal? Something that one wants to describe but cannot] (p. 9); 'Insecten' [insects] – 'Ein undeutsches Wort' [an un-German word] (p. 235); and 'Phantome' [phantoms] – 'denn wir haben keine Gespenster' [for we have no ghosts] (p. 335).

63 The *Sendbrief vom Dolmetschen* [*An Open Letter on Translating*] contains many of the maxims which had governed Luther's translation of the Bible and

Collective attempts among the educated, meanwhile, to 'improve' the condition of the German language, and to purify and standardize its literary idiom in the context of the continuing rise of the vernacular and wide-spread linguistic innovation, were not altogether new. Over the course of the seventeenth century clubs and societies dedicated to the purpose of 'Sprachpflege' [cultivation of language] had been founded all over the German-speaking states.[64] In 1727 Gottsched was elected 'Senior' of the *Teutschübende poetische Gesellschaft* in Leipzig, the roots of which reached back into the late seventeenth century; he promptly renamed it the 'Deutsche Gesellschaft'.[65] At the same time, the society remained conscious of the strong tradition of 'Sprachpflege' of which it was part. Its new statutes contained a list of similar institutions which had been established in the previous century 'zur Verbesserung unsrer Muttersprache' [for the improvement of our mother tongue]: the 'Fruchtbringende Gesellschaft', the 'Aufrichtige Tannen-Gesellschafft', the 'Pegnitzische Schäfer-Gesellschafft' [more commonly known as the 'Pegnesischer

remained influential throughout the centuries. In a famous passage, Luther describes the form of language by which the translator should be guided: 'Denn man mus nicht die buchstaben inn der lateinischen sprachen fragen, wie man sol Deutsch reden, [...] sondern, man mus die mutter jhm hause, die kinder auff der gassen, den gemeinen man auff dem marckt drumb fragen, und den selbigen auff das maul sehen, wie sie reden, und darnach dolmetzschen, so verstehen sie es den und mercken, das man Deutsch mit jn redet [For one should not ask the Latin letters how to speak German, [...] but one should ask the mother in the home, the children in the street, and the common man at the market, and look at their mouths, at how they talk, and translate accordingly, so they will comprehend it and realize that one is speaking German to them] ('Ein Sendbrief vom Dolmetschen', in Martin Luther, *Werke*, 127 vols (Weimar: Böhlau, 1883–2009), xxx (1909), 632–46 (p. 637)). A transcription with English translation is available online: Martin Luther, *Ein Sendbrief vom Dolmetschen / An Open Letter on Translating*, trans. by Howard Jones, Treasures of the Taylorian: Reformation Pamphlets (Oxford: Taylor Institution Library, 2017) <https://ora.ox.ac.uk/objects/uuid:61dd3bfe-bd7d-48a2-adca-79e28d5cc63d/download_file?file_format=pdf&safe_filename=Reformation%2BPamphlets_Martin%2BLuther.pdf&type_of_work=Book> [accessed 14 December 2020].

64 For an overview of the linguistic development in Germany in the period, see Hans Eggers, *Deutsche Sprachgeschichte*, 2 vols (Reinbek: Rowohlt, 1986), II, *Das Frühneuhochdeutsche und Neuhochdeutsche*.

65 See, e.g., Blackall, *The Emergence of German*, pp. 107–09. As an account of the linguistic innovation in this period, Blackall is somewhat dated and reductive, but his monograph still manages to convey a sense of the forcefulness with which the German literary idiom evolved in the eighteenth century.

Blumenorden'] and several others.[66] Among the new statutes, the practice of translation is specifically mentioned as one of the tasks typically undertaken by members of the society. More importantly, however, they contained an exhortation to use only pure and correct German:

> Man soll sich allezeit der Reinigkeit und Richtigkeit der Sprache befleißigen; das ist, nicht nur alle ausländische Wörter, sondern auch alle Deutsche unrichtige Ausdrückungen und Provinzial-Redensarten vermeiden; so daß man weder Schlesisch noch Meißnisch, weder Fränckisch noch Niedersächisch, sondern rein Hochdeutsch schreibe; so wie man es in gantz Deutschland verstehen kan.[67]

> [At all times the purity and correctness of the language shall be observed; that means not only to avoid all foreign words, but all incorrect German expressions and regional idioms as well; so that you write neither Silesian nor in the Meißen dialect, neither Franconian nor Lower Saxon, but pure High German as can be understood in all of Germany.]

What this excerpt shows is that early in the century the fragmentation of the German language into its regional varieties had been regarded by writers such as Gottsched as no less a threat to a standardized, proper German literary idiom than foreign influences. This would change somewhat over the course of the century, when the repulsion of especially French and English influences once more took centre stage. Weiße himself would later join the 'Deutsche Gesellschaft', but at a time when Gottsched had already left it following his conflict with the Swiss, which again plays a role in the next chapter. For the time being, it should be noted that even in the eyes of much more open-minded theorists and practitioners of translation such as Lessing, foreign idioms and grammatical constructions posed a certain danger to the stylistic unity of the German text. In his *Rettungen des Horaz* (1754), Lessing placed the latter above indiscriminate literal faithfulness to the form of the original, asserting that 'Die Treue eines Uebersetzers wird zur Untreue, wann er seine Urschrift dadurch verdunkelt' [The faithfulness of a translator turns into faithlessness if he thereby obscures his original].[68]

66 [Anon.], *Nachricht von der erneuerten Deutschen Gesellschafft in Leipzig und ihrer ietzigen Verfassung* (Leipzig: Breitkopf, 1727), pp. 8–9.

67 [Anon.], *Nachricht von der erneuerten Deutschen Gesellschafft*, p. 14.

68 Gotthold Ephraim Lessing, *Rettungen des Horaz*, in *Sämmtliche Schriften*, ed. by Karl Lachmann, 13 vols (Berlin: Voß, 1838–40), IV (1838), 5–43 (p. 37).

In all its prescriptivism, eighteenth-century theory of translation reflects the position from which the translators looked at the texts themselves. As Helmut Knufmann observes in his survey of translators' prefaces in the period, with few exceptions the Enlightenment interest in translated texts was less aesthetic-poetical than content-oriented, pedagogical, or determined by educational policies:[69] so much seemed to hinge on these questions, not least because Enlightenment attitudes to translation always emphasized the *prodesse* rather than the *delectare*.[70] Therefore, the applicability of these ideas to the popular (i.e., entertaining) literature that rose to prominence only a few decades later was limited to begin with.[71] Most commercial translators (and, by extension, publishers) made the German reader their first concern; faithfulness to the original author's style and cultural peculiarity remained a secondary concern for many, if not most of them. Even a translator such as Weiße in his early work often translated in an acculturating way, changing the names of literary characters as well as place-names to more German-sounding ones, and he was by no means an exception in this regard. Nonetheless, because translation took place in a literary industry in which the theoretical animosities between Leipzig and Zurich translated into an impact on all sorts of publishing networks, it was virtually impossible for a translator of Weiße's standing, who from the 1760s onwards occupied an increasingly prominent position in this industry, not to engage with these discussions. Moreover, while Weiße never published an extended contribution to the theory of translation himself, the following chapters investigate how he engaged with these problems in his practice as a translator.

Translators and their Practice

Who were the translators? Most of them came from the educated middle classes, people who, once they had completed their academic training, often lacked regular income and had limited professional prospects.[72] An increasing number of them were women, including one of the most influential and prolific translators of the period, Luise

69 Knufmann, 'Das deutsche Übersetzungswesen', p. 2681.

70 Walter Fränzel, *Geschichte des Übersetzens im 18. Jahrhundert* (Leipzig: Voigtländer, 1913), pp. 25–30.

71 Cf. also Senger, *Deutsche Übersetzungstheorie*, p. 60; and Willenberg, *Distribution und Übersetzung*, p. 274.

72 Willenberg, *Distribution und Übersetzung*, p. 242.

Gottsched.[73] For most commercial translators, the working conditions were hard. Despite the fact that information about their remuneration remains scarce even for the second half of the eighteenth century, we know that, compared to those of original writers, translators' fees decreased in relative terms. While in the first half of the century writers and translators were paid approximately the same, in the second half of the century translators' pay generally remained below the average honorarium for original German works.[74] In their dealings with publishers, translators were often in a rather vulnerable position.

Given their precarious economic situation (as well as the public perception of their work, discussed below), it is not surprising that for almost all translators this was a sideline. Most of them did not publish more than a handful of translations, which were often a by-product of their main literary employment.[75] Of course, there always was a spectrum ranging from the well-informed, ambitious, 'highbrow' translators such as Bode, Gottsched, or Herder to the 'anonymous hack-writers' whose work 'was almost exclusively commissioned by publishers'.[76] Most of them lived in the centres of publishing, chief among them Leipzig, home to the firms of Crusius, Dyck, Junius, Schwickert, Weidmanns Erben und Reich and Weygand, all well-known for their focus on translated literature.[77] Like Weiße, who regularly worked for four out of these six publisher-booksellers, most translators had no exclusive affiliation with any given employer. Those among them who lived in provincial towns or cities far from the northern and central German capitals of publishing and intercultural communication often found it difficult to obtain original works in time to secure a commission from a publisher. A later chapter in this study will feature Weiße's correspondence with Christian Garve

73 See *Übersetzungskultur im 18. Jahrhundert. Übersetzerinnen in Deutschland, Frankreich und der Schweiz*, ed. by Brunhilde Wehinger and Hilary Brown (Hanover: Wehrhahn, 2008); as well as Willenberg, *Distribution und Übersetzung*, pp. 233–34.

74 Harald Steiner, *Das Autorenhonorar. Seine Entwicklungsgeschichte vom 17. bis 19. Jahrhundert*, Buchwissenschaftliche Beiträge aus dem deutschen Bucharchiv München, 59 (Wiesbaden: Harrassowitz, 1998), pp. 250–52.

75 Willenberg, *Distribution und Übersetzung*, pp. 222–23.

76 Fabian, *The English Book*, p. 79.

77 Willenberg, *Distribution und Übersetzung*, p. 190. The perspective of publishers will not be discussed here because the chapter that examines Weiße's work with and for Weidmanns Erben und Reich presents what can be considered the exemplary case.

in Breslau, whose work exemplifies the difficulties faced by the provincial translator. Especially in the cities, collaboration among translators was also quite common, increasingly so towards the end of the century.[78] There was a general trend from the amateur translator, whose importance declined over the course of the century, towards the occasional translator, whose main occupation might be writing or teaching; meanwhile, the type of the professional or semi-professional translator established itself especially in the realm of popular novels, travel literature and medicine.[79]

With few exceptions, the work of the translator was held in low regard. As Jennifer Willenberg points out, translation ranked at the bottom of the hierarchy of literary activities.[80] The general understanding was that translation required neither intellect nor originality and that translators performed a mechanical, reproductive task.[81] The practitioners themselves did little to dispel this notion. Weiße himself is a good example: as he confessed to his friend and colleague Karl Wilhelm Ramler in a letter from 1787, '[I]ch [fülle] die Zeit, wo mein Kopf nichts taugt, oder ich ihn nicht anstrengen mag, und doch mit der Feder gern spielen möchte, mit einer Übersetzung aus' [I fill the time when my mind is useless or I do not wish to exert it, and yet want to play with the quill, with a translation].[82] Similarly, Weiße's friend and colleague, Christian Garve, complained: 'Der Titel eines Uebersetzers von Profession, den ich mir vielleicht zuziehen werde, gefällt mir nicht ganz' [I do not quite like the title of professional translator, which I shall perhaps bring upon myself].[83]

Almost regardless of the frequency and seriousness with which they translated, many translators used prefaces to remind readers that the translation in question was only a product of their 'Nebenstunden' [spare hours] to avoid the stigma of being associated with the 'factory translators', the most indiscriminately prolific professionals.[84] Largely for this reason, many translations, especially of popular fiction, were

78 Cf. Willenberg, *Distribution und Übersetzung*, p. 232.

79 Willenberg, *Distribution und Übersetzung*, p. 225.

80 Willenberg, *Distribution und Übersetzung*, p. 255.

81 Cf. Willenberg, *Distribution und Übersetzung*, pp. 254–57.

82 C. F. Weiße, Letter to K. W. Ramler, 18 May 1787 (GSA 75/229,4 (103)).

83 Chr. Garve, Letter to C. F. Weiße, 15 August 1786, in Christian Garve, *Briefe an Christian Felix Weiße und einige andere Freunde*, 2 vols (Breslau: Korn, 1802–03), I, 289.

84 Willenberg, *Distribution und Übersetzung*, p. 219.

published anonymously.[85] Most of these developments became most pronounced only in the second half of the eighteenth century, with the rise of popular fiction and the spread of Anglophilia. Before the middle of the century the great majority of dramatic texts translated into German were French, not least because of Gottsched's censure of 'irregular' English drama, which would have a profound impact on Weiße's early literary career.[86] In the second half of the century and at the height of German Anglophilia, popular fiction became the genre most commonly translated from the English, followed by travel writing and medical treatises.[87]

As mentioned before in this chapter, well into the second half of the century knowledge of modern foreign languages usually remained limited to French, even among the educated. Bernhard Fabian has proposed that translations from the English which appeared before 1770 are 'at best of historical interest', but even later in the century we find that many English-German translations are seriously marred by their translator's limited knowledge of the source language.[88] Towards the beginning of the eighteenth century French had begun to replace Latin as the European 'lingua Franca'; and French books were ubiquitous in Germany when a working knowledge of English was still a niche phenomenon. Especially in the first half of the century, the great Dutch publisher-booksellers such as Elzevier in Leiden, who had previously provided Latin books to the whole of Europe, now produced reprints of French literature, as well as French translations of English books, for a market which included the German-speaking states.[89]

The French language therefore remained an important medium of foreign literatures. Up until the middle of the century German versions of English works were often based on the French translation rather than the original. This was the case, for instance, with the first German translation of Addison and Steele's *Spectator* in 1719, which was a re-translation from the French.[90] When Luise Gottsched

85 Of course, this was also still a relatively common practice for original works and Weiße, for instance, rarely allowed his name to appear on the title page of anything which he had produced, including his plays and poetry, though admittedly he was rather an extreme case.

86 Cf. Willenberg, *Distribution und Übersetzung*, pp. 179ff.

87 Willenberg, *Distribution und Übersetzung*, pp. 181–82.

88 Fabian, *The English Book*, p. 57.

89 Willenberg, *Distribution und Übersetzung*, p. 161.

90 Blassneck, *Frankreich als Vermittler*, pp. 54–67.

published her own translation of the *Spectator* twenty years later, she could cite many reasons to justify her decision to go back to the English original, including serious errors and omissions in the earlier one.[91] The criticism of the French practice of the 'belle infidèle' in translation became a recurring trope in the discourse around re-translation; and the ideal of 'faithfulness' is often invoked in a specifically anti-French way.[92] Marce Blassneck's survey of sixty-three works of English literature translated into German using the French version as an 'intermediary' finds that in almost half these cases the French translation was the only source, whereas a little more than a quarter of these translations had used French sources alongside the English ones they were translating. Nonetheless, with the end of the 'linguistic and cultural supremacy' of French in Germany, the reliance of translators on French versions of English works declined sharply around the middle of the century.[93]

When it comes to their attitude to the integrity of the text they were translating, eighteenth-century translators still took much greater editorial liberties than did those in later periods. The duty to be 'faithful' to the original might collide with a perceived duty to shield readers from supposedly offensive, indecent, or simply tedious passages, in which case abridgement and expurgation were common practices. The same held true for content judged to be too nationally specific to be relatable to the German reader, a problem with which, as we shall see, Christian Felix Weiße struggled as much as any of his colleagues.[94] Another standard response to the challenges posed by such elements of the original was editorial comment provided by the translator, usually in footnotes or translators' prefaces, a genre more common in the eighteenth century than perhaps any other period in German literary history. Footnotes often served to explain vocabulary or idioms that translated badly, or to comment

91 Blassneck, *Frankreich als Vermittler*, pp. 67–70.

92 Knufmann, 'Das deutsche Übersetzungswesen', p. 2688. More recent studies have occasionally classed the 'belles infidèles' as adaptations rather than translations in the narrow sense of the word (Bastin, 'Adaptation', p. 10).

93 Blassneck, *Frankreich als Vermittler*, p. 151. Jürgen von Stackelberg has analysed a selection of these mediated translations in greater detail: those of Joseph Addison's *Drummer* (1716), George Lillo's popular *London Merchant* (1731) and Alexander Pope's *Essay on Man* (1733–34) among them (Jürgen von Stackelberg, *Übersetzungen aus zweiter Hand. Rezeptionsvorgänge in der europäischen Literatur vom 14. bis zum 18. Jahrhundert* (Berlin/New York: de Gruyter, 1984)).

94 Cf. Knufmann, 'Das deutsche Übersetzungswesen', p. 2696; Willenberg, *Distribution und Übersetzung*, pp. 286–87.

on cultural peculiarities which might impede the German reader's comprehension of the text.[95]

With the growth of the reading public and the rise of popular literature, the market for translations started to grow exponentially: midway through the century critics began to complain about the vast 'flood' of translations and many noted a decline in the quality of literary translations in the second half of the century.[96] The aforementioned proverbial 'translation factories', a phenomenon whereby well-connected translators subcontracted commissions commercially, became a target of universal criticism. Regardless of their position on the theory of translation, especially with translators from English an unreflecting literalism became the mark of those equipped with insufficient knowledge of the source language. As the philosopher Moses Mendelssohn put it in 1757, in a review of a German translation of Akenside's *The Pleasures of Imagination*:

> Der größte Haufen von unsern Uebersetzern [...], und besonders diejenige, welche für die Uebersetzungsfabriken arbeiten, lassen es ihr erstes Gesetz seyn, sich nicht von den Worten der Urschrift zu entfernen. Sie glauben getreulich übersetzt zu haben, wenn der Leser die Uebersetzung eben so wenig versteht, als er die Urschrift verstanden hätte.[97]
>
> [The great bulk of our translators [...], and especially those who work for the translation factories, make it their first rule not to stray from the words of the original. They believe they have translated faithfully if the reader is as unable to understand the translation as the original.]

The image of the 'flood' was an appropriate one. After the Seven Years' War, Leipzig was one of the motors driving the economic recovery of Saxony and the book business flourished. The share which translations enjoyed of the overall production peaked in the mid-1770s; and in the last third of the century over eighty per cent of the translations from modern European languages were from French and English.[98] It has already been mentioned that scarcely

95 Willenberg, *Distribution und Übersetzung*, p. 297; Knufmann, 'Das deutsche Übersetzungswesen', pp. 2697–99.

96 Cf. Fränzel, *Geschichte des Übersetzens*, pp. 72–100; Willenberg, *Distribution und Übersetzung*, pp. 315–18 and passim.

97 Moses Mendelssohn, review of *The Pleasures of Imagination / Die Vergnügungen der Einbildungskraft*, by [Mark] Akenside, *Bibliothek der schönen Wissenschaften und der freyen Künste*, 2.1 (1757), 91–124 (p. 92). The German translation to which Mendelssohn refers was published by Weitbrecht (Greifswald/Leipzig) in 1757.

98 Willenberg, *Distribution und Übersetzung*, p. 174.

an important or successful novel written in either of these languages escaped the attention of German translators and publishers. Christian Felix Weiße puts it less flatteringly when he speaks of the 'Raubsucht der Übersetzer' [rapacity of the translators] in a letter to his friend and colleague Friedrich Justin Bertuch in 1775.[99] Bertuch himself, in a preface written in 1779, vividly describes what the market forces did to the profession:

> [U]nd wer kann izt ohne Ekel und Unwillen den Unfug ansehen, der mit der Uebersetzerey getrieben wird? Kein schaaler Roman, kein elender Wisch darf in Paris oder London erscheinen, und gleich ist er auch ins Teutsche übersetzt. Knaben, die noch lange nicht vom Sprachmeister entlassen sind, machen sich mit der frechsten Stirn entweder an wissenschaftliche Werke, wovon sie noch nicht einmal die Anfangsgründe und Kunstsprache verstehen, oder an Werke des Genies, Geschmacks und Witzes, davon ihrem hohlen Kopfe nie etwas träumte. Doch so lange unser liebes Publikum noch solchen Fabrikenplunder kauft, unsre Buchhändler mit diesen Artikeln ihr Capital erträglich benutzen, und gewisse Amphibien von Gelehrten und Tagelöhnern ihr Leben noch so mittelmäßig mit dieser Sudeley hinbringen können, wird diesem Unwesen schwerlich zu steuern seyn.[100]

> [And who can look upon the way in which translation is now being abused without disdain and indignation? As soon as any vapid novel, any wretched scrap is published in Paris or London, it is translated into German forthwith. Boys who have not yet graduated from the lessons with their tutor brazenly have the nerve to approach scholarly works of which they understand not even the basics and artistic language, or works of genius, taste and wit of which their empty heads have never dreamt. Yet as long as our dear public buy such factory trash, and our booksellers employ their capital gainfully with these items and certain amphibians of scholars and peons can make a middling living with this waste, it will scarcely be possible to rein in this mischief.]

With English literature in particular, positive prejudice regarding every product of the British Isles was a precondition of the process whereby, after the middle of the century, the originally selective reception of English writing increasingly became a quantitative one, seemingly without market saturation in sight.[101] Many enduringly

99 C. F. Weiße, Letter to F. J. Bertuch [March 1775] (GSA06/2093 (27))

100 F. J. Bertuch, Preface [1779] to *Magazin der spanischen und portugiesischen Literatur*, 1 (1780), iv.

101 Willenberg, *Distribution und Übersetzung*, p. 320.

popular works were translated numerous times within that period: because the very act of translation contributed to the evolution of the German literary idiom, translations 'aged' very quickly and were often considered stylistically obsolete mere decades after their first publication.[102]

Aside from the sheer mass of the production, the speed with which translations were produced after the publication of the original (sometimes even before, as we see in later chapters) increased markedly in the second half of the century. The modernization of the book trade, which led to translation's increasingly taking place within the competition of an early capital-driven business (which Weiße's main partner for translations, Philipp Erasmus Reich at Weidmann's, helped to create), and the absence of universal copyright laws meant that publishers raced to be the first to announce the translation of a new work of fiction or travel writing.[103] An interval of less than a year between the publication of the original and the translation was not uncommon. Even translations which took the longer route via the French version were often published in the year after the original had come out.[104] In the eyes of many, this competitive speed was the reason for the perceived decline in the quality of translation. As early as 1762 the prolific Leipzig-based translator from the French and English Johann Gottfried Gellius expressed a common sentiment when he complained: 'Uebersetzungen sind, bey der gegenwärtigen Verfassung der Dinge, nichts als frühzeitige Früchte, die oft halb unreif aufgetragen werden, um nur die Lüsternheit der Leser zu stillen' [As things stand now, translations are nothing but unseasonably early fruit which are often served unripe if only so that the readers' appetite may be satisfied].[105] Christian Felix Weiße entered the literary world in the mid-1740s, at a time when many of the above-mentioned developments began to speed up. In which ways he exemplified them, and in which ways he actively came to shape them, the following chapters will show.

102 Fabian, *The English Book*, p. 55.

103 Cf. Willenberg, *Distribution und Übersetzung*, p. 188.

104 Willenberg, *Distribution und Übersetzung*, p. 165. In Willenberg's survey, between 1710 and 1740 an average of seven to nine years passed between the English original and the German translation; between 1740 and 1770 this dropped to an average of approximately five years; and in the last third of the century the average interval was barely two years (p. 206).

105 Johann Gottfried Gellius, *Anmerkungen zum Gebrauche deutscher Kunstrichter* (Leipzig: n. pub., 1762), p. 4.

2. Early Translations

This chapter is devoted to the first phase of Weiße's literary career, the 1740s and 1750s. Weiße started translating at the same time as he composed his first original works and his career as a translator was always bound up with that as a poet and dramatist. Weiße's work as a dramatist and his involvement in the evolution of German theatre in the second half of the century have been the object of many a study and are beyond the scope of the present investigation. Nevertheless, because translations of dramatic texts were particularly prominent among Weiße's early production as a translator and some of them sparked considerable controversy, the context of Weiße's involvement in the disputes about German theatre around the middle of the century need to be sketched briefly alongside the survey of his early translations.

Translation for the Stage and the Collaboration with Lessing

Christian Felix Weiße was born in Annaberg, Saxony, in 1726, into a family that had produced a number of minor men of letters.[1] He grew up in Altenburg, where his father, Christian Heinrich Weiße, was director of a *Gymnasium* [grammar school]. Weiße Senior taught classical and modern languages and occasionally wrote plays or translated foreign works. Christian Felix developed poetic talents early and even in school read not just classical, but modern writers as well, including translations of French and English works. In 1745 he enrolled at the University of Leipzig to study Classics and

1 The standard biographical source is still Weiße's autobiography: Christian Felix Weiße, *Selbstbiographie*, ed. by Christian Ernst Weiße and Samuel Gottlob Frisch (Leipzig: Voß, 1806). It should be complemented by Minor, *Christian Felix Weiße*.

Divinity. As mentioned in the previous chapter, the city had been evolving into the printing, publishing and bookselling capital of Germany since the early eighteenth century.[2] Leipzig had an ancient university (founded in 1409) and thrice a year – at New Year, Easter and Michaelmas – the great trade fairs, which lasted for two weeks each, served as a stock exchange for goods and ideas from all over Germany and Europe. In a letter to the Bavarian writer of the Enlightenment, Lorenz Westenrieder, Weiße would later describe the city as follows: 'Der grosse Handel macht den Ort lebhaft, die Messen und die vortheilhafte Lage zieht eine Menge von Fremde beynahe aus allen Theilen der Welt hieher, der grosse Buchhandel bringt die Produkte des menschlichen Verstandes von jeder Nation sogleich hieher [The thriving trade makes it a busy place, the Fairs and the advantageous location attract many foreigners from almost all quarters of the globe, the extensive book trade quickly conveys to us the products of the human mind from all nations].[3] We can confidently say that only in a city which so very closely combined commercial enterprise with intellectual attractions could Weiße's career have taken the shape it did.

It was at the University of Leipzig that Weiße met Gotthold Ephraim Lessing (1729–1781), with whom he shared a passion for the theatre; their friendship would have a lasting impact on his literary career. According to Weiße's autobiography, it was Lessing who introduced him to the English language and many of Weiße's early translations were collaborations with him. In the 1740s theatrical life in Leipzig was dominated by the theatrical troupe of Friederike Caroline Neuber (1697–1760), whose numerous attempts to set up a permanent theatrical stage did much to call time on itinerant theatre. In order to gain free entrance to Neuber's theatre, Weiße and Lessing translated French plays for her, starting with Pierre de Marivaux's *Annibal* (*Hannibal*; cf. Bibliography of Translations [72]), of which each

2 Cf. Hazel Rosenstrauch, 'Leipzig als "Centralplatz" des deutschen Buchhandels', in *Zentren der Aufklärung III. Leipzig. Aufklärung und Bürgerlichkeit*, ed. by Wolfgang Martens, Wolfenbütteler Studien zur Aufklärung, 17 (Heidelberg: Schneider, 1990), pp. 103–24.

3 C. F. Weiße, Letter to L. Westenrieder, 19 May 1781, in 'Briefe von Christian Felix Weiße und Friedrich Jacobi an Lorenz Westenrieder aus den Jahren 1781–1783', ed. by A. Kluckhohn, *Sitzungsberichte der philosophisch-philologischen und historischen Classe der K.B. Akademie der Wissenschaften zu München* (1889), 2 vols, I, 237–70 (p. 246).

Figure 1 Johann August Rossmaesler, *Auerbachs Hof in Leipzig* (1778) © Stadtgeschichtliches Museum Leipzig, Inventar-Nr. 1624 b. Auerbachs Hof was one of the hotspots of the trade fairs

of the two fledgling playwrights translated half.[4] Other collaborative translations included Prosper de Crébillon's *Catilina* (*Catilina*, 1749 [68]) and Jean Regnard's *Le joueur* (*Der Spieler*, *c*. 1748–50 [79]). Many of these early translations are lost; and even with those that survive, the share which either of the two translators had in them is, of course, difficult to determine. This has not discouraged many later bibliographers from naming only Lessing as the translator.[5]

At the same time as working together with Lessing, Weiße produced his first own translations, initially for Neuber's stage

4 Cf. Karl Gotthelf Lessing, *Gotthold Ephraim Lessings Leben*, 3 vols (Berlin: Voß, 1793–95), I (1793), 62–63.

5 In the same way, later critics usually (and perhaps justifiably) assume that, given his superior stature in the canon, Lessing probably had more of an influence on Weiße than the other way round – which sometimes leads to questionable scholarly intentions, such as Minor's wish 'Weiße auf Lessing zurückzuführen' [to derive Weiße from Lessing] (Minor, *Christian Felix Weiße*, p. vi.).

as well, including one – apparently his first English-to-German translation – of James Thomson's *Sophonisba* (*Sophonisbe, c.* 1748 [58]). In 1750 Neuber's theatrical establishment had dissolved and the troupe of Heinrich Gottfried Koch (1703–1775) effectively became its successor. This was the year in which Weiße left the university. He continued to translate and adapt French plays for Koch, such as Voltaire's *Mariamne* (*Marianne,* 1752 [84]) and another play by Regnard, *Le distrait* (*Der Zerstreute,* 1752 [78]). Around this time he also made the acquaintance of the famous actor Conrad Ekhof (1720–1778), something of a German David Garrick, on whom Weiße would sometimes rely to comment on his own original plays and to help with their revision. During the 1750s Weiße's main occupation was as a private tutor to the young Graf Johann Heinrich von Geyersberg in Leipzig; and translating remained a side occupation, as it would throughout his life. At university he had met and befriended Christian Fürchtegott Gellert (1715–1769), poet and, from 1751, Professor of Philosophy, a leading figure in the city's literary life. Another friendship which originated in this early period was that with Gottlieb Wilhelm Rabener (1714–1771), the satirist.

In 1752 one of Weiße's adaptations of foreign plays for Koch's theatre provoked some controversy. While its literary-historical significance has sometimes been overstated, it both exemplifies some of the period's discussions about foreign models in the theatre and may have been among the events which contributed to Weiße's lifelong aversion to intellectual conflict. In October 1752 his adaptation of Charles Coffey's hugely popular ballad opera *The Devil to Pay* (*Die verwandelten Weiber oder Der Teufel ist los* [11]) was first performed in Leipzig and immediately drew the ire of Gottsched.[6] The professor, who had set himself up as the 'linguistic [and literary] mentor of all Germany', had long been imposing his deep distrust of English theatre on the German literary world.[7] This partly reached back to the dispute between Leipzig and Zürich, one element of which has already been mentioned in the preceding chapter. The main bone of contention was, however, the form and purpose of the theatre; and from the earliest beginnings discussion of this had revolved around foreign models. Milton's *Paradise Lost*, championed by its translator Bodmer (the German version was published in 1732),

6 The original was itself an adaptation of Thomas Shadwell's *The Devil of a Wife* (Alfred E. Richards, 'A Literary Link between Thomas Shadwell and Christian Felix Weisse', *PMLA*, 21 (1906), 808–30).

7 Blackall, *The Emergence of German*, p. 107.

had been attacked by Gottsched on the grounds of its 'irregularity' and uncontrolled imagination, which in the latter's view contrasted unfavourably with the 'regularity' of French drama; similar views would later be held about Shakespeare, whose mainstream German reception was not yet underway at that point. Another contentious question was which kind of audience the theatre should serve, with Gottsched firmly in favour of an exclusive target group.[8] Unsurprisingly, Coffey's *Devil*, a musical farce the plot of which involves the highly improbable transformation of a cobbler's wife into a Lady, quickly became a prime target of Gottsched's criticism. However, even though Gottsched included the translator in his attack, Weiße by and large remained on the margins of the dispute, with the theatre director, Koch, becoming the main target of Gottsched's faction.

In the end, the controversy irreparably damaged the reputation of Gottsched as the doyen of the theatre in Leipzig while doing little harm to Weiße.[9] *Der Teufel ist los* became the most frequently performed German play based on an English original in the whole of the eighteenth century. Part of the reason Weiße's adaptation was so particularly successful may have been its 'commercial' character, as Gerd Nover calls it: Weiße replaced everything that was typically 'English' in the play, i.e., any cultural barrier to the audience's understanding of the plot and characters, with references comprehensible to a German audience.[10] The version of this comic opera created by Weiße and his collaborators (the music was written by Johann Georg Standfuß and Johann Adam Hiller) became highly influential in the genesis of the German *Singspiel*.[11] It was enlarged and revised numerous times and in 1759 Weiße also adapted Coffey's

8 For a summary of the whole conflict, which took place over several decades, see Jürgen Wilke, 'Der deutsch-schweizerische Literaturstreit', in *Formen und Formgeschichte des Streitens: Der Literaturstreit*, Kontroversen, alte und neue, 2, ed. by Franz Josef Worstbrock and Helmut Koopmann (Tübingen: Niemeyer, 1986), pp. 140–51.

9 See Minor, *Christian Felix Weiße*, pp. 147–57. See Gerd Nover, *Die deutschen Übersetzungen und Bearbeitungen englischer Komödien im 18. Jahrhundert*, Europäische Hochschulschriften, I/462 (Frankfurt am Main: Lang, 1981), pp. 58–60, for a summary of the debate about English theatre following the controversy; and Price, *English Literature in Germany*, pp. 226–27.

10 Nover, *Die deutschen Übersetzungen*, p. 55.

11 Cf. Walter Henry Marshall, '"The Devil to Pay" and its Influence on Eighteenth-Century German Singspiel' (unpublished doctoral thesis, The Open University, 1985).

sequel, *The Merry Cobbler*, for the German stage (*Der lustige Schuster* [12]). Weiße's own comedy, *Die Poeten nach der Mode* (written in 1751 and first performed in Hamburg in 1756), ridiculed the excesses of both Gottsched's faction and the Swiss.

Throughout his own career as a dramatist, Weiße's stance on the dichotomy of French vs. English theatre remained complicated. He shared his contemporaries' belief that in order to develop a native tradition, Germany needed inspiration from foreign models. In the prefaces to the editions of his own plays he regularly took a middle position that sought to combine the effects of the classical regularity of French drama with those of the imaginative freedom of English theatre to create an original German theatre superior to both – always remembering, of course, to stress the innate superiority of ancient drama over either of these:

> Ohne die großen Muster der Alten zu erwähnen, haben wir die Exempel unsrer Nachbarn der Engländer und Franzosen vor uns, die uns in der dramatischen Dichtkunst weit hinter sich gelassen haben. Bloße Nachahmer sollten wir freylich nicht seyn […]! würden wir nicht wohl thun, wenn wir zwischen ihnen die Mittelstrasse nähmen, von beyden lernten, und einen eignen Weg beträten? Von Engländern könnten wir die großen tragischen Situationen, die Bearbeitung und Abstechung der Charaktere, den edlen, kühnen und erhabnen Ausdruck, und die Sprache der Leidenschaften: von Franzosen die Wohlanständigkeit der einzelnen Theile zum Ganzen, die gezüchtigte und feine Sprache des Hofes, der Gefälligkeit und der Liebe, und endlich die Regelmäßigkeit und Ordnung lernen; durch eine solche Vereinigung würden wir den Schwulst und das Uebertriebene der einen, und das Leere und Geistlose der andern; das Zügellose, Unregelmäßige, und oft in eine Wildheit ausartende der Engländer, und das lächerliche, galante, coquettenmäßige und seichte der Franzosen vermeiden. Noch besser aber thäten wir, wenn wir die Natur des menschlichen Herzens und der Leidenschaften kennen lernten, und blos dem Pfade der Alten nachgiengen.[12]

> [Leaving aside the model of the ancients, we have before us the example of our neighbours, the English and French, who have left us far behind in the art of dramatic writing. Of course, we should not be mere imitators […]! Would we not do well to travel the middle road between them, learning from both and forging our own path? From the English we could learn the great tragic situations, the treatment and differentiation of characters, noble, bold, and sublime

12 C. F. Weiße, *Beytrag zum deutschen Theater*, [1], 2nd edn (Leipzig: Dyck, 1765), pp. 3–4.

expression and the language of passion; from the French the proper relation of the parts to the whole, the chaste and refined language of the court, of courtesy and love and, lastly, order and regularity. Through such a combination we would avoid the bombast and exaggeration of the former and the vacuousness and vapidity of the latter; the extravagance, the irregularity, that which often degenerates into savagery in the English; and that which is ludicrous, gallant, coquettish and shallow in the French. However, we would do even better if we became acquainted with the nature of the human heart and the passions and only followed the path of the Ancients.]

While Weiße would spend the remainder of his career translating mostly works written in English, this early phase is dominated by translations of French drama. While Weiße's own dramatic production regularly relied on English inspiration for its subject matter, the form always remained a compromise. His first volume of plays, *Beytrag zum deutschen Theater*, published in 1759, contained two plays based on English history: *Eduard III* and *Richard III*. The latter created a plagiarism debate which kept critics busy for a century after Weiße's death. Suffice it to say at this point that Weiße's own assertion he had not read Shakespeare's *Richard the Third* until after his own play was finished seems to have been true.[13] A more direct engagement with Shakespeare was Weiße's successful tragedy *Romeo und Julie* (1767). All these plays, however, kept to the classical unities, which resulted in a 'rule-bound neoclassical rigidity' criticized by many.[14] Most painfully for Weiße, these included his former collaborator, Lessing. As Weiße confessed to Ramler, the comparison with Shakespeare frightened him: '[E]r [Lessing] hält mir unaufhörlich den Shakespear vor: dieser Spiegel erschreckt mich, und ich sehe darinnen einen Zwerg, der nur Gelächter erreget' [He [Lessing] always holds Shakespeare up to me: this mirror frightens me and in it I see a dwarf

13 Weiße, *Beytrag zum deutschen Theater* [1], p. 123; F. W. Meisnest, 'Die Quellen zu Christian Felix Weißes Richard III.', *Euphorion*, 17 (1910), 538–56; Sabine Durchholz, 'Im "lebenden Labyrinth der Literatur": Shakespeares "Richard der Dritte" in Versionen von Christian Felix Weiße und Carl Steinberg; mit einem Blick auf Lessings Weiße-Rezeption', *Lessing Yearbook*, 38 (2008–09), 169–91 (pp. 170–71).

14 Francis Lamport, '"Des Menschen Herz, o Gott! welch Elend kann es stiften!": The Tragedies of Christian Felix Weisse', *Publications of the English Goethe Society*, 82 (2013), 1–15 (p. 14). In this context, see also Elsa Jaubert, '"Richard III" et "Roméo et Juliette" de Christian Felix Weiße: une voie médiane entre la barbarie anglaise et la superficialité française?', *Revue germanique internationale*, 5 (2007), 23–35.

who elicits only laughter].[15] In the preface to the second volume of his plays, Weiße defends his formal choices, including his attempts at carving out a middle space between the French and English models:

> Der Verfasser glaubte dem deutschen Trauerspiele einen Originalcharakter zu geben, wenn er das große Tragische der Engländer mit der französischen Ordnung [...] zu verbinden suchte: er würde sich inzwischen kein Gewissen machen, eine schöne Situation durch eine Sünde wider die drey Einheiten, und auf Kosten der Regelmäßigkeit zu erkaufen: sein Grundsatz ist nur, diese nicht ohne Noth zu beleidigen, oder eine Schönheit in der Unordnung zu suchen.[16]
>
> [The author believed he was giving German tragedy an original character by striving to combine the tragic greatness of the English with French order [...]. Meanwhile, he would feel no remorse about paying for a beautiful scene with a sin against the classical unities and at the cost of regularity: his only precept is not to offend either without need, nor to seek for beauty in disorder.]

In the mid-1750s Weiße also began translating poetry and prose, initially also in collaboration with Lessing. Their first venture was the joint translation of Elizabeth Rowe's devotional collection *Devout Exercises of the Heart* (*Geheiligte Andachts-Uebungen*, 1754 [52]), which featured extensive poetic selections from some of the most popular Early Modern and contemporary British poets, including Joseph Addison, John Dryden, John Milton, Alexander Pope, Matthew Prior and Edward Young.[17] Their second joint prose translation was

15 C. F. Weiße, Letter to K. W. Ramler, 4/11 May, 1768 (GSA 75/229,2 (29)). Weiße's letters to Ramler have in part been published: 'Briefe von Ch. F. Weisse an K. W. Ramler, im Auszuge mitgeteilt (I–III)', ed. by Karl Schüddekopf, *Archiv für das Studium der neueren Sprachen und Litteraturen*, 77 (1887), 1–46; 79 (1887), 149–216; 82 (1889), 241–90. However, the transcriptions are often unreliable, which is why the present study will cite the original letters. Lessing had unfavourably compared Weiße's *Richard* with Shakespeare's in the seventy-third number of his *Hamburgische Dramaturgie* (cf., e.g., Price, *English Literature in Germany*, pp. 230–34).

16 C. F. Weiße, *Beytrag zum deutschen Theater*, 2 (Leipzig: Dyck, 1763), unpag. preface.

17 Wilkie doubts that Weiße was involved in the Rowe translation based on its unusual place of publication (Erfurt) and Lessing's absence from Leipzig at the time (Wilkie, 'Christian Felix Weisze', pp. 29–31). However, given the fact that other translations by Weiße in this period were also published outside Leipzig and that he would regularly work with collaborators all over Germany later in his career, we see no reason to contradict the existing bibliographical evidence.

another devotional treatise: William Law's *Serious Call to a Devout and Holy Life* (1729), translated as *Eine ernsthafte Ermunterung an alle Christen* (1756 [34]). On this occasion the collaboration seems to have been motivated by expediency rather than opportunity. Lessing had originally planned to translate the book but broke off his work after providing only a few print sheets, at which point Weiße stepped in to complete the translation on his behalf.[18] Finally, the last collaboration between Weiße and Lessing showed Weiße the translator his further path in more ways than one. It was a collection of snippets of wisdom culled from Samuel Richardson's works (*Gemeinnützige Lehren der Tugend, und der guten Sitten*, 1757 [51]). In terms of its genre, this was much closer to the type of text he would routinely translate in the following decades. More importantly, Lessing had introduced him to Philipp Erasmus Reich at Weidmann's, a company which published both the Law and Richardson translations. A separate chapter is devoted to Weiße's formative work for and with Reich.

The Making of a Translator

Like so many translators of his age, Weiße taught himself English. The biographer of the writer Moritz August von Thümmel (1738–1817) relates the advice the latter received from his friend Weiße:

> Thümmel fragte bei Weissen an, wie er am leichtesten zur Kenntniss der englischen Sprache gelangen könne? Und Weisse lehrte ihn, wie er selbst zu dieser Sprache gelangt sei. 'Sie sollen, schrieb er ihm, englisch nicht zum Reden, sondern zum Lesen lernen, und da wird Ihnen nichts heilsamer seyn, als wenn Sie im Anfang, um sich nicht durch das Aufschlagen der Wörter verdriesslich zu machen, englische Bücher als den Tristram Shandy, Tom Jones u.s.w. mit einer guten Übersetzung in der Hand durchlesen. So habe ich es gelernt, und wenn man etliche Bücher durchlaufen, so weiss man schon viel.'[19]

18 As told in Karl Gotthelf Lessing, *Gotthold Ephraim Lessings Leben*, I, 198–99. Curtis Vail doubts Weiße's involvement based on the stylistic unity of the work (Curtis Vail, *Lessing's Relation to the English Language and Literature*, Columbia University Germanic Studies, n.s., 3 (New York: Columbia University Press, 1936), p. 41). The tendency among older scholars to eliminate Weiße from the translations has already been noted; admittedly, as Wilkie points out, both this and the fact that only Lessing received payment from the publishers for this translation are a 'slight argument' against Weiße's involvement (Wilkie, 'Christian Felix Weisze', pp. 31–33).

19 Johann Ernst von Gruner, *Leben M. A. von Thümmels* (Leipzig: Göschen, 1819), pp. 159–60.

> [Thümmel enquired of Weiße how he could most easily acquire a knowledge of the English language. And Weiße taught him how he himself had come to such knowledge. 'You should', he wrote to him, 'learn English not to speak it, but to read it; and for that nothing will be more beneficial than if, in the beginning and lest the looking up of words make you morose, you were to read such English books as Tristram Shandy, Tom Jones, etc. with a good translation to hand. This is how I learnt it; and when one has gone through a few books, one already knows a lot.']

If this was indeed the way Weiße had first taught himself to read English, proficiency would have been achieved by different means. The practice of translation itself probably contributed most to Weiße's progress in the English language, but his library, which at the time of his death comprised over ten thousand volumes, was also exceptionally well stocked with books which would have helped.[20] It included several histories of 'England' (which often meant Britain); numerous translations of literary and scholarly works, many of which Weiße had received as gifts from the authors or as review copies; travel accounts, including those of German travellers to Britain; books on the geography and history of European nations; and the works of Hugh Blair, John Locke, Edmund Burke and many other important Enlightenment thinkers. Apart from books in German and English, Weiße owned numerous French and Italian books, as well, of course, as classical texts.

In his library the oldest English dictionary published during his own lifetime was the eighth edition of Dyche's *New General English Dictionary* (London: Ware, 1754), a book which besides explanations of the usual 'difficult terms' contained a short English grammar and a list of proper names which might have been useful to non-native speakers.[21] Most of the dictionaries Weiße owned, however, were published after he had already completed dozens of translations and unfortunately his letters and autobiography provide no insight into how frequently he consulted these. They included Adelung's *Neues grammatisch-kritisches Wörterbuch der englischen Sprache für die Deutschen* (1783), which was based on Samuel Johnson's *Dictionary*; Karl Philipp Moritz's *Englische Sprachlehre für die Deutschen* (1784); and Robert Lowth's *Introduction to English Grammar* (in a Basel edition

20 The auction catalogue of Weiße's library printed after his death remains the most comprehensive and reliable source regarding his ownership of books: *Verzeichniß der Bibliothek Hrn. Christian Felix Weiße* (Leipzig: n. pub., 1806).

21 *Verzeichniß der Bibliothek*, 3787. The number is that of the entry.

from 1794).[22] Finally, Karl Gustav Friedrich Schwalbe's *Lesebuch für Anfänger in der englischen Sprache* (1793), which may well have been a presentation copy from its Leipzig-based author, probably earned its place in the library based on Weiße's pedagogical interests rather than his own linguistic needs.[23] Weiße also owned numerous volumes of the *Critical Review* published in the 1760s and 1770s which, as will be discussed below, played a key role in his activities as a translator as well.

While Weiße's encounters with the English language were thus limited to what he could find in books, his knowledge of French culture was enriched by a journey to Paris with Graf Geyersberg, whose tutor Weiße remained throughout the 1750s. From November 1759 until May 1760 the two of them stayed in Paris together.[24] After translating French plays for the Leipzig theatre for years, Weiße finally had an opportunity to see the Paris stage in action. He discovered the Opéra Comique, something which later resulted in his adaptation of plays by Charles Simon Favart.[25] While in Paris Weiße started adapting an operetta by Sedain, *Le Savetier* (*Der Dorfbalbier*). The visit also provided an opportunity to develop his literary networks further. Weiße and his master shared quarters with Louis-Esaïe Pajon de Moncets (1725–1796), a reconvalescent preacher of the Reformed Church in Leipzig, and the translator Johann Jakob Volkmann (1732–1803), who introduced Weiße to Paris intellectual society. He would remain friends with both of these after his return to Leipzig.

Among the leading intellectuals of the French Enlightenment, he made the acquaintance of, among others, Jean-Baptiste d'Alembert, Jean-Antoine Nollet and, most excitingly for Weiße, the pedagogical writer and philosopher Jean-Jacques Rousseau. Weiße and Pajon visited the latter in Montmorency in April 1760 and Weiße presented the philosopher with the *Essai sur l'Inégalité*, the French translation of a text by Moses Mendelssohn. Another notable acquaintance during the stay in Paris was Michael Huber (1727–1804), a translator of

22 *Verzeichniß der Bibliothek*, 3786, 1390 and 4817. There were also two dictionaries which had been published before Weiße was born and would have been completely outdated by the time he started translating. See nos. 645 and 3045.

23 *Verzeichniß der Bibliothek*, 5700.

24 Weiße, *Selbstbiographie*, pp. 64–75; cf. Minor, *Christian Felix Weiße*, pp. 34–37.

25 Michel Espagne, 'Christian Felix Weiße und Paris – Literarische Aufklärung und Kunstgeschichte', in *Sächsische Aufklärung*, ed. by Klingenberg and others, pp. 161–72 (pp. 166–67).

French literature and contributor to the *Journal étranger*, whom Weiße helped to return to Germany by securing an appointment for him in Leipzig. While these six months would remain Weiße's only period of residence in Paris, it was a formative time. The trip allowed him to become better acquainted with contemporary French theatre and, at least equally importantly, to make new connections in the Republic of Letters on whom he could draw for the rest of his career.

Editor of the *Bibliothek der schönen Wissenschaften und der freyen Künste*

In 1759, the year his journey to Paris began, Weiße was appointed editor of the journal *Bibliothek der schönen Wissenschaften und der freyen Künste*.[26] Founded two years earlier by Friedrich Nicolai, published by Dyck in Leipzig and edited by Nicolai together with Mendelssohn, the periodical published reviews and essays about German and European art and literature and quickly came to have an impact on some of the most important discourses of the Enlightenment 'Republic of Letters'.[27] The preface of the first volume in the *Bibliothek* outlines an aesthetic-didactic programme to which Weiße would also subscribe during his over twenty years as active editor:[28]

> Unser Zweck, ist die Beförderung der schönen Wissenschaften, und des guten Geschmacks unter den Deutschen, und wir werden also nichts unterlassen, was uns zu diesem Zwecke dienlich scheinen wird. Wir nehmen uns daher vor, alles, was uns zur Kenntniß der Geschichte und der Verbesserung der schönen Künste, bey den Ausländern so wohl als besonders in Deutschland, dienliches vorkommen wird, beyzubringen. [...] Wir werden zu Erreichung des gedachten Zwecks

26 For the circumstances of the transition from Nicolai to Weiße, see Minor, *Christian Felix Weiße*, pp. 26–30.

27 The significance of this journal has only relatively recently begun to attract attention: cf. the landmark conference proceedings *Sächsische Aufklärung*, ed. by Klingenberg and others. The role played by this journal in one of the most influential cultural transfers of the period, the German reception of Ossian, is discussed in Chapter 5. For a detailed analysis of the journal's intellectual programme and its contribution to the 'Saxon Enlightenment', see Ludwig Stockinger, 'Die Sächsische Aufklärung als Modell deutscher Aufklärungsvarianten', in *Sächsische Aufklärung*, pp. 23–48.

28 In 1783, vol. 29 was the last to be published under Weiße's active editorship (Richard F. Wilkie, 'Weisse's Borrowings for the "Bibliothek der schönen Wissenschaften"', *Modern Philology*, 53 (1955), 1–7 (p. 2)).

> von allen Büchern, die in die schönen Wissenschaften einschlagen, Nachricht geben, und zwar so wohl von denen die bey unsern Nachbaren, sonderlich den Engländern, Franzosen und Italiänern, als auch von denen, die bey uns in Deutschland herauskommen.[29]
>
> [Our aim is to promote *belles lettres* and good taste among the Germans; and we shall spare no effort which promises to serve this end. We therefore intend to supply everything that – whether taken from foreign sources or, especially, also from German ones – seems conducive to enlarging our knowledge of history and enhancing the *beaux arts*. [...] To accomplish the intended purpose, we shall furnish information on all books pertaining to the *belles lettres*, both those published by our neighbours, especially the English, French and Italians, and those published here in Germany.]

After Weiße took over editorship in 1759, he restructured the standard issue of the journal. The section dedicated to 'Vermischte Nachrichten' [miscellaneous news] at the end of each issue, which reported news on European art, music and literature, grew from between five and eight pages in the previous issues to between forty and fifty in the new ones; starting with volume 7.2 (1762), Weiße also introduced the subsections of 'Aus Engelland' [From England], 'Aus Frankreich' [From France], etc. In volume 12 he announced that from 1765 onwards the journal would be continued as the *Neue Bibliothek der schönen Wissenschaften und der freyen Künste*. Over the years the journal's focus on the arts increased, but it also remained an important venue for the publication of reviews of English, French and Italian works.[30]

As Weiße explains in his autobiography, the financial rewards in editing the journal were slim at best.[31] What the *Bibliothek* offered were primarily networking opportunities. The recurring contributors over the following decades, usually personal friends of Weiße's, included many of the leading literary and intellectual lights of the period: Christian Garve, Heinrich Wilhelm von Gerstenberg, Christian Ludwig von Hagedorn, Moses Mendelssohn, Rudolf Erich Raspe, Moritz August von Thümmel and Johann Joachim Winckelmann, to name but a few. What the editorship of a journal

29 Anon., 'Vorläufige Nachricht', *BSWFK*, 1.1 (1757), 4–5.

30 Anneliese Klingenberg, 'Die "Neue Bibliothek der schönen Wissenschaften und der freyen Künste" – Programm für eine europäische République des Lettres', in *Sächsische Aufklärung*, ed. by Klingenberg and others, pp. 173–96 (p. 178).

31 Weiße, *Selbstbiographie*, p. 81.

with an established focus on foreign art and literature also allowed Weiße to do was actively to shape the intercultural transfer that was so characteristic of the German Enlightenment. The engagement with British culture once more took centre stage in this process. As Klaus Rek observes, the reception of British culture in the *Bibliothek* performed a key function in the conception of the Enlightenment realized by the journal. For example, the *Bibliothek* reviewed more English books than works in any other foreign language.[32]

The reviews of English books in the journal have attracted a great deal of critical attention based on the fact that a great many of them are unacknowledged translations. This is first observed by Charles Paul Giessing in 1918, who notes that many of the reviews were free translations of reviews printed in the *Monthly Review*: Weiße would 'read whatever the *Monthly Review* had to say, pick out words, phrases, and whole sentences, add a little material of his own, and finally wind up with a quotation'.[33] Richard Wilkie's more elaborate investigation in 1955 demonstrates that of the 823 notices and reviews of English books which appeared in the 'Miscellaneous News' section of the *Bibliothek* during Weiße's time as editor, 492 were based on texts in the *Critical Review*, 247 could be traced to the *Monthly Review* and seventeen were based on both.[34] As Wilkie notes, the practice was fairly common in German journals and despite the stigma of plagiarism had a positive effect, especially 'when one considers the large number of English and French books which Weiße brought to the attention of his countrymen, usually within a year of their publication'.[35] All this notwithstanding, the reviews have not been included in the bibliography of Weiße's translations at the end of this volume, mainly because there is no definite proof that the editor himself saw to the translation of these reviews.[36] Nevertheless, the

32 Klaus Rek, 'Englandrezeption und Aufklärungskonzeption in der "Neuen Bibliothek der schönen Wissenschaften und der freyen Künste"', in *Sächsische Aufklärung*, ed. by Klingenberg and others, pp. 197–210 (pp. 197, 202).

33 Charles Paul Giessing, 'The Plagiarized Book Reviews of C. F. Weisse in the "Bibliothek der schönen Wissenschaften"', *Modern Philology*, 16 (1918), 77–88 (p. 85).

34 Wilkie, 'Weisse's Borrowings', p. 3. A complete list of these borrowings can be found in Appendix II of Wilkie, 'Christian Felix Weisze'.

35 Wilkie, 'Weisse's Borrowings', p. 7.

36 A similar case is a review of Wieland's translation of Shakespeare published in the journal in 1763, which has attracted some attention in the context of the German reception of Shakespeare (review of William Shakespeare, *Theatralische*

'borrowings' exemplify one form of cultural transfer which, as a broader phenomenon, has received little scholarly attention.

The plagiarized book reviews were not the only significant engagement with British (and other foreign) literature and art in Weiße's (*Neue*) *Bibliothek*, of course. Under his editorship, the interest which the journal took in European art increased continually. It devoted a singular amount of space to reviews and notices of newly published prints from England, France and Italy and had a reputation for being a reliable catalogue.[37] More pertinent to his work as a translator, Weiße continued the practice established by Nicolai of opening volumes with long art-historical or literary-theoretical treatises translated from the English, French or Italian. For instance, with the help of Adam Friedrich Oeser, Weiße himself translated Joshua Reynolds's *Discourses* (*Reden* [49]), the annual lectures delivered by Reynolds as President of the Royal Academy. Between 1773 and 1788 eight of these lectures were published in the *Neue Bibliothek*, with five of them as the opening texts of the volume in which they appeared (a practice which continued after Weiße had relinquished control of the journal in the early 1780s). Similarly, Weiße translated William Haley's *Poetical Epistle to an Eminent Painter*, a long poem dedicated to George Romney, which was published

Werke, I, trans. by Christoph Martin Wieland, *BSWFK*, 9 (1763), 257–70). In the review the translation, which had simultaneously elicited harsh criticism of Wieland and wild enthusiasm for Shakespeare, was attacked for its many weaknesses (Münzberg, *Die Darstellungsfunktion*, p. 301). Largely based on Weiße's role as editor, some have attributed the review to him (e.g. Minor, *Christian Felix Weiße*, p. 314, n. 2). However, it seems at least equally likely that it was the work of another frequent contributor, Johann Nicolaus Meinhard (Hüttemann, *Christian Felix Weiße*, p. 64, based partly on the authority of Johann Joachim Eschenburg, *Ueber W. Shakspeare* (Zürich: Orell, Geßner, Füßli, 1787), p. 506, n. 1); cf. also F. W. Meisnest, 'Wieland's Translation of Shakespeare', *Modern Language Review*, 9 (1914), 12–40 (p. 14, n. 3).

37 Timothy Clayton, 'Reviews of English Art in the Neue Bibliothek', in *Sächsische Aufklärung*, ed. by Klingenberg and others, pp. 231–37; cf. Anneliese Klingenberg, 'Sächsische Aufklärung und europäische "République des Lettres" – die "Neue Bibliothek der schönen Wissenschaften und der freyen Künste"', in *Christian Felix Weiße und die Leipziger Aufklärung*, ed. by Katrin Löffler and Ludwig Stockinger, pp. 9–30 (pp. 17–18). Helmut Peitsch, in his survey of reviews of English travel accounts in the *Neue Bibliothek*, has suggested that the way in which the journal prefers 'picturesque' travel accounts for its reviews is connected to the focus on English engravings (Helmut Peitsch, 'Englische Reisebeschreibungen in der *Neuen Bibliothek der schönen Wissenschaften und der freyen Künste*', *Internationales Archiv für Sozialgeschichte der deutschen Literatur*, 31 (2006), 1–50 (especially pp. 14–29)).

in two parts in the *Neue Bibliothek* (*Gedichte über die Malerey* [28]). With subjects ranging from style in painting or taste in art to the imitation of nature, these texts were not only further illustrations of the exceptional interest taken in contemporary art by Weiße and his journal: with their publication Weiße also assumed an important role in introducing German readers to the thoughts of some of the leading English painters and art theorists of the eighteenth century.[38]

As this brief examination of Weiße's editorship of the *Bibliothek* has already shown, from the point at which he became responsible for the journal in 1759, in many ways this position intersected with his work as a translator. As we shall see, his intimate (and early) knowledge of the latest publications advertised and reviewed in the *Critical* and *Monthly Review*, as well as the connections with which the position as editor of the *Bibliothek* equipped him, would give him a competitive advantage both as a translator and as an entrepreneur of translations, particularly during the 1760s and 1770s.

38 It should be noted that besides its primary interest in art and literature, the intercultural information offered by the journal could refer to far more obscure areas and pursuits – in fact, whatever piqued its authors' and editor's interest. To name a particularly obscure example: Raspe, having met Benjamin Franklin during the latter's visit to Germany in 1766, would publish an article on Franklin's glass armonica in the *Neue Bibliothek* (Rudolf Erich Raspe, 'Beschreibung der Armonica des Hrn. Franklins', *NBSWFK*, 4.1 (1767), 116–27). See, e.g., Robert L. Kahn, 'Three Franklin-Raspe Letters', *Proceedings of the American Philosophical Society*, 99 (1955), 397–400.

3. Early Translations of Poetry

Alongside his translations for the theatre Weiße produced numerous translations and adaptations of classical and modern poetry throughout the 1750s and 1760s, the first extensive selection of which was printed in the third edition of his collection *Scherzhafte Lieder* in 1763.[1] In terms of Weiße's role in the emergence of the professional translator and his contribution to cultural transfer in the Enlightenment, his mostly minor translations of poetry might not be particularly significant; yet because the classically-educated Weiße always held his poetic production – including the translations – in higher regard than most other parts of his oeuvre, he frequently went back and revised his translations of poetry, sometimes even embracing the possibility of variant translations of the same text. Therefore, a brief survey of his early poetic translations and their later revisions provides a rare opportunity to see how these reworkings reflect Weiße's development both as a poet and a translator.

A reflection of both his education and the literary models of the German Enlightenment, almost half the translations contained in the third edition of *Scherzhafte Lieder* are classical in origin – Homer, Horace and Martial. For the most part these are adaptations rather than translations in the narrow sense. Because they are significant only within the context of Weiße's own body of work, and because the present study focuses on translations from the modern languages, they are surveyed only briefly here. First, Weiße adapts a short passage from Book 6 of Homer's *Iliad* which tells the story of how Lykourgos once attacked Dionysos and his followers and was struck with blindness as divine retribution. Weiße frames it as a 'Romance' ('Romanze. Der bestrafte Verächter des Weins' [86]). In keeping with the overall theme of the collection, the passage is entertainingly

1 C. F. Weiße, *Scherzhafte Lieder*, 3rd edn (Leipzig: Weidmanns Erben und Reich, 1763 [1758]).

didactic, but for his ballad-style adaptation Weiße chooses a folk-tale tone which seems a poor match for the original. A footnote mentions Alexander Pope's translation of the *Iliad* and it seems likely that the latter provided the immediate inspiration for Weiße's rendering of the passage.[2] At the same time Weiße significantly embellishes the story: while it comprises barely a dozen lines in the original and fourteen in Pope's translation, Weiße's adaptation is no less than seventeen quatrains long.

The extensive translations from Horace's odes are presented as an appendix under the heading of 'Imitations and Translations' ('Nachahmungen und Uebersetzungen' [87]) and are, indeed, often rather free renderings of the selected passages. As Weiße wrote to his friend and colleague Karl Wilhelm Ramler, 'Ich bin mit dem Horatz sehr verwegen umgegangen, u. habe ihm oft Gedanken angedichtet, die er nicht gehabt: deswegen aber wollte ich sie auch lieber Nachahmungen, als Übersetzungen genannt wissen' [I have dealt very boldly with the Horace and often ascribed to him ideas which he did not have; this is why I would like them to be called adaptations rather than translations].[3] Walther Killy, who has analysed Weiße's version of the Fifth Horatian Ode, harshly but aptly characterizes it as a 'domesticated', 'verbose' and 'one-dimensional' adaptation which turns an accomplished love poem into a simple 'song' within eighteenth-century conventions.[4] Thus, 'Auf ein untreues Mägdchen' transposes the poem not only into a different style, but into an altogether different romantic situation. A few lines from the original along with Weiße's rendering and a modern English translation by Niall Rudd will suffice to illustrate this shift:

> Quis multa gracilis te puer in rosa
> perfusus liquidis urget odoribus
> grato, Pyrrha, sub antro?
> cui flavam religas comam,
> simplex munditiis? (ll. 1–5)

2 Weiße, *Scherzhafte Lieder*, p. 217.

3 C. F. Weiße, Letter to K. W. Ramler, *c.* April 1763 (GSA 75/229,1 (5)).

4 Walther Killy, 'Über den deutschen Horaz', in *Geschichte des Textverständnisses am Beispiel von Pindar und Horaz. Vorträge gehalten anläßlich des 6. Wolfenbütteler Symposions vom 18. bis 22. September 1978 in der Herzog-August-Bibliothek*, ed. by Walther Killy, Wolfenbütteler Forschungen, 12 (München: Kraus, 1981), pp. 243–59 (pp. 248–49). Killy's analysis is based on a reprint from 1778 which has almost exactly the same text as the 1763 version.

[To a Flirt
Pyrrha, what slender youngster, soaked with perfume, holds you in his arms, lying on a heap of roses in a delightful grotto? For whom are you tying up your flaxen hair, so simple, so elegant?][5]

Welch schöner Jüngling salbet sich
Mit süßen Salben itzt für dich,
Um dir auf Lilien und Rosen
Aufs neue liebzukosen?

Für wen läßt du dein blondes Haar
Nachlässig schön, doch voll Gefahr
Und sicher, ohne Schmuck zu siegen,
Um weiße Schultern fliegen. – (ll. 1–8)[6]

When the adaptations of Homer and Horace were reprinted in Weiße's three-volume collected poems (*Kleine lyrische Gedichte*) in 1772, the revisions were mostly negligible.[7] The contrast is provided by his variant translations of classical poetry. The first consists of two different translations of no. 47 ('Vitam quae faciant beatiorem') from Book 10 of Martial's epigrams ('Aus dem Martial' [88]), one a rather literal translation, the other a freer rendering. The latter suffers from the same weaknesses as the Homeric and Horatian adaptations – evidently, combining his own poetic style with the classical subject matter did not come easily to Weiße – but the former is still readable. Of course, even the literal translations still impose new formal features on the poem, for instance, the simple rhyme, which is particularly prevalent in his classical translations. The second example was printed as part of a review by Weiße of Christian August Clodius's *Versuche aus der Litteratur und Moral* in Weiße's *Bibliothek*. Appalled by the choice of translations of Sappho's poetry which Clodius cites, Weiße provides two translations of Fragment 31 ('Fragment einer Ode' [89]): again, one that is relatively literal (though marred by the rigid iambic tetrameter that Weiße applies); one less faithful to the original wording, but which maintains the original metre. The former, which we have to consider the more successful, was reprinted in the *Anthologie der Deutschen* in 1771, though it could not be determined whether Weiße had a hand in that selection.

5 Horace, *Odes and Epodes*, ed. and trans. by Niall Rudd, Loeb Classical Library, 33 (Cambridge, MA: Harvard University Press, 2004), pp. 34–35.

6 Weiße, *Scherzhafte Lieder*, p. 170.

7 C. F. Weiße, *Kleine lyrische Gedichte* (Leipzig: Weidmanns Erben und Reich, 1772 [87]).

The last classical translation to be mentioned here, albeit briefly, is the highly popular rendering of Tyrtaeus's *Πόλεμιστηρια* (*Kriegslieder* [*War Songs*] [90]), which Weiße began during his stay in Gotha in 1761 and first published in the second edition of his standalone volume of poetry, *Amazonen-Lieder*.[8] Despite the rigid formal frame which Weiße once more chooses (iambic verse with alternate rhyme), he is more successful in matching the heroic tone of the original. Not only was the translation reprinted multiple times; published in 1762, towards the end of the Seven Years' War, it had a topicality that certainly contributed to its success. In a review of the *Amazonen-Lieder*, Nicolai singles this translation out for comment, since it is 'so getreu[] als glücklich[]' [as faithful as it is successful] and lauds a particular 'Stück das man beinahe ohne Aenderung in diesem Kriege dem Preußischen Heere, zuruffen könte' [passage which, in the current war, one could recite to the Prussian Army with barely any alterations].[9] A look at two of Weiße's quatrains demonstrates what Nicolai refers to; for the sake of comparison, a modern English translation by Douglas Gerber is printed alongside the original:

ἀλλ᾽, Ἡρακλῆος γὰρ ἀνικήτου γένος ἐστέ,
θαρσεῖτ᾽· – οὔπω Ζεὺς αὐχένα λοξὸν ἔχει –
μηδ᾽ ἀνδρῶν πληθὺν δειμαίνετε, μηδὲ φοβεῖσθε,
ἰθὺς δ᾽ ἐς προμάχους ἀσπίδ᾽ ἀνὴρ ἐχέτω,
ἐχθρὴν μὲν ψυχὴν θέμενος, θανάτου δὲ μελαίνας
κῆρας <ὁμῶς> αὐγαῖς ἠελίοιο φίλας.

[Come, take courage, for your stock is from unconquered
Heracles – not yet does Zeus hold his neck
aslant – and do not fear throngs of men or run in
flight, but let a man hold his shield straight toward
the front ranks, despising life and loving the black
death-spirits no less than the rays of the sun.][10]

Stammt Ihr von dem Alcides nicht,
Ein unbesiegt Geschlecht?

8 C. F. Weiße, *Amazonen-Lieder* (Leipzig: Weidmanns Erben und Reich, 1762), pp. 153–80; cf. Weiße, *Selbstbiographie*, p. 85.

9 Friedrich Nicolai, review of C. F. Weiße, *Amazonen-Lieder*, 2nd edn [1762], *Briefe, die neueste Litteratur betreffend*, 17 (1764), 3–16 (p. 11). Nicolai also recommends that the Greek text be printed alongside the German, a suggestion which Weiße would adopt in later editions of the translation.

10 *Greek Elegiac Poetry*, ed. and trans. by Douglas E. Gerber, Loeb Classical Library, 258 (Cambridge, MA: Harvard University Press, 1999), p. 54.

Noch gönnt Euch Zeus sein Angesicht,
Traut auf ein göttliches Recht!

Was ist die Menge, die Euch droht?
Erzittert nicht vor ihr!
Ergreift den Schild, und sucht den Tod
Und kämft voll Ruhmbegier.

Ist Euch das Leben nicht verhaßt?[11]

While Weiße obviously adopts a tone more suited to eighteenth-century sensibilities, he matches the rousing tone of the original in his concise and, above all, noticeably singable rendering – one of his great talents as a translator (as well as a poet and playwright, of course) and one which we shall encounter again in this study.

The second significant group of translated poems contained in the third edition of *Scherzhafte Lieder* (1763) are translations from the English.[12] Weiße groups together three odes: William Congreve's 'Hymn to Harmony' (1701) (Ode auf die Harmonie [13]); John Dryden's 'Alexander's Feast' (1697) (Alexanders-Fest [17]), now best known for the musical adaptation by Händel; and Alexander Pope's 'Ode for Musick' (1708) (Ode auf die Musik [48]). The precise rationale for this combination could not be determined, but the three odes are united by a common theme – music – and both Congreve's and Pope's poems were written for St Cecilia's Day.[13] All three texts were later revised by Weiße and republished in his *Kleine lyrische Gedichte* (1772). The revisions demonstrate not only how much Weiße's understanding of the original English poems had evolved, but also how his ability adequately to render them in German had grown. The first stanza of the translation of Congreve's 'Hymn to Harmony' will serve as an example.

In many passages, the version from 1772 appears more concise and to the point than the original translation. In this first stanza the phrasing 'es schallen unsre Lieder, | Von deiner Macht, die wir erflehen, wieder!' is less verbose and more poignant than the earlier

11 Weiße, *Amazonen-Lieder*, pp. 169–70.

12 The collection also contains a translation from the French, Jean-Baptiste Rousseau's cantata *Cephale* (*Cephalus und Aurore* [80]), which is not looked at here because at the time Weiße's engagement with French literature was focused on the theatre.

13 Cf. Price, who notes that 'Pope's "Ode on St. Cecilia's Day" received attention in Germany chiefly as a companion piece to Dryden's "Alexander's Feast"' (Price, *English Literature*, p. 71).

Table 1 Weiße's Translations of Congreve's 'Hymn to Harmony'

Original 'A Hymn to Harmony, written in Honour of St Cecilia's Day' (1701)[a]	1763 Version 'Ode auf die Harmonie, an eben dem Feste'	1772 Version 'Ode auf die Harmonie, an eben dem Feste'
O Harmony, to thee we sing, To thee the grateful tribute bring Of sacred verse, and sweet resounding lays; Thy aid invoking while thy pow'r we praise.	O Harmonie! wir singen Dir! In heilgen Tönen bringen wir Dir unsers Dankes Zoll! es schallen unsre Lieder, Indem wir Dich um Hülfe flehn, von Deinem Lobe wieder!	O Harmonie! wir singen Dir! In heilgen Tönen bringen wir Dir unsers Dankes Zoll! es schallen unsre Lieder, Von deiner Macht, die wir erflehen, wieder!
All Hail to thee All-pow'rful Harmony! Wise Nature owns thy undisputed sway, Her wond'rous Works resigning to thy care: The planetary orbs thy rule obey,	Dir singen wir Allmächtge Harmonie! Heil Dir! Die Weisheit der Natur erkennet Deine Stärke, Und Deiner Sorgen Theil sind ihre großen Werke: Planeten rollen hier auf auf [*sic*] Dein erschallend Wort	Dir singen wir Allmächt'ge Harmonie! Heil Dir! Dein mächtiges Gebot erkennet die Natur, In seiner ganzen Stärke: Und folgsam überläßt sie Deiner Sorge nur Hier ihre wundervollen Werke. Planeten rollen schnell auf Dein erschallend Wort
And tuneful roll, unerring in their way, Thy voice informing each melodious Sphere.	In angewießnen Bahnen fort! So bald sie Deine Stimme hören, Ertönen weit umher die Sphären.	In angewiesnen Bahnen fort. Melodisch tönen alle Sphären, So bald sie Deine Stimme hören

[a] Since Weiße's source for the original could not be determined, a contemporary collection of Congreve's poems is cited here: 'A Hymn to Harmony, written in Honour of St Cecilia's Day', in *Poems Upon Several Occasions* (Glasgow: Foulis, 1752), pp. 51–56.

'es schallen unsre Lieder, | Indem wir Dich um Hülfe flehn, von Deinem Lobe wieder!'. Weiße's decision to make the 'Lieder' the core of this phrase in both versions already shows he is not wedded to the original syntax; it avoids the problem of having to find a German match for Congreve's participle ('invoking') where the German grammatical equivalent would seem uncommon. In lines 7–8 ('Wise Nature owns thy undisputed sway, | Her wond'rous Works resigning to thy care') Weiße's initial translation – 'Die Weisheit der Natur erkennet Deine Stärke, | Und Deiner Sorgen Theil sind ihre großen Werke' – manages to keep to the number of lines but is also syntactically baffling and ambiguous to boot. The revised version needs four lines to produce clarity:

> Dein mächtiges Gebot erkennet die Natur,
> In seiner ganzen Stärke:
> Und folgsam überläßt sie Deiner Sorge nur
> Hier ihre wundervollen Werke. (ll. 7–10)

Despite its length, this translation expresses the sentiment of the original far more clearly and unambiguously. In numerous passages such as these, the 1772 version demonstrates Weiße's progress as a translator from English.

While Weiße's translation of Dryden's popular ode 'Alexander's Feast' saw fewer revisions between the versions published in 1763 and 1772, it offers a rare opportunity for comparison with another contemporary translation. In an act of remarkable literary parallelism, the above-mentioned Ramler published his own revised translation of the ode in a collection of his poetry also called *Kleine lyrische Gedichte*.[14] However, a comparison between the respective first stanzas of their 1772 versions shows that the similarities do not extend beyond this.

The most notable difference between the two versions is that, unlike Weiße, Ramler does not attempt to reproduce the rhyme scheme of the original. Although both maintain the iambic metre of the original, they take different liberties with the text. While Weiße extends the refrain – his 'Nur der Held ists! Er allein!' is a much

14 John Dryden, 'Alexanders Fest, oder Die Gewalt der Musik', in Karl Wilhelm Ramler, *Kleine lyrische Gedichte* (Berlin: Voss, 1772), pp. 303–16. Earlier translations of the ode by Ramler had been published separately in 1766 (Berlin: n. pub.) and 1770 (Berlin: Voß). There is some evidence that Weiße and Ramler took inspiration from each other's translations at various points between 1763 and 1772, but an investigation into this would go beyond the limits of the present study.

Table 2 Weiße and Ramler's Translations of Dryden's 'Alexander's Feast'

1697 Original 'Alexander's Feast; or, The Power of Musique'[a]	Weiße's 1772 Version 'Alexanders-Fest, oder Die Gewalt der Musik'	Ramler's 1772 Version 'Alexanders Fest, oder Die Gewalt der Musik'
'T was at the royal feast, for Persia won By Philip's warlike son: Aloft in awful state The godlike hero sate On his imperial throne; His valiant peers were plac'd around; Their brows with roses and with myrtles bound: (So should desert in arms be crown'd.) The lovely Thais, by his side, Sate like a blooming Eastern bride In flow'r of youth and beauty's pride. Happy, happy, happy pair! None but the brave, None but the brave, None but the brave deserves the fair.	Am königlichen Fest, als Philipps kriegerischer Sohn Der Perser Reich an sich gebracht, Saß hoch, den Göttern gleich an Macht, Der Held in feyerlicher Pracht Auf seinem furchtbar'n Thron: Die Feldherrn saßen um Ihn her Mit Ros' und Myrth' umkränzt wie Er, Ein würd'ger Schmuck für solch ein Helden-Heer! Die Thais blüht' an seiner Seite: An Jugend Glanz, an Schönheit wich ihr heute, Die Schönste morgenländ'scher Bräute. Glücklich! Glücklich! Glücklich Paar! Nur der Held ists! Er allein! Nur der Held ists! Er allein! Nur der Held ists! Er allein! Der der Schönen würdig war!	Am königlichen Fest, als Persis fiel Durch Philipps tapfern Sohn, Sass hoch, in stolzem Pomp, Der göttergleiche Held Auf seinem furchtbarn Thron: Der Feldherrn Trupp rund um ihn her, Im Haare Rosen, Myrten um den Schlaf, (Der Sieger Haupt verdient den Kranz!) Die holde Thais neben ihm, Des Aufgangs bluhmengleiche Braut, Wie Hebe jung, wie Hebe schön. Selig, selig, selig Paar! Nur unser Held, Nur unser Held, Nur unser Held Verdient die Braut.

[a] Again, Weiße's source for the original text could not be determined: the edition of *The Works of Dryden* which he owned was published two years prior to the first publication of the ode (see *Verzeichniß der Bibliothek*, 3033–3035). Therefore, the first edition of John Dryden's *Alexander's Feast* (London: Tonson, 1697) is cited here.

less straightforward translation of Dryden's 'None but the brave' than is Ramler's 'Nur unser Held' – Ramler replaces the original description of Thais as '[i]n flow'r of youth and beauty's pride' with a more specific reference to the goddess Hebe. Weiße's rendering of 'blooming' as 'blüht' might be a slightly better match than Ramler's 'bluhmengleich[]'; and 'morgendländ'sch[]' is certainly a better translation of 'Eastern' than Ramler's stilted 'Des Aufgangs', yet Ramler, on the other hand, manages to be more economical when Weiße's version once more seems unnecessarily verbose in parts. Overall, the two versions seem about equally accomplished. As has been mentioned before, Weiße's early translations of poetry are but a minor part of his body of work; nevertheless, his ability to produce a version of this ode which is on a par with that by the famed 'Deutscher Horaz' [German Horace], Ramler, speaks for his development as both a poet and a translator.[15] Unlike his 'imitations' of classical poetry, Weiße's German renderings of Congreve, Dryden and Pope have the character of genuine translations. In terms of impact on the literary world, however, Weiße's most significant project in the realm of foreign poetry revolved around Ossian and 'Bardic' poetry, the German reception of which he came to shape considerably, as discussed in Chapter 5.

15 For a critical survey of this contemporary trope, cf. Alexander Košenina, 'Ein deutscher Horaz? Karl Wilhelm Ramler in der zeitgenössischen Rezeption', in *Urbanität als Aufklärung. Karl Wilhelm Ramler und die Kultur des 18. Jahrhunderts*, ed. by Laurenz Lütteken, Ute Pott and Carsten Zelle (Göttingen: Wallstein, 2003), pp. 129–52. Weiße himself was certainly aware of the epithet: see, e.g., his mention of Ramler as 'unser deutscher Horaz' [our German Horace] in a letter to Benedict Maria von Werkmeister, 30 April 1774 (C. F. Weiße, 'Briefe des Herrn Kreissteuer-Einnehmers Christian Felix Weisse in Leipzig an Benedict Maria von Werkmeister', *Jahrschrift für Theologie und Kirchenrecht der Katholiken*, 6 (1824), 276–303 (p. 277)).

4. Professionalization: Weiße at Weidmann's

After his return from Paris in 1760 Weiße's professional situation changed. In 1762 he took office as *Kreissteuereinnehmer* [District Tax Collector] in Leipzig, a post which would remain his main occupation to the end of his life. In the course of his induction he also met Christian Ludwig von Hagedorn (1712–1780), soon-to-be Director of the Saxon Academy of Arts in Dresden, who would become one of his most important correspondents and collaborators. Most importantly for his career as a translator, however, this is the period in which a singular co-operation between Weiße and his Leipzig-based publisher, Philipp Erasmus Reich, begins. More than any other factor, it would shape the emergence of Weiße as a professional and highly prolific translator – and, in turn, Weiße's contribution would have a profound impact on the catalogue of the firm of Weidmanns Erben und Reich.

Philipp Erasmus Reich and Translation in the Eighteenth Century

If we assume that, as Mark Lehmstedt suggests in his study of the firm of Weidmann's, the evolution in the eighteenth century of structurally new conditions of production, distribution, communication and reception in the book trade and publishing industry was essential for the formation and development of the German Enlightenment, then Philipp Erasmus Reich was definitely a major figure in this Enlightenment.[1] Were it not for the fact that the list of authors published by him reads like a *Who's Who* of the German, English and

1 Mark Lehmstedt, 'Struktur und Arbeitsweise eines Verlages der Deutschen Aufklärung. Die Weidmannsche Buchhandlung in Leipzig unter der Leitung von Philipp Erasmus Reich zwischen 1745 und 1787' (unpublished doctoral thesis, Karl-Marx-University, Leipzig, 1990), p. 1.

French Enlightenment in the second half of the century, his reforms of the book industry alone would have secured him that status.[2]

Having learnt the bookseller's trade in Frankfurt, Reich joined the Weidmannsche Buchhandlung in Leipzig in 1744, the year before Weiße enrolled at the university.[3] Founded in Frankfurt in 1680 by Moritz Georg Weidmann Senior, the business had been based in Leipzig since 1682 or 1683. Weidmann's son of the same name, who was at the helm of the firm between 1717 and 1743, rose to become a prominent bookseller and prolific publisher with outstanding regional and international contacts. After his death, Reich became chief executive of the business in 1745, employed by the widow Weidmann. From 1759 onwards, the firm published the catalogues of the Leipzig book fairs, a highly profitable enterprise. During the Seven Years' War Reich pushed for higher prices for books published in Saxony to combat war-induced inflation and secured not only the survival of the firm but also its continuing growth. Consequently, in 1762 the proprietor Johanna Marie Weidmann made Reich a co-owner of the business, which henceforth (until Reich's death in 1787) traded under the name of 'Weidmanns Erben und Reich'.

After the war Reich continued to be a force for reform in the German book trade. In 1764 he and the other Leipzig-based publisher-booksellers attended the Frankfurt fair for the last time, marking the final step in Leipzig's ascendancy to being the capital of the German book trade.[4] The following year Reich founded a German booksellers' association (*Buchhandlungsgesellschaft*) in Leipzig, of which he became secretary and which became a significant political lobbying force on behalf of the industry.[5] In this role Reich also led the fight against unauthorized reprints in an age when copyright was still largely uncodified. A mandate issued in Saxony in 1773 would eventually guarantee a form of copyright that also barred unauthorized reprints from being traded at the Leipzig fairs.[6] Publishers who were planning a translation could enter it into a 'Bücherprotokoll' to enjoy the benefits of this law. Originally intended to protect the home

2 Lehmstedt, 'Struktur und Arbeitsweise', p. 32.

3 For all information on Reich's biography this chapter relies on Mark Lehmstedt, *Philipp Erasmus Reich (1717–1787). Verleger der Aufklärung und Reformer des deutschen Buchhandels* (Leipzig: Karl-Marx-Universität, 1989).

4 Cf. Rosenstrauch, 'Leipzig als "Centralplatz"', pp. 106–12.

5 Mark Lehmstedt, 'Die erste Buchhandlungsgesellschaft in Deutschland', *Börsenblatt*, 157.19 (1990), Beiheft, 2–12.

6 Cf. also Rosenstrauch, 'Leipzig als "Centralplatz"', p. 116.

market from reprints, this measure effectively also ensured that no retranslations could be presented in Leipzig as long as the earlier translation was still on sale, a problem we shall encounter again.[7] This did not prevent the South German and Austrian publisher-booksellers from reprinting such books – both original titles and translations – without permission: two of the leading firms in the field of such reprints, Schmieder in Carlsruhe and Trattner in Vienna, reprinted numerous of Weiße's works, for instance.

In his capacity as business director of Weidmann's, Reich became one of the most productive publishers in the second half of the century.[8] Bernhard Fabian even goes so far as to call him the 'leading publisher of the age' and in terms of his influence on the market this was certainly true.[9] In terms of languages, the portfolio of the company was broad from the beginning: under Reich, Weidmann's original publications could be in German, French or the classical languages, sometimes in co-operation with foreign publishers to whose print sheets the Weidmann title page only needed to be added.[10] While any genre might be included in its catalogue, Weidmanns Erben und Reich was characterized by a focus on prose – especially novels – and non-fiction in the arts and philosophy. The company's production in the realm of *belles lettres*, pedagogy and the arts was particularly considerable.[11] However, the most remarkable feature of Reich's work, at least in the context of the present study, was the publisher's focus on translations.

In 1754 the first major English novel Reich introduced to a German audience was Samuel Richardson's *Sir Charles Grandison*, the original of which had been published the year before. The book went through numerous editions and Weidmann's published a French translation of it as well. In 1756 Reich even travelled to England to visit Richardson and his family, on which occasion he presented the

7 Lehmstedt, *Philipp Erasmus Reich*, pp. 98–101; cf. also Willenberg, *Distribution and Übersetzung*, pp. 195 and 209–12. For a comprehensive study of Reich's reforms of the industry, see Hazel Rosenstrauch, 'Buchhandelsmanufaktur und Aufklärung. Die Reformen des Buchhändlers und Verlegers Ph. E. Reich (1717–1787). Sozialgeschichtliche Studie zur Entwicklung des literarischen Marktes', *Archiv für Geschichte des Buchwesens*, 26 (1986), 1–129.

8 Lehmstedt, *Philipp Erasmus Reich*, p. 7; 'Struktur und Arbeitsweise', p. 7.

9 Bernhard Fabian , 'Die Meßkataloge und der Import englischer Bücher nach Deutschland im achtzehnten Jahrhundert', in Fabian, *Selecta Anglicana*, pp. 141–53 (p. 148).

10 Lehmstedt, 'Struktur und Arbeitsweise', pp. 11–12.

11 Lehmstedt, 'Struktur und Arbeitsweise', pp. 13–15.

writer with a panegyric in several versions which Gellert had written and Weiße had translated into English. Weiße and Lessing's joint translation of Richardson's *Gemeinnützige Lehren der Tugend* (1757 [51]) was produced in the context of Reich's dedication to the works of Richardson.

Almost half of all titles published by Weidmanns Erben und Reich were translations from modern languages – at a time when the proportion of translations in an average German publisher's catalogue was well below ten per cent.[12] The publisher not only embraced the wave of Anglophilia that swept Germany in the second half of the century, but anticipated it.[13] This went beyond the company's successful business of importing English books. While with most German publishers the proportion between translations from the French and from the English was between 3:2 and 2:1, Reich turned this relation on its head: under his management almost two thirds of the translations published by Weidmann's were from the English and fewer than a third from the French. Thanks to the large proportion of translations in the firm's catalogue, thirty per cent of all the titles published by them were translations from the English, while those from the French accounted for only fifteen per cent of all titles. As Lehmstedt, basing his remarks on these numbers, observes, Reich began turning Weidmann's into an 'English' publishing company in the mid-1750s, well ahead of mainstream Anglophilia and at a time when the German book industry was still largely dominated by French influences.[14]

Reich's instinct for the demands of the market is illustrated by the series of novels he began publishing in the late 1750s. With a new instalment published usually every half a year for the next Leipzig book fair, the series were successful enough to be relaunched every couple of years. They included *Gesammelte Frauenzimmer-Briefe zum Unterrichte und Vergnügen* (12 vols, 1759–64); *Landbibliothek zu einem angenehmen und lehrreichen Zeitvertreibe* (30 vols, 1762–78); *Unterricht und Zeitvertreib für das schöne Geschlecht* (30 vols, 1765–76); *Sammlung*

12 Lehmstedt, 'Struktur und Arbeitsweise', p. 18.

13 A concise summary of existing research of Reich's role in the cultural transfer between Britain and Germany in the period can be found in Martin Munke, 'Philipp Erasmus Reich und die Verbreitung britischer Literatur in Deutschland. Import und Übersetzung', in *Britisch-Deutscher Literaturtransfer 1756–1832*, ed. by Lore Knapp and Eike Kronshage (Berlin/Boston, MA: de Gruyter, 2016), pp. 21–38.

14 Lehmstedt, 'Struktur und Arbeitsweise', p. 19.

vom Briefen und Geschichten (8 vols, 1776–78); and the *Lesecabinett zum Nutzen und Vergnügen* (12 vols, 1779–85).[15] The texts published through this channel were usually at the extremely popular end of the market and it is not surprising that Weiße, who translated a number of novels for several of these series, foregoes naming any of their titles in his autobiography.

As with most German publishers, Weidmann's translations from the English peaked during the 1770s.[16] By this time Reich had assembled a network of agents and contributors that spanned the European Continent and gave him a competitive edge over other German publishers when it came to acquiring foreign texts for translation. In Leipzig itself a group of writers, scholars and artists – all of whom were authors published by Weidmann's – served as editors and advisors to the publisher himself.[17] Among his German networks the Göttingen connection was particularly important because of the university's long-established links with Britain. Georg Friedrich Brandes (1719–1791), responsible for book orders at the University Library in Göttingen, provided Reich with information about new English books since the 1750s, recommended titles for translation and sent Reich copies of imported English books for which the Library had no need. So did the Library's director, Christian Gottlob Heyne (1729–1812). Internationally, Reich was particularly interested in maintaining networks in London. His agents there included Paul Henry Maty (1744–1787), a librarian at the British Museum, and Rudolf Erich Raspe (1736–1794). A former librarian at the University Library in Göttingen and the Royal Library in Hanover, and later curator of the collections of the Landgrave of Hesse-Cassel, Raspe had fled to England to escape prosecution for embezzlement at the latter institution.[18] Reich's most important contact in London was

15 Lehmstedt, 'Struktur und Arbeitsweise', p. 30.

16 Lehmstedt, 'Struktur und Arbeitsweise', p. 20.

17 Lehmstedt, 'Struktur und Arbeitsweise', pp. 89–92.

18 Willenberg, *Distribution und Übersetzung*, p. 205. For Raspe's biography see Uwe Meier, 'Raspe, Rudolf Erich', in *Neue Deutsche Biographie*, 28 vols (Berlin: Duncker & Humblot, 1953–2020), xxi (2003), 164–66. In 1785 the same Raspe published an English translation of several of the well-known, anonymous Münchhausen stories, the second edition of which (1786) was translated back into German by the poet Gottfried August Bürger. In the well-known episode featuring a postilion who is unable to sound his horn on a winter journey, only to find later that the sounds have been 'frozen' inside the horn and are released by 'thawing', Raspe mentions that the two songs which left the horn during the 'thawing entertainment' were 'The King of Prussia's March' and 'Over the

Johann Friedrich Schiller (a cousin of the poet's), who during the 1770s was a vital part of his strategy to dominate the market. Schiller, who was well-connected among the London *literati* and publishers, not only provided Reich with information on translatable new works so that Reich could immediately procure an entry for them in the 'Bücherprotokoll', but could also procure fresh print sheets of new works so that the translation could be underway before the English original had even been published. An occasional translator, Schiller was also in a unique position to secure such commissions for himself.[19]

The year of Reich's death, 1787, is also the last time imported English books were listed in Weidmann's catalogue for the fair.[20] Translations continued to play a role in the firm's catalogue, but with decreasing importance. However, during the 1760s and 1770s, at the height of their power, Weidmanns Erben und Reich dominated the German publication of translations from the English. It is, of course, no coincidence that the publisher with the highest proportion of translations from the English among their offerings should attract the period's most prolific translator from that language. As the remainder of this chapter will show, however, Weiße's work for and with Reich went far beyond the conventional relationship between translator and publisher. It seems likely that without the extraordinarily close cooperation between the two, both would have struggled to maintain their singular level of productivity.

Hill and over the Dale'. In an attempt to match the popularity of these musical references in his German translation, Bürger let his postilion play no fewer than five named pieces of music, including 'Ohne Lieb' und ohne Wein' and 'Als ich auf meiner Bleiche', songs which had originally featured in two of the musical comedies for which Weiße had provided the libretto and Johann Adam Hiller the music: the aforementioned *Der Teufel ist los* (set to music by Hiller in 1766) and *Die Jagd* (1770). Bürger's choice in his translation thus attests to the enduring popularity of these songs (Frieder von Ammon, 'Tereng! Tereng! teng! teng! Was der Postillion auf Münchhausens Posthorn geblasen hat', in *Das Phänomen Münchhausen*, ed. by Stefan Howald and Bernhard Wiebel (Kassel: Kassel University Press, 2020), pp. 110–23 (pp. 116–20)). First published in 1770, *Die Jagd* became the most successful collaboration between Weiße and Hiller and one of the most popular *Singspiele* of the eighteenth century. For a comprehensive analysis along with a look at the tradition of which the play was a part, see Jörg Krämer, *Deutschsprachiges Musiktheater im späten 18. Jahrhundert*, Studien zur deutschen Literatur, 149 (Tübingen: Niemeyer, 1998), pp. 130–201.

19 Willenberg, *Distribution und Übersetzung*, pp. 203–04; Lehmstedt, 'Struktur und Arbeitsweise', pp. 130–31.

20 Fabian, 'Die Meßkataloge', p. 152.

Weiße as a Translator for Weidmann's

We have already mentioned the two collaborative translations which Weiße and Lessing produced for Weidmann's in the 1750s: William Law's devotional treatise, the *Serious Call to a Devout and Holy Life* (translated as *Eine ernsthafte Ermunterung an alle Christen*); and the collected moral sentiments from Richardson, the *Gemeinnützige Lehren der Tugend, und der guten Sitten*. Weiße had introduced Lessing to Philipp Erasmus Reich, probably at some point in the early 1750s.[21] After Lessing had left Leipzig for Berlin in 1758, Weiße left off translating for Weidmann's for several years, even though he served as an advisor to Reich from approximately 1754 onwards.[22] It was not until 1762, the year Reich became co-owner of the firm and changed its name to 'Weidmanns Erben und Reich', that Weiße's next translation for them was published. From that point onwards, however, this publisher more than any other would serve as the venue for Weiße's work as 'the most industrious translator of his period'.[23] Of the ninety titles listed in the bibliography of Weiße's translations at the end of this book, forty-two – almost half – were published (or, in a few cases, republished) by Weidmanns Erben und Reich. Almost all of them are translations from the English.

One of the genres which was prominent both in Weidmann's catalogue and Weiße's own production as a translator were didactic titles – books on the conduct of young men and women, especially. During the 1760s almost all the titles Weiße translated for the firm belonged in this category. In 1762, the year Reich had his own name affixed to that of the firm, he published Weiße's translation of Edward Moore's *Fables for the Female Sex* (*Fabeln für das schöne Geschlecht* [40]), a collection which cloaks moral lessons in sub-par rhymes about vain panthers and monkish owls. More commonly, however, the conduct books which Weiße translated in this early phase were written by English or Scottish clergymen. These included such titles as Wetenhall Wilkes's *Letter of Genteel and Moral Advice to a Young Lady* (1740) (*Erinnerungen an ein junges Frauenzimmer* [63]), published by Weidmann's in 1763; and James Fordyce's *Sermons to Young Women* (*Predigten für junge Frauenzimmer* [18]) in 1767. Around this

21 Karl Buchner, *Aus dem Verkehr einer deutschen Buchhandlung mit ihren Schriftstellern* (Berlin: Weidmann, 1873), p. xx.

22 Lehmstedt, 'Struktur und Arbeitsweise', p. 91.

23 Wilkie, 'Christian Felix Weisze', p. 34.

time Weiße probably also began translating for the series of popular novels which Reich published, two of which originated in the 1760s.

While the growing proportion of English titles among Weidmann's catalogue in this period was linked to the rise of Anglophilia in Germany, Weiße's increasing productivity as a translator had mundane economic reasons as well. In 1763 he had married Christiana Platner (sister of the philosopher and physician Ernst Platner) and the couple would have five children: Christiana Henriette (b. 1765), Christian Ernst (b. 1766), Christian August (b. 1771, d. 1773), Carolina Sophia (b. 1774) and Juliana Dorothea (b. 1776). Weiße's earnings as a tax collector no longer sufficed to support this growing family. As he writes about the birth of their fourth child in 1774: 'In diesem Zuwachs seiner Familie und dem vermehrten Aufwande, den seine älteren Kinder verursachten, lag auch ein Grund, warum Weiße mehrere Zeit auf Übersetzungen verwendete' [This growth of his family, as well as the increased expense caused by his older children, were among the reasons Weiße devoted more time to translations].[24] The conditions under which he worked became ever more frantic, meanwhile. In a letter to Christian Ludwig von Hagedorn he mentions the translation of Fordyce's *Sermons*: 'Wie sehr schmeichelt es mir nicht, mein Theuerster Freund, daß Ihnen die Übersetzung der Frauenzimmerpredigten nicht mißfallen: Gott weiß unter was für Schmerzen und Zerstreuungen ich sie aufs Papier geworfen!' [I am so very pleased, my dear friend, that you do not disapprove of the translation of the *Sermons to Young Women*: God knows under what pains and distractions I dashed it off!].[25] The translation of titles such as Fordyce's stern admonitions to young women served to support children who, in time, might even become their target audience. That same year, Weiße also mentions this book to Karl Wilhelm Ramler, declaring that:

> H. Reich hat mir gestanden, daß er Ihnen den Übersetzer entdeckt, und ich kann mirs gefallen laßen, wenn es wahr ist, was er hinzusezt, daß Sie nicht unzufrieden damit wären: Ich muß für mein Mädchen in Zeiten sorgen, weil noch die Hand gesund ist, und sie allen möglichen Ansatz hat, ein leichtfertiges Mädchen zu werden.[26]

24 Weiße, *Selbstbiographie*, p. 181.

25 C. F. Weiße, Letter to Christian Ludwig von Hagedorn, 17 May 1767 (UBL Ms.0670u (25)).

26 C. F. Weiße, Letter to Karl Wilhelm Ramler, 25 May 1767 (GSA 75/229,1 (21)). Weiße also occasionally referred to his Muse as his 'girl', but in the context a reference to Henriette is much more likely, especially since her 'recklessness' is also mentioned in a letter to Gleim in 1766 (cited in Mai, *Christian Felix Weiße*, p. 44).

> [Herr Reich has confessed to me that he discovered the translator to you; and I can acquiesce in that if what he adds is true, namely, that you were not dissatisfied with it. I have to take care of my girl in the times when my hand still works and because she has every tendency to become a reckless girl.]

The year 1767 was also the one in which Weidmanns Erben und Reich published Weiße's *Lieder für Kinder*, a title which may be regarded as the nucleus of his career as a children's writer. From the very beginning, then, his didactic translations and original writing were closely connected.[27] Despite his enormous output Weiße seems to have maintained a balance between his professional and family life from which his image as a children's writer would eventually benefit. In another letter to Ramler in 1767 he describes his typical day as follows: 'Von früh 8. Uhr sitze ich bis abends um 6. Uhr, die Mittagsmahlzeit ausgenommen ununterbrochen auf meiner *Expedition*: dann eile ich auf Flügeln der Liebe zu meiner kleinen Familie und vergesse Witz und Welt' [From 8 in the morning to 6 in the evening I sit in my office, with the exception of the lunch break: then the wings of love carry me to my small family and I forget wit and world].[28] While it would certainly be justified to see the 1750s and early 1760s as Weiße's apprenticeship as a literary translator, his work became far more methodical over the following decade. The 1770s see Weiße's speed of translating accelerate to about two volumes a year, an extraordinary level which he was able to maintain and even surpass in the years to come – all the while continuing to write for the stage, editing the *Neue Bibliothek* and fulfilling his time-consuming (and oft-lamented) duties as tax collector.

During the 1770s the range of genres translated by Weiße for Weidmann's gradually broadens. To be sure, education and conduct books remain important. In 1778 another Fordyce is published, this time the translation of his *Addresses to Young Men* (*Reden an Jünglinge* [19]). In the same year Weiße completes the translation of a volume of essays aimed at newly married young women and containing texts by Hester Chapone, Hannah More and a Mrs. Cartwright (*Versuche mancherley Inhalts für junge Frauenzimmer* [41]). However, increasingly Weiße begins to translate essays and novels as well, especially the latter, a genre fully embraced by Reich. In the

27 Chapter 9 of the present study is devoted to Weiße's translations of children's literature.

28 C. F. Weiße, Letter to Karl Wilhelm Ramler, 12 December 1767 (GSA 75/229,1 (25)).

Figure 2 Adolf Eltzner, *Thomaskirchhof* (*c.* 1860), public domain: The 'Amtshaus' in Leipzig (centre), where Weiße's office as tax collector was located, next to St Thomas's Church

wake of Laurence Sterne and his exceptional impact on the German readership and literature, 'sentimental' literature makes up a significant fraction of Weiße's translations in the 1770s, with such titles as the *Sentimental Lucubrations* of 'Peter Pennyless' (*Empfindsame Gedanken* [43]), Samuel Pratt's comprehensive *Liberal Opinions upon Animals, Man, and Providence* (*Freymüthige Gedanken über die Thiere, den Menschen und die Fürsehung* [49]) and a collection of Sterne's own letters.[29] The most important sentimental novel translated by Weiße was the four-volume *Rambles of Mr. Frankly* (*Die Wanderungen des Herrn Frankly* [4]) by Elizabeth Bonhote, better known for her later novel *Bungay Castle*. As late as 1779, George Keate's *Sketches from Nature Taken and Coloured in a Journey to Margate*, translated by Weiße in 1780 as *Skizzen aus der Natur* [32], was influenced by the sentimental movement. All these titles are listed in Michelsen's bibliography of German translations of English imitations of Sterne and Weiße may thus be assumed to have made some impact on

29 For the influence of Sterne, see, e.g., Peter Michelsen, *Laurence Sterne und der deutsche Roman des 18. Jahrhunderts*, 2nd edn, Palaestra 232 (Göttingen: Vandenhoeck & Ruprecht, 1972 [1962]).

German *Empfindsamkeit* – though not all his translations were as successful as the English originals.[30]

On average these titles were published within a year of the original English publication; and while Weiße as a translator certainly benefited from Reich's networks, which enabled such speed, the quality of his translations sometimes suffered from this extraordinary haste and some certainly have to be grouped among the 'flood' of hastily manufactured translations so often criticized in the second half of the century. His own letters in this period are full of reference to the 'yokels' who besieged his tax office during the day, keeping him from his literary work. Weiße certainly felt the strain. For example, in a letter to Ramler written in 1778 he complains that:

> ich hatte diesen Winter so viel zu übersetzen angenommen Z. B. Courtney Melmoths freymüthige Gedanken in 3. Th. Miß Moore Abhandlungen für junge Frauenzimmer, andere kleinere Arbeiten ungerechnet, daß ich, da mich meine Krankheit beÿnahe 6. Wochen gekostet, kaum fertig werden konnte. Sie werden sagen, liebster Freund, daß ich als Übersetzer wenig Lorbeern einärndten werde, Sie haben Recht: wäre ich ledig, so hätte ich gewiß ein besserer Dichter u. größerer Gelehrter werden wollen: aber wo der Kreis der Familie sich sich [*sic*] so erweitert hat, daß die Ausgabe die Einnahme übersteigt, muß man bisweilen mehr auf Gewinnst als auf Ehre sehen.[31]

> [this winter I had taken on so many translations, e.g. Courtney Melmoth's Liberal Opinions in 3 parts, Miss Moore Essays on Various Subjects, not to mention other, smaller projects, that I could scarcely finish everything after my illness cost me nearly six weeks. You will say, my dear friend, that I shall garner few laurels as a translator and you are right: were I alone, I surely should have become a better poet and greater scholar: yet as the family circle has grown so much that expenses exceed income, one sometimes has to look for profit rather than honour.]

Weiße managed to maintain this level of output throughout the 1780s, the last years of Reich's management of Weidmann's. The educational works in this period included a volume of *Dramen zur Belehrung junger Frauenzimmer* (possibly by Elizabeth Pinchard [46]) and John Aikin's *Calendar of Nature* (*Naturkalender zum Unterrichte*

30 See Michelsen, *Laurence Sterne*, pp. 79–81.

31 C. F. Weiße, Letter to Karl Wilhelm Ramler, 25 May 1778 (GSA 75/229,4 (78)). Courtney Melmoth was a pseudonym used by the poet, dramatist and novelist Samuel Jackson Pratt (1749–1814). The work to which Weiße refers is: *Liberal Opinions, upon Animals, Man, and Providence*, 6 vols (London: Robinson & Bew, 1775–77).

und Vergnügen junger Leute [2], discussed in Chapter 9). Despite his pace Weiße occasionally seems to have taken his time with a text he enjoyed – as seems to have been the case with William Hayley's impressively wide-ranging *Philosophical, Historical, and Moral Essay on Old Maids* (*Ein philosophischer, historischer, und moralischer Versuch über die alten Jungfern* [29]), which does exactly what the title promises. Weiße added more extensive translator's notes than was his wont, explaining Hayley's literary and historical references. As soon as it was finished, he also sent copies of the translation to Ramler and Christian Garve in Breslau, explaining to Ramler that '[d]as Buch [...] mir den Sommer über, wo ich es meistens auf dem Lande übersetzt, manche angenehme Stunde gemacht [hat]' [This summer, the book, which I have translated mainly in the country, has brought me many a pleasant hour] – a rare statement from Weiße.[32] While contemporary reviewers rarely commented on the quality of a translation unless there was something with which to find fault, the anonymous reviewer for the *Allgemeine deutsche Bibliothek* commended it, saying 'An der Uebersetzung ist kein Fleiß gespart, man liest sie gern' [No industry has been spared on the translation, which we enjoyed reading].[33]

Especially the translations of multi-volume English novels which Weiße completed for Weidmann's in the 1780s, however, often attracted criticism for their linguistic 'sloppiness'. *Clare und Emmeline* (1789 [30]) by Elizabeth Helme (herself a translator of German literature), for instance, attracted a harsh review in the *Allgemeine Literatur-Zeitung*. The reviewer finds that '[d]er Uebersetzer [...] öfters zu buchstäblich übersetzt [hat]' [the translator has often translated too literally], listing a number of cases in which Weiße had failed to find idiomatic German equivalents for English expressions. For example, Weiße regularly translates the phrase 'reject somebody' as 'einen verweigern' (rather than 'abweisen'), which results in awkward sentences such as, 'Sie träumt von verweigerten Anbetern' (in the original, it is 'to dream of [...] rejected coronets').[34] Similarly,

32 C. F. Weiße, Letter to Karl Wilhelm Ramler, *c.* late 1786 (GSA 75/229,4 (100)). Cf. his letter to Christian Garve, 31 December 1786 (in Garve, *Briefe an Christian Felix Weiße*, I, 266).

33 Anon., review of William Hayley, *Ein philosophischer, moralischer und historischer Versuch über die alten Jungfern*, trans. by C. F. Weiße, *Allgemeine deutsche Bibliothek*, 75 (1787), 305–10 (p. 307).

34 Anon., review of Elizabeth Helme, *Clare und Emmeline, oder, Der mütterliche Seegen* [1789], trans. by C. F. Weiße, *Allgemeine Literatur-Zeitung*, 1.52 (1790), 414–15. Cf. Elizabeth Helme, *Clara and Emmeline*, 2 vols (London: Kearsley, 1788), I, p. 42. A more extensive discussion of such issues and their context can be found in Chapter 6.

the review of Weiße's translation of Cassandra Hawke's *Julia de Gramont* (*Julie de Gramont* [27]) in the same journal (and quite possibly by the same reviewer) lists instances of stilted expressions and unidiomatic translations, concluding that the translator both worked in haste and wrestled with the purple prose of the original.[35] While this criticism is entirely justified, it should be pointed out that it was a staple feature of reviews in an age anxious about the development of the German literary idiom, when complaints about the decline of literary standards – and those in translation – were almost a cliché. Nevertheless, the effects of the haste with which Weiße worked are visible in such instances.

A look at the numbers reveals Weiße's singular share in the publication of translations of English books by Weidmann's in the years of Reich's management.

Table 3 Weiße's translations for Weidmann's / Weidmanns Erben und Reich (from 1762) in proportion to the total number of English-to-German translations published by the company under Ph. E. Reich's management, 1747–87.[a]

	Total no. of translations		No. of translations by Weiße		Percentage	
Years	Titles	Volumes	Titles	Volumes	Titles	Volumes
1747–52	3	7	0	0	0	0
1753–57	11	20	2	2	18.2	10
1758–62	7	21	1	1	14.3	4.8
1763–67	28	49	2	2	7.1	4.1
1768–72	26	53	1	2	3.8	3.8
1773–77	58	99	4	7	6.9	7.1
1778–82	51	85	6	8	11.8	9.4
1783–87	21	60	4	9	19	15
Total	**205**	**394**	**20**	**31**	**9.8**	**7.9**

[a] Only book-length translations from the English have been included; multi-volume titles are listed in the year of the publication of the first volume. Only first editions and only securely attributable translations have been included. The numbers on Weidmann's total production of translations listed in the first column are taken from Lehmstedt, 'Struktur und Arbeitsweise', p. 18, Table 6. In order to make the numbers comparable, the segmentation into five-year intervals has also been adopted from Lehmstedt.

35 Anon., review of Cassandra Hawke, *Julie de Grammont, Eine rührende Geschichte*, trans. by C. F. Weiße, *Allgemeine Literatur-Zeitung*, 3.219 (1790), 295–96.

As this table shows, the number of volumes translated by Weiße for Weidmann's in each five-year interval grew steadily throughout the 1770s and 1780s. He was responsible for almost ten per cent of the translations from the English published by the firm during the years of Reich's management between 1747 and 1787; during the last years of his co-operation with Reich the proportion was even higher than this average. What these numbers also demonstrate is that throughout this time Weiße remained selective about the works he translated. His preference for educational works is reflected in the fact that, fairly consistently, his share of the titles among Weidmann's output remains higher than that of the actual volumes translated, meaning that despite the fact that translators were paid per print sheet, Weiße frequently picked 'slimmer' (i.e., single-volume) works rather than multi-volume popular novels.

After Reich's death in 1787 Weiße's contribution to Weidmann's catalogue decreased. As already discussed, the firm became less focused on English books, but Weiße had changed his own literary priorities as well. His cooperation with Reich had partly been based on the fact that the latter also published Weiße's original poetry. Now in his sixties, Weiße increasingly turned towards children's writing and translations of children's literature and the Leipzig publisher Crusius became a more important partner for him. Throughout the 1790s Weiße translated two more novels for Weidmann's (now again trading under its old name): Phebe Gibbes's colonial fiction *Hartly House, Calcutta* (*Hartlyhaus* [20]) and Helen Maria Williams's novel *Julia* (*Julie* [61]). Only six years after the death of Reich, Weiße's last translation for the company was Richard Cumberland's essayistic *Observer* (*Beobachter* [15]).

Weiße as Editor and Agent for Weidmann's

Weiße's role as an agent and 'entrepreneur' of the translating business is a recurring subject of this book, of course, especially in the two chapters dedicated to his networks. His close co-operation with Philipp Erasmus Reich, however, is a special case and as such deserves a separate discussion. From the 1760s at the latest, Weiße had a special place in Reich's extensive network. Mark Lehmstedt has called Reich a 'strangely inactive' publisher as far as editorial decisions were concerned, for which he often relied on the advice of others.[36] An author such as Weiße, whose editorship of the

36 Lehmstedt, 'Struktur und Arbeitsweise', pp. 89–90.

Neue Bibliothek meant that he read foreign journals and was more than commonly well-connected in the literary world, was almost predestined to become one of his agents, a kind of 'sub-contractor' even.[37] Beyond Weiße's role as an advisor on all editorial matters, a friendship evolved between the two men. Reich was wont to pay daily visits to the members of his network in Leipzig to share information.[38] Many of Weiße's letters mention the literary news their author had received that very day during Reich's latest visit. For a time Weiße and Reich even shared a house, a situation which aided communication, even though it is one of the reasons few records of their exchanges survive.[39] Perhaps the best illustration of how close they had become by the mid-1760s is provided by an incident Weiße relates in his autobiography: during the Easter Fair in 1766 one of his scribes absconded after embezzling part of the tax money that Weiße's office collected, some 2,100 Reichsthaler. Reich helped to find money to make up the losses and stood surety for Weiße until they could be repaid.[40]

Aside from being an original writer and translator published by Weidmann's, Weiße's duties there were manifold. He assessed manuscripts, suggested new titles for publication or translation, recommended translators and illustrators to Reich and negotiated on his behalf with the various agents involved in book production. As Lehmstedt points out, the fact that Reich had most of Weidmann's books printed in Leipzig meant that the task of copy-editing was also in the hands of his Leipzig-based agents – Weiße himself and Georg Joachim Zollikofer, probably Johann Joachim Schwabe and Johann Gottfried Gellius as well.[41] In this area as in many others, Weiße's activities as an agent for Weidmann's intersected with his more personal networks. To cite but one example: in 1773 his friend Ramler's translation of Batteux's influential *Cours de belles lettres*

37 Willenberg, *Distribution und Übersetzung*, p. 227.

38 Lehmstedt, 'Struktur und Arbeitsweise', pp. 94–95.

39 Weiße, *Selbstbiographie*, p. 214. Reich's epistolary exchanges with other writers and thinkers have attracted increasing attention in recent years. See, e.g., Thomas Bremer and Christine Haug, with Helga Meise, *Verlegerische Geschäftskorrespondenz im 18. Jahrhundert. Das Kommunikationsfeld zwischen Autor, Herausgeber und Verleger in der deutschsprachigen Aufklärung*, Buchwissenschaftliche Beiträge, 96 (Wiesbaden: Harrassowitz, 2018), a volume which contains several essays on the subject.

40 Weiße, *Selbstbiographie*, pp. 130–31.

41 Lehmstedt, 'Struktur und Arbeitsweise', p. 128.

(*Einleitung in die schönen Wissenschaften*) was to be substantially revised for a fourth edition published by Weidmann's (in 1756 the first edition had been an early project of Reich's at the firm). To initiate the revision, Reich wrote to Ramler directly.[42] After that, however, Weiße seems to have been in charge of the revisions. His first letter to Ramler about this business suggests that this might well have been an act of friendship, the same way as Weiße and his other fellow writers (many of whom were published elsewhere) looked over one another's texts as a courtesy: 'Die Revision bey dem Drucke Ihres neuen Batteux will ich mit Freuden hier übernehmen u. ich verspreche Ihnen auch alle mögliche Sorgfalt: Was könnte ich weniger für Sie thun?' [I will happily take over the revision of the new edition of your Batteux and I promise due diligence: surely that is the least I could do for you?].[43] A few months later Weiße suggested to Ramler that he could help to advertise the book, albeit in a capacity which had nothing to do with his work for Reich. Even though his career as a children's and educational writer would only gather pace towards the end of the 1770s, his hugely popular *Neues A, B, C Buch* (first published by Crusius in 1772) had made him a minor authority on education; and the letter to Ramler, written in January 1774, points out how much he could do to advance the book:

> Eilen Sie immer mit Ihrem Batteux. Sie wissen die grossen Veränderungen, die man itzt in Katholischen Schulen machet. Von verschiedenen Orten, namentlich Wien, Würzburg und München bin ich seit Kurzen von neu ernannten Lehrern und Direktoren angegangen worden ein Lesebuch über die schönen Wissenschaften vorzuschlagen: und was konnte ich bessers empfehlen, als meines liebsten Rammlers Batteux.[44]
>
> [Be quick with your Batteux. You know of the great changes that are now being implemented in Catholic schools. I have received enquiries from newly appointed teachers and headmasters in various places, namely Vienna, Würzburg and Munich, asking me to recommend a textbook on the *belles lettres*: and what better to recommend than my dear Ramler's Batteux?]

42 Cf. Lehmstedt, 'Struktur und Arbeitsweise', pp. 120–21.

43 C. F. Weiße, Letter to Karl Wilhem Ramler, 17 October 1773 (GSA 75/229,3 (56)). Cf. the letter dated 18 March 1774 (GSA 75/229,3 (58)), in which the progress of the revision is discussed.

44 C. F. Weiße, Letter to Karl Wilhem Ramler, 3 January 1774 (GSA 75/229,3 (57)).

In this case, as in many others, the line between Weiße's acting as an agent for Reich and as a friend and colleague of the author in question is blurred.

Meanwhile, Weiße's broader networks were also fully utilized by the publisher. His connections to France were particularly important because Reich does not seem to have had a permanent agent in Paris.[45] Like other editors of journals within Reich's environment, Weiße could be called upon to launch reviews of works published by Weidmann's.[46] The strong focus of the *Neue Bibliothek* on English literature and reviews thereof meant that Weiße had his own channels for obtaining English books that he could then propose to Reich for translation:

> Unter einigen engl. Büchern, die ich ganz neuerlich erhalten, finde ich eines, das ein Anhang zu Ihrem Magazin des Enfants abgeben könnte u. ein artges Bändchen ausmachen würde: es heißt Die Gouvernante, oder die kleine weibl. Akademie (The Governess or the little Female Academy), von der Schwester des Fieldings, die den David Simple geschrieben hat: es stehet Ihnen zubefehl wenn sie es haben wollen, geben Sie mir ein andres Büchelchen dafür.[47]
>
> [Among some English books that I recently received, there is one which might serve as an addition to your *Magazin des Enfants* [i.e., the translation of Beaumont's work of that title at Weidmann's, translated by the above-mentioned Schwabe] and which would make a nice volume: it is called The Governess or the little Female Academy, by Fielding's sister, who wrote David Simple: it is yours if you want it, just give me another little book for it.]

The book by Sarah Fielding mentioned here, for instance, was published by Weidmann's less than a year later, as *Die Hofmeisterinn, oder Die kleine Akademie für das Frauenzimmer*. Weiße by no means exclusively recommended pedagogical works to Reich, but Weidmann's strong focus on children's and 'young people's' literature was almost certainly a product of Weiße's influence.[48] Of course, his role as a mediator between the company and the literary world was not limited to translations: Weiße was responsible for many original works' finding their way to Weidmann's. In the realm

45 Lehmstedt, 'Struktur und Arbeitsweise', p. 133.

46 Lehmstedt, 'Struktur und Arbeitsweise', p. 134.

47 C. F. Weiße, Letter to Philipp Erasmus Reich, 22 November 1760 (this was written during Weiße's stay in Gotha, hence the rare correspondence by letter; cited in Lehmstedt, 'Struktur und Arbeitsweise', p. 112).

48 Lehmstedt, 'Struktur und Arbeitsweise', p. 114.

of children's literature, for example, he provided the inspiration for Johann Matthias Schröckh's four-volume *Allgemeine Weltgeschichte für Kinder* (1779–84), recommended the author to Reich and found an illustrator for the book.[49] As far as canonical reputation is concerned, the most significant original writer brought to Weidmann's by Weiße was Christoph Martin Wieland, whose *Musarion* he ensured was published there in 1768.[50] The catalogue of Weiße's library shows that he often owned multiple copies of the same book, which was probably the result of activities such as these: as the leading intermediary facilitating literary communication between Reich and his writers and translators, Weiße would have been sent more proof and presentation copies even than for his role as editor of the *Bibliothek*.[51]

Weiße had, in a way, 'inherited' his role as the literary manager to whom young writers and translators would turn for commissions and other forms of advancement from Gellert, who in turn had succeeded Gottsched in the role as the doyen of the literary establishment in Leipzig.[52] With Reich, however, he had a congenial partner in the publishing business; and Weiße's influential role at Weidmann's allowed him to distribute work among the struggling young scholars and writers – whose economic situation mirrored the one in which he had found himself when he enrolled at the university – more methodically than most professional networkers could have. There seems always to have been enough work to go around. Aside from the fact that his role as editor and agent for Reich occasionally provided additional income, it also allowed him to shape the publisher's output and to help fledgling writers and translators.[53] A great many of them were poor students at the University of Leipzig. Christian Ernst Wünsch (1744–1828), who later became a well-known natural philosopher, applied to Weiße for help in order to be able to pursue his academic career:

49 Lehmstedt, 'Struktur und Arbeitsweise', p. 105.

50 Cf. C. F. Weiße, Letter to Karl Wilhelm Ramler, 21 July 1768 (GSA 75/229,2 (30)). See also Weiße, Letter to Johann Peter Uz, 15 April 1768, cited in 'Felix Christian [*sic*] Weisse an Johann Peter Uz', *Morgenblatt für gebildete Leser*, 284 (1840), 1134–35 (p. 1135).

51 Cf. *Verzeichniß der Bibliothek*.

52 Lehmstedt, 'Struktur und Arbeitsweise', pp. 102–21.

53 Cf. Lehmstedt, 'Struktur und Arbeitsweise', pp. 138–39.

> Als ich diesen jungen Mann die vorige Woche sehr niedergeschlagen fand, drang ich in ihn, mir sein Anliegen zu sagen: u. es war nichts anders, als daß er gern itzt mit Magister geworden wäre, um sich zu habilitiren und Collegia zu lesen, aber nicht mehr als 10 rt. dazu gesammelt habe: ich suchte den andern Tag sogleich ein französisches Buch, die *Observationes* de Physique von M. Rozier zur Übersetzung für ihn auf, gieng zu Reichen und ließ mir 20 rt. darauf für ihn, die er nach und nach abarbeiten kann, vorschießen, und so war ihm und auch meinem mitleidigen Herzen geholfen.[54]
>
> [When I found this young man all downcast last week, I asked him what his wish was: and it was nothing more than that he wanted to become a *Magister* in order to acquire his habilitation and teach at the university, but he had collected no more than 10 Reichsthaler for that purpose. The following day I quickly chose a French book, the *Observationes de Physique* by M. Rozier, for him to translate; I went to Reich and had him advance me 20 Reichsthaler for him which he can work off in time and in this way I helped both him and my own compassionate heart.]

Less than a year later the first volume of Wünsch's translation was published by Weidmann's.[55]

For many a poor young writer such commissions were an important means of winning their daily bread, but the pool of supplicants consisted by no means exclusively of them. At the same time as Wünsch, a *Legationsrat* [Legation Councillor] named Albert wrote to Weiße pleading his case; Weiße sent him some money directly and then tried to obtain a commission for the unknown petitioner. Weidmann's offered a French book for translation on the condition that Weiße guarantee the quality of the translation, something which, however, he did not feel able to do; and in this case the translation never saw the light of day.[56] Seasoned authors and translators for Weidmann's knew that even when they dealt with Reich directly, Weiße was among the people who would have

54 C. F. Weiße, Letter to Christian Ludwig von Hagedorn, *c.* late 1774 (UBL Ms.0670u). Cf. also the letter dated 5 February 1775.

55 François Rozier, *Sammlung brauchbarer Abhandlungen aus des Herrn Abt Rozier Beobachtungen über die Natur und Kunst*, trans. by Christian Ernst Wünsch, 2 vols (Leipzig: Weidmanns Erben und Reich, 1775–76).

56 Cf. C. F. Weiße, Letter to Johann Peter Uz, 2 January 1775; cited in Lehmstedt, 'Struktur und Arbeitsweise', p. 104.

a say in any final decision on the publication. When Christian Garve (1742–1798), the Breslau-based philosopher who was among Weiße's most frequent correspondents, wrote to Reich in 1785 suggesting that he might translate William Mitford's monumental *History of Greece* for the firm, he characteristically added: 'Sie werden so gütig seyn mit meinen und Ihren Freunden, den Herrn Weise [*sic*] u. Zollikofer darüber zu rathschlagen, und mich alsdann, sobald es Ihre Geschäfte erlauben Ihren Entschluß [...] wissen lassen' [You will be so kind as to discuss this with your friends, Messrs. Weise [*sic*] and Zollikofer, and to let me know your decision [...] at your earliest convenience].[57]

Weiße seems to have been a favourite go-between of Reich's when persuasion was needed to initiate a project. A prime example is Guthrie and Gray's *General History of the World*, which had been published in English in twenty-six volumes between 1736 and 1765.[58] Reich had originally intended the Göttingen professor Christian Gottlob Heyne (1729–1812) to write a history of the world for Weidmann's, a commission which Heyne declined. When Guthrie and Gray's *History* was finished, Reich decided to have it translated. Weiße interceded on Heyne's behalf and soon after the latter was appointed general editor of a monumental project that would eventually become tiresome for everybody involved. Further references to it in Weiße's letters are discussed in later chapters.[59] Suffice it to say at this point that during the 1770s Weiße would spend much time spurring on the various translators, editors and authors involved in a multi-volume translation that had quickly turned into an original work of historiography. In this case, as in many others, Weiße's own literary networks could scarcely be separated from those he established in his role as editor and agent for Reich. Many of the writers he approached about projects at Weidmann's also contributed to his (*Neue*) *Bibliothek*

57 Christian Garve, Letter to Philipp Erasmus Reich, 3 April 1785; cited in Lehmstedt, 'Struktur und Arbeitsweise', p. 97.

58 For the German publication history of this fascinating project, see Marianne Heidenreich, *Christian Gottlob Heyne und die alte Geschichte*, Beiträge zur Altertumskunde, 229 (München/Leipzig: Saur, 2006), pp. 149–83; Monika Baár, 'From General History to National History: The Transformations of William Guthrie's and John Gray's *A General History of the World* (1736–1765) in Continental Europe', in *Cultural Transfer through Translation*, ed. by Stockhorst, pp. 61–82.

59 Cf. also Buchner, *Aus dem Verkehr*, p. 4.

and his various other projects. Nonetheless, his position as advisor to the leading publisher of translations from the English allowed him to influence the introduction especially of English literature to a German readership in an even more impactful way than his role as editor of a review journal did.

5. Weiße and the German Reception of Ossian

The German reception of Ossian was one of the most remarkable instances of cultural transfer between Britain and Germany in the second half of the eighteenth century.[1] In 1760 the Scottish poet James Macpherson published the *Fragments of Ancient Poetry, Collected in the Highlands of Scotland*, the first of his purported translations of the 'rediscovered' works of the mythical ancient Gaelic bard Ossian, followed by the epics *Fingal* (1761) and *Temora* (1763) and the collected *Works of Ossian* in 1765. As enthusiasm for the supposedly ancient Bardic prose poetry swept through Europe, translators set to work with astonishing zeal. It was particularly the elegiac tone of the rhythmical prose and its author's yearning for a glorious, primeval past, exemplified by the deeds of his father, the warrior Fingal, that lent itself to being linked to the emergent cultural nationalism in the German-speaking states and therefore hit a nerve with intellectuals and artists alike.[2] As Wolf Gerhard Schmidt points out, there are more translations of Ossian's poetry into German than any other language.[3] Almost as soon as these English 'translations' had been

1 For a comprehensive overview of the reception of Ossian in Germany, see Wolf Gerhard Schmidt's wide-ranging study, *'Homer des Nordens' und 'Mutter der Romantik'. James Macphersons Ossian und seine Rezeption in der deutschsprachigen Literatur*, 4 vols (Berlin: de Gruyter, 2003–04).

2 Georg-Michael Schulz, 'Ossian', in *Handbuch Sturm und Drang*, ed. by Matthias Luserke-Jaqui (Berlin/Boston, MA: de Gruyter, 2017), pp. 64–68. A similar effect could be observed in Britain: see Jeff Strabone, *Poetry and British Nationalisms in the Bardic Eighteenth Century: Imagined Antiquities*, Palgrave Studies in the Enlightenment, Romanticism and Cultures of Print (London: Palgrave Macmillan, 2018).

3 Schmidt, *'Homer des Nordens'*, II, 1133. The reception of Ossian is also remarkable for the speed of this process, which illustrates how closely interconnected the agents in the European 'Republic of Letters' had become: while, for instance, it had taken over two centuries for the poetry of Petrarch to be received all over

published, a fiercely contentious debate about the authenticity of these poems sprung up that would last for decades: Macpherson had combined the translation of authentic material with free adaptation, imitation, compilation and his own additions in the Bardic style into something the authenticity of which still proves difficult to judge.[4] Regardless of this debate, however, Ossian had a lasting impact on German literature in the second half of the eighteenth and in the early nineteenth century; until well into the latter, these works were generally and without much dispute counted among the great works of world literature, ranked alongside Shakespeare and Homer.[5] While Weiße was always critical of such excesses, he was no exception inasmuch as the poetry of Ossian as he saw it made a deep impression on him. As should be expected, he took an active (and lifelong) interest in shaping the reception of these works, both as a translator and as an editor and reviewer at the *Neue Bibliothek*.[6]

The *Bibliothek*'s Influence on the Reception of Bardic Poetry

As editor of the *Bibliothek*, Weiße was at the helm of a journal that would quickly become an important forum for the publication and review of Bardic poetry, even before the first German translations of Ossian began to be published. As Rudolf Tombo observes, the journal 'for a number of years [...] assumed a leading rôle in Ossianic criticisms and discussions'.[7] The speed with which the *Bibliothek* took notice of the above-mentioned works was remarkable. The

Europe, it took a mere two decades for Ossian's poetry to spread to the farthest corners of the Continent and to exert its influence there.

4 Schmidt, *'Homer des Nordens'*, I, 3–4.

5 Schmidt, *'Homer des Nordens'*, I, 1. In the wake of such developments, the same period saw the revaluation of Homer as an ancient 'bard' (Maike Oergel, 'Die "Verurtümlichung" Homers – ein Beispiel transnationaler Antiketransformation: Die Rezeption des Homerischen Barden in Großbritannien und Deutschland im 18. Jh.', in *Topographien der Antike in der literarischen Aufklärung*, ed. by Annika Hildebrandt, Charlotte Kurbjuhn and Steffen Martus, Publikationen zur Zeitschrift für Germanistik, n.s., 30 (Berlin: Lang, 2017), pp. 181–200.

6 Cf. Rudolf Tombo, *Ossian in Germany: Bibliography, General Survey, Ossian's Influence upon Klopstock and the Bards*, Columbia University Germanic Studies, 1 (New York: Columbia University Press, 1901), p. 79.

7 Tombo, *Ossian in Germany*, p. 79.

first German notice of *Fingal* (which may well have had Weiße as its author) appeared in the *Bibliothek* in 1762. The English edition had appeared in December 1761, even though the year stated in its title page was 1762;[8] since the notice printed in the *Bibliothek* gives 1761 as the date of publication as well, it seems that, as so often, Weiße had received notice of the book even before it had been published. The notice itself is extremely short, but its emphatic praise for the 'kühnen poetischen Ausdruck' [bold poetic expression] of the poetry anticipates the tenor of much later German criticism.[9]

In 1763 a review of *Temora* appeared in the *Bibliothek*.[10] It seems highly likely that it was written by Weiße himself. The critic praises 'die Größe und Hoheit der Gedanken, [...] das Feuer des Genies, [...] die Kraft des Ausdrucks, [...] die Kühnheit der Metapher, [...] die schnellen Uebergänge, die unwiderstehlichen Züge des Pathetischen und Zärtlichen' [the grandeur and sublimity of the ideas, [...] the flame of genius, [...] the power of expression, [...] the boldness of the metaphors, [...] the swift transitions, the irresistible tenderness and pathos throughout it all].[11] These are phrases that would reappear (sometimes almost verbatim) in Weiße's later review of the *Works of Ossian*. Another element which makes this attribution plausible is the reference to Hugh Blair's *Critical Dissertation on the Poems of Ossian*, which had been published that same year and in the popularizing of which Weiße would be instrumental. While, in this early review, he mistakenly identifies Macpherson himself as the author of the *Dissertation*, he regards both it and 'die Natur der Poesie selbst' [the nature of the poetry itself] as sufficient argument for the authenticity of these poems.[12] The controversy about the authenticity of the Ossianic prose poems which raged in Britain would become widely known in Germany after Christian Heinrich Schmid published, in the *Hamburger Unterhaltungen* in 1766, his partial translation of 'a sceptical essay' by John O'Brien, the (Catholic) Bishop of Cloyne, which had originally been published under a pseudonym in

8 Tombo, *Ossian in Germany*, p. 3, n. 1.

9 Anon., review of Ossian [James Macpherson], *Fingal, an Ancient Epic Poem*, *BSWFK*, 8 (1762), 349.

10 C. F. Weiße [?], review of Ossian [James Macpherson], *Temora, an ancient Epic Poem*, *BSWFK*, 9 (1763), 315–16.

11 Weiße [?], review of *Temora*, p. 316.

12 Weiße [?], review of *Temora*, pp. 315–16.

the *Journal des Sçavants*.[13] As far as his published comments on the matter are concerned, however, Weiße persisted in his belief in the authenticity of the texts.

Judging from the contents of his private library, Weiße seems to have paid attention to the early German translations of Ossian as well. Among other texts, he owned copies of Albrecht Wittenberg's translation of *Fingal* from 1764 and Johann Andreas Engelbrecht's translation of Macpherson's *Fragments* (*Fragmente der alten hochschottländischen Dichtkunst*), also published in 1764.[14] As his reviews and translations demonstrate, however, he mainly engaged directly with the original works. In 1766 he reviewed the edition of the *Works of Ossian* which, styled as the '3rd edition', had been published the year before.[15] The extensive review was published in two parts in successive volumes of the *Neue Bibliothek* and in some ways it can be regarded as Weiße's most important contribution to the German reception of Ossian.[16] The original edition of the *Works* was prefaced by Blair's *Dissertation*; and since he finds the authenticity of Ossian's works has been widely challenged, Weiße regards it as worth defending by citing some of Blair's thoughts and arguments (in translation, of course), which then essentially make up the whole review. By presenting excerpts from Blair which had not been published in translation before, he significantly contributes to making the former's seminal *Dissertation* known in the German literary world.[17] As in his previous review, Weiße himself argues aesthetically rather than philologically, as Wolf Gerhard Schmidt observes.[18] Commenting on the range of authorities which Blair cites for the authenticity of Ossian's poems, Weiße says: 'Wir haben

13 Price, *English Literature*, p. 125; Diarmaid Ó Catháin, 'An Irish Scholar Abroad: Bishop John O'Brien of Cloyne and the Macpherson Controversy', in *Cork. History and Society*, ed. by Patrick O'Flanagan and Cornelius G. Buttimer (Dublin: Geography Publications, 1993), pp. 499–533.

14 *Verzeichniß der Bibliothek*, 2524 and 2616.

15 Also among Weiße's books (*Verzeichniß der Bibliothek*, 3457–58).

16 [C. F. Weiße], review of [James Macpherson], *The Works of Ossian* [3rd edn, 1765], *NBSWFK*, 2.2 (1766), 245–61, continued in 3.1 (1766), 13–38; attributed to Weiße in Tombo, *Ossian in Germany*, p. 6; cf. pp. 79–80. See also [Hugh] Blair, 'Kritische Abhandlung über die Gedichte Ossians', in [James Macpherson], *Ossians und Sineds Lieder* [trans. by Michael Denis], 6 vols (Vienna: Alberti, 1791–92), III (1791), unpag. Here Denis writes in a footnote that he believes the review probably has the same author as the *Amazonenlieder*, i.e., Weiße.

17 Cf. Price, *English Literature in Germany*, p. 126.

18 Schmidt, *'Homer des Nordens'*, I, 264.

immer den größten Beweis in ihrem Charakter selbst gefunden, und sind überzeugt, daß man ohne blinde Partheylichkeit schwerlich das Gegentheil behaupten könne' [We have always regarded their character itself as the best proof for it and we believe that, unless one were blindly partisan, one could hardly claim the opposite].[19] Until well into the 1790s the *Neue Bibliothek* continued to publish reviews of Ossianic translations and Bardic poetry, as well as dissertations on the authenticity debate in both Britain and Germany. Weiße's own further contributions to the reception, however, are mainly to be found in his work as a translator.

Translations as Part of the Reception

In 1768 the Viennese Jesuit Michael Denis had published the first two volumes of his translation of the *Works of Ossian* (*Die Gedichte Ossians*).[20] The seminal translation would be immensely popular, contributing to an ever-growing demand for publications that would satisfy the Ossian-crazed German readership. Weiße, who exchanged letters with Denis, produced his own first, book-length contribution to the discourse in 1770.[21] *Von den Barden, nebst etlichen Bardenliedern* was published by Dyck in Leipzig.[22] It consists of Weiße's translation of John [*sic*] Macpherson's 'Dissertation XIV, Of the Bards' from his collection of *Critical Dissertations on* [...] *the Ancient Caledonians* (1768), to which had been added a number of so-called 'Bardenlieder', translations of poems by Thomas Gray which had been republished in an English collection that same year and fitted the overall topic of the Celts: 'Der Barde', 'Die Schwestern des Todes', 'Die Höllenfahrt des Odin' and 'Die Triumphe Owens'.[23]

While, unfortunately, it seems impossible to determine whose editorial decision it was to collect these texts in a single volume, the rather idiosyncratic choice suggests that the translator himself at least had a hand in it. At the same time, Weiße showed himself severely critical of the whole publication, calling it 'ein sehr seichtes Werkchen' [a trivial piece of work].[24] This assessment seems to have

19 Weiße, review of *The Works of Ossian*, p. 38.

20 In Weiße's library: *Verzeichniß der Bibliothek*, 2909.

21 Cf. Minor, *Christian Felix Weiße*, p. 326.

22 Bibliography of Translations [38].

23 Thomas Gray, *Poems* (London: Dodsley, 1768).

24 John Macpherson, *Von den Barden, nebst etlichen Bardenliedern, a.d.E.* (Leipig: Dyck, 1770), unpag. preface.

derived from his disappointment in the focus of Macpherson's study, which lies with the social history rather than the poetic style of the bards: 'Von den Bardentönen selbst, von der Einrichtung ihrer Gesänge, von ihrem [*sic*] Sylbenmaaßen [...] sagt er uns gar nichts' [We learn nothing of the Bardic tones themselves, of the arrangement of their songs, and their metre].[25] As to Thomas Gray's poems, the translator judges them no less harshly, writing of 'Der Barde' that '[w]ir zweifeln, daß er darinnen den wahren Bardenton getroffen' [we doubt that with this he matched the true Bardic tone].[26] All this is very much in keeping with the focus on the aesthetics of Bardic poetry that had characterized Weiße's reviews of the 1760s.

The generally increased interest in Celtic poetry and culture which came in the wake of Ossian's German reception occasioned an extensive review of Weiße's translation of *Von den Barden* in the journal *Deutsche Bibliothek der schönen Wissenschaften*. In it the anonymous reviewer not only echoes Weiße's criticism of both Macpherson's dissertation and Gray's poems, but also finds fault with one specific choice of word in the translation of the poem 'Der Barde': 'Ich weiß nicht, warum S. 60 *prow* durch Prora übersetzt ist, Vordertheil des Schiffes ist zwar etwas weitschweifig, aber warum muste ein lateinisches Wort eingemischt werden?' [I do not see why p. 60 *prow* has been translated as *prora*; front end of a ship may be a little awkward, but why did a Latin word have to be inserted?].[27] This might seem a minor point, but as the summary of contemporary discussions about translation in Chapter 1 has shown, the 'purity' of the target idiom was a bone of contention between various major theorists. As we shall see in subsequent chapters, the choice criticized here is rather characteristic of Weiße's approach. While he was by no means perfectly consistent in this, he generally preferred Germanized expressions over outright Anglicisms and Gallicisms and a certain tendency towards Latin vocabulary is one of the few features that set him apart from Bodmer and Breitinger's faction.[28]

What this choice also exemplifies is Weiße's comparative timidity when it comes to deviation from the original wording. From time to time, however, he could turn this faithfulness into a

25 Macpherson, *Von den Barden*.

26 Macpherson, *Von den Barden*.

27 Anon., review of *Von den Barden, nebst etlichen Bardenliedern*, *Deutsche Bibliothek der schönen Wissenschaften*, 4 (1770), 727.

28 More examples of Weiße's stance on the assimilation of foreign expressions are discussed at length in the following chapter.

virtue. Such was the case with his translation of John Smith's *Galic Antiquities*, published in German by Weidmanns Erben und Reich in 1781 as *Gallische Alterthümer* [56]. The preface contains one of few programmatic passages in which Weiße details his own approach to the translation of a text:

> Wenn übrigens der Uebersetzer sich sehr genau an die Worte des Originals gehalten, so hofft er dießfalls völlige Vergebung, gesetzt, daß auch ein deutsches Ohr die Metaphern und den Ausdruck zu kühn, und die Bindung der Wörter dem gewöhnlichen Gebrauch der Muttersprache nicht ganz gemäß fände. Er glaubt, daß man bey Uebersetzung eines ausländischen, und so alten Dichters nothwendig nicht bloß mit dem Gedanken, sondern hauptsächlich auch mit dem Gange der Ursprache, ihrer Natur und ihrem Umfange bekannt seyn wolle. Ossian würde nicht mehr Ossian seyn, wenn man statt der oft vorkommenden kühnen Metaphern, ihm gelindere oder unsern Sitten, unserer Lebensart und unserer Sprache gemäßere unterschieben, oder seinen fremden Gang nach dem unsrigen abmessen wollte. Der engländische Uebersetzer hat dieß in seiner Uebersetzung gethan, und sollte der deutsche diesem Muster nicht folgen?[29]
>
> [If the translator has kept closely to the wording of the original, he hopes for complete forgiveness in this regard, even if a German ear may find the expression and metaphors too bold and the collocations uncommon compared to the usual usage. He believes that the translator of such a foreign and ancient poet must be acquainted not just with the substance, but also with the flow of the source language, its character and compass as well. Ossian would no longer be Ossian were we to replace his frequently bold metaphors with such that are gentler or more agreeable to our language and way of life, or if we measured his foreign gait by our own. The English translator has acted upon this premise in his translation, and should the German one not follow his example?]

In the way it prioritizes the stylistic equivalency between original and translation over adherence to the 'gewöhnlichen Gebrauch der Muttersprache' [common usage in the mother tongue], this stance would have been considered controversial in Leipzig only a few decades earlier; and while there is little evidence that Weiße had followed developments in the theory of translation after the middle of the century and Gottsched was long dead, it marks the evolution in Weiße's approach. As we have seen, his early translations of both

29 C. F. Weiße, 'Vorrede des Uebersetzers', in John Smith, *Gallische Alterthümer oder Eine Sammlung alter Gedichte,* trans. by C. F. Weiße (Leipzig: Weidmanns Erben und Reich, 1781), unpag.

plays and poetry had tended to impose German settings and forms on the content matter of the original. Unlike with English drama, however, the 'foreignness' of the supposedly ancient Gaelic poetry of Ossian was embraced wholeheartedly by Weiße, as by many other German literati. Moreover, in poetic terms this particular translation was certainly a success.

Gallische Alterthümer oder Eine Sammlung alter Gedichte aus dem Gallischen des Ulin, Ossian, Orran usw. – thus the full title – was Weiße's last major contribution to the reception of Bardic poetry in Germany. The English original, published the year before, was the work of a Scottish minister who had been inspired by Macpherson's collection to produce his own, 'authentic' Celtic prose poetry alongside its English translation.[30] Weiße's rendering manages to find a German match for the rhythm and lexicon of the original:

See! Dargo rests beneath his lonely tree, and listens to the breeze in its rustling leaf. The ghost of Crimoina rises on the blue lake below: the deer see it, and stalk, without fear, on the upland rock.	Siehe! Dargo ruht unter seinem einsamen Baume, und horcht auf den Wind in seinem rasselnden Laube. Der Geist Crimoinens erhebt sich über dem blauen See unter ihm: das Wild sieht es, und schreitet ohne Furcht auf emporragenden Felsen umher.
No hunter, when the sign is seen, disturbs their peace; for the soul of Dargo is sad, and the swift-bounding companion of his chace howls beside him.[31]	Kein Jäger, wann die Erscheinung gesehen wird, stört seine Ruh: denn die Seele des Dargo ist traurig, und der schnell hüpfende Gefährte seiner Jagd heult ihm zur Seite.[32]

For his translation, Weiße chooses to employ a rhythmical prose rather similar to the 'freie Rhythmen' [free verse] which Klopstock

30 John Smith, *Galic Antiquities* (London: Cadell; Edinburgh: Elliot, 1780). See Donald E. Meek, 'The sublime Gael: The Impact of Macpherson's Ossian on Literary Creativity and Cultural Perception in Gaelic Scotland', in *The Reception of Ossian in Europe*, ed. by Howard Gaskill (London: Thoemmes Continuum, 2004), pp. 40–66 (p. 52). The book had been reviewed in the *Neue Bibliothek* the year it was published (*NBSWFK*, 25.1 (1780), 172–73).

31 Smith, *Galic Antiquities*, pp. 133–34 (layout adjusted to aid comparison).

32 Smith, *Gallische Alterthümer*, I, 3. Weiße changed the order of the elements of the collection so that in the German version the poems precede the critical dissertations.

had introduced into German poetry (minus the verse form, of course). This choice may have been a response to a minor controversy over Michael Denis's Ossian translation. Denis had used hexameters when translating the Ossianic prose poetry, declaring: 'Kein Sylbenmaass schien mir meinem Gegenstande angemessener' [No metre seemed more appropriate to my object].[33] Notwithstanding the otherwise universal praise the translation received, this decision met with harsh criticism, among others from Herder, who explicitly recommended that Denis rework his translation 'nach dem freyen Klopstockischen Sylbenmaaße' [in the free metres of Klopstock].[34] Evidently, Weiße did not subscribe to Denis's reasoning about the hexameter.

Weiße's translation includes the author's 'Dissertation on the Authenticity of the Poems of Ossian' and at least in this respect the book can also be seen as the translator's final attempt to weigh in on the authenticity issue. As Weiße himself writes in his preface:

> Was die Aechtheit der Gedichte selbst anbetrifft, so bezweifelt sie zwar Niemand mehr unter uns; indem die Einwürfe, die dießfalls Dr. Johnson und einige andere englische Kunstrichter gemacht haben, von Lord Kaims, Dr. Blair und Herrn Macpherson genugsam widerlegt worden.[35]
>
> [As for the authenticity of the poems themselves, it may no longer be contested by anyone among us; for the objections made in this case by Dr. Johnson and some other English critics have been entirely refuted by Lord Kames, Dr. Blair and Mr. Macpherson.]

If Weiße at some point realized he was on the losing side, he certainly never showed it. At least the critical reaction was more positive than with *Von den Barden*. The anonymous reviewer in the *Göttingische Anzeigen* found no fault with the fact that '[d]er Verf. [...] sich sehr an den originellen kühnen, bildervollen Ausdruck gehalten [hat], so wie das Englische ihn dargestellt hat' [the author [i.e., the translator]

33 James Macpherson, *Die Gedichte Ossians, eines alten celtischen Dichters*, trans. by Michael Denis, 3 vols (Vienna: Trattner, 1768–69), I (1768), unpag. translator's preface. In the same place Denis also mentions the review of Albrecht Wittenberg's translation of *Fingal* (1764) which had appeared in Weiße's *Bibliothek* and expresses the hope that his own translation would meet with similar approval.

34 Johann Gottfried von Herder, review of *Die Gedichte Ossians*, I, trans. by Michael Denis, *Allgemeine deutsche Bibliothek*, 10.1 (1769), 63–69 (p. 69); cf. Tombo, *Ossian in Germany*, pp. 120–23.

35 Smith, 'Vorrede des Uebersetzers', in *Gallische Alterthümer*, unpag.

has closely followed the original, bold, vivid style which he found in the English].[36]

Weiße and Bardic Poetry

In the wake of his engagement with Ossian, Weiße, like many German writers, embraced a fascination with all sorts of ancient Nordic and Gaelic poetry. In his *Critical Dissertation* Hugh Blair had cited the funeral song of King Regner Lodbrok from the Danish antiquary Olaus Wormius's collection *Runir seu danica literatura antiquissima* (where the text is entitled *Regis Regneri Lodbrog epicedium*).[37] Despite the fact that for Blair the *epicedium* only serves as an illustration of what 'barbarous' poetry that did not possess the beauties of Ossian looked like,[38] in his summary of Blair in the *Neue Bibliothek* in 1766 Weiße includes a translation of no fewer than eight stanzas. This translation would be reprinted in Schmid's *Anthologie der Deutschen* in 1771 and Weiße lightly revised it for republication in his collected *Kleine lyrische Gedichte* (1772; cf. [85]).

While the interest in Ossian led to the rediscovery of collections such as that by Wormius, the most important contemporary project it inspired also had an impact on Weiße's work as a translator: Thomas Percy's *Reliques of Ancient English Poetry*, first published in 1765, of which Weiße owned a first edition.[39] The fact that this anthology had been inspired by Macpherson's Ossian is reflected in the extent to which the German reception of the former went hand in hand with that of the latter. While Percy's eclectic collection never quite inspired the same delirious craze as Ossian, the list of its German admirers was certainly impressive: the group of translators who collaborated on the first German translation of part of the *Reliques* in 1777 included Joachim Heinrich Campe, Johann Joachim Eschenburg and Johann Gottfried Herder.[40] Weiße's friend and protégé, Heinrich

36 Anon., review of John Smith, *Gallische Alterthümer*, trans. by C. F. Weiße, *Zugabe zu den Göttingischen Anzeigen von gelehrten Sachen*, 1.28 (1781), 442–47 (p. 447).

37 See Hugh Blair, *A Critical Dissertation on the Poems of Ossian, the Son of Fingal* (London: Becket and De Hondt, 1763), pp. 5–11.

38 Blair, *Critical Dissertation*, p. 11.

39 Thomas Percy, *Reliques of Ancient English Poetry*, 3 vols (London: Dodsley, 1765) (*Verzeichniß der Bibliothek*, 3473–3475).

40 Thomas Percy (ed.), *Balladen und Lieder altenglischer und altschottischer Dichtart*, ed. by August Friedrich Ursinus (Berlin: Himburg, 1777).

Wilhelm von Gerstenberg, also translated individual poems from the *Reliques*.[41]

Weiße's own translations were mostly published in journals and anthologies before he included them in his volumes of poetry. One of them was a traditional ballad, 'Fair Rosamond', Weiße's translation of which first appeared as part of Raspe's review of the *Reliques* in his *Neue Bibliothek* in 1766 (cf. [1]), an indication of Weiße's early interest in the collection. The same review contained his translation of the English Renaissance poet George Wither's 'The Shepherd's Resolution' ('Der entschloßne Schäfer' [64]), which was reprinted in various venues before being substantially revised and republished under a new title, *Antiseladon*, in Ramler's popular anthology, *Lyrische Bluhmenlese*, in 1774. Beyond the poems contained in Percy's *Reliques*, it is possible that Weiße's interest in an otherwise obscure poem by Percy's friend, William Shenstone, 'In den moosbewachsnen Zellen' [53], (orig. 'Here in cool grot and mossy cell') owes its translation to that connection, though another possibility is suggested in Chapter 9 below.

Unbroken though his fascination with Ossian and Percy's *Reliques* remained throughout the 1770s, Weiße quickly became critical of the effect which the craze for Bardic poetry had on German literature. Most prominently, Friedrich Gottlieb Klopstock (1724–1803; another alumnus of Leipzig University), broke ground for the *Sturm und Drang* [Storm and Stress] movement not least in the way in which he identified himself as part of a supposedly ur-Germanic tradition of native 'Bardic' poetry. Like Ossian, Klopstock's *Bardendichtung* proved a useful element in the cultural nationalism embraced by German writers of the period.[42] At the same time, much of the over-enthusiastic poetry published in the wake of such sentiments could overshoot the mark, particularly in the eyes of Weiße, always sceptical of literary fads. As early as 1766, a new poem by Gerstenberg occasions a lament about the increasing introduction of Norse mythology into German literature in a letter Weiße writes to Johann Peter Uz.[43] Five years later, when Karl Friedrich Kretschmann's song *Der Barde an dem Grabe des Majors von Kleist* is sent to him, Weiße decides he does not want to risk the ire of 'das ganze nordische Reich'

41 Cf. Schmidt, *'Homer des Nordens'*, I, 532.

42 See Grit Dommes, 'Klopstock, Friedrich Gottlieb', in *Handbuch Sturm und Drang*, ed. by Luserke-Jaqui, pp. 130–34.

43 C. F. Weiße, Letter to Johann Peter Uz, 5 February 1766; cited in Anon., 'Felix Christian [*sic*] Weisse an Johann Peter Uz', *Morgenblatt für gebildete Leser*, 282 (1840), 1125–26 (p. 1126).

[the whole Nordic Empire] by criticizing the song.[44] Numerous other letters contain similar sentiments.[45] On the other hand, Weiße himself had by this time become something of a figurehead of the German 'bards', whose tendency (in true Bardic style) to praise one another in song (while using their 'Bardic' names as pseudonyms) he could not escape. Kretschmann (1738–1809), who styled himself *Der Barde Rhingulph*, was one of nine German 'bards' who had songs dedicated to them in Michael 'Sined der Barde' Denis's collection *Die Lieder Sineds des Barden* (1772).[46] So was Weiße's friend Ramler; another was Weiße himself. And it is difficult to imagine that he was not at least a little flattered as Denis, in the poem 'An den Oberbarden der Pleisse', described him as a literal 'star' among poets:[47]

Du glänzest in den Hunderten
Der Barden Manas,* wie der Stern,
Der Abendführer, der die Glut
Der Sommermonden dämpft.

Druiden locket er hervor
Aus ihrer Höhle, freudig sieht
Der braune Sohn der Arbeit ihn,
Und trocknet seinen Schweiß.

*) Mana der Deutschen zweiter Stammvater nach dem Tuito oder Teut.

[Thou shinest among the Centuries
Of Mana's* poets like the Star,
The evening guide, that tempers
The glow of summer moons.

44 C. F. Weiße, Letter to Johann Peter Uz, 25 March 1771; cited in Anon., 'Felix Christian [*sic*] Weisse an Johann Peter Uz', *Morgenblatt für gebildete Leser*, 286 (1840), 1142–43 (p. 1143). The review in the *NBSWFK* nevertheless features harsh criticism of the way the poet's enthusiasm had led him to gloss over formal imperfections (*NBSWFK*, 12.2 (1771), 241–53).

45 E.g., his aforementioned letter to Benedict Maria von Werkmeister, 30 April 1774 (Weiße, 'Briefe an Werkmeister', p. 278).

46 Michael Denis, *Die Lieder Sineds des Barden* (Vienna: Trattner, 1772) (in Weiße's library: *Verzeichniß der Bibliothek*, 2910). Weiße owned at least two of 'Ringulph's' volumes of poetry (*Verzeichniß*, 2594 and 2595).

47 Denis, 'An den Oberbarden der Pleisse', in *Die Lieder Sineds des Barden*, pp. 194–97 (p. 195). The River Pleiße, which runs through Leipzig, was a popular poetic symbol for the city in the eighteenth century.

Druids he lures
From their caves, smiling
The brown son of work looks upon him
And dries his sweat.

*) Mana, the second forefather of the Germans after Tuito or Teut.]

For all his habitual self-deprecation, this poem illustrates Weiße's rank in a literary discourse that he himself might have considered relatively marginal. However, regardless of his scepticism towards Bardic German poetry, Ossian ranked as high in his estimation as in that of many others. Weiße's contributions to the German reception of these works were as much a labour of love as they were part of his commercial translating and the prestige of Ossian guaranteed a sustained critical interest in his translations and reviews. As we have seen, the latter had, to some extent, been true of his translations of plays and poems as well. However, from an early point in his career he had also been translating popular prose, including that highly controversial genre, the novel. In order fully to understand the intersection between literary and commercial concerns in Weiße's translating, therefore, a closer look at these works is necessary.

6. Translations of Novels and Other Prose

While translations of novels and various forms of essay make up a considerable section of Weiße's oeuvre as a translator, in some ways they stand apart. Most obviously, Weiße did not produce original writing in these genres, hence the absence of the connection between his translating and original writing that characterized, for instance, his work in drama. Like many of his colleagues, Weiße seems to have held the genre of the popular novel in comparatively low regard. The catalogue of his library features few copies of novels aside from those he himself had translated and, judging from his letters, novels were not part of his regular reading. Of course, there are exceptions to this – such as the case of Mercier's utopian novel *L'An 2440*, which is discussed below. Because the translation of novels and essayistic prose often involved less of a concern with specificities of form, however, these texts offer an abundance of examples of the lexical choices Weiße made when unfettered by metre or rhyme, thus allowing us to assess his command of the source language at the time of the translation as well as his stance on the ongoing debate about neologisms, Anglicisms, Gallicisms and the shape of the German literary idiom. Especially his translations of non-fiction also provide examples of what editorial techniques Weiße relied on to bridge gaps in cultural knowledge.

Language and Form in the Prose Translations

As we have seen in the chapters on Weiße's early translations of plays and poetry, his initial practice often involved heavy 'Germanization' of literary forms and settings, paired with a readiness to invent German matches for foreign idioms which, even while Gottsched still reigned supreme in Leipzig, created a commonality with the Swiss theorists Bodmer and Breitinger. While the latter tendency became more pronounced as Weiße developed his abilities as a translator, his translations of prose generally exhibit the same respect for the stylistic peculiarity of the original which characterized his engagement with Ossian and Bardic poetry. Unlike with the early translations, Weiße's prose translations of the 1770s and 1780s often aim to retain those features of the original which made it peculiar and culturally specific.

As one would expect, the genre of the translation nearly always automatically matched that of the original. The rare exception to this rule demonstrates that the attitude described above pertained first and foremost to language, however. In 1771 Weiße translated Jean-François de Saint-Lambert's long poem *Les saisons* (*Jahreszeiten* [81]), which had been published in French two years previously. In the translator's preface he explains that the poem certainly deserves a translation, yet the question remains:

> eine freye oder eine mehr wörtliche? Bey der ersten hat man den Vortheil, des Verfassers Gedanken harmonischer auszudrücken, und seiner Muttersprache weniger Gewalt anzuthun: bey der zweyten aber kann man mehr die Farbe und das poetische Kolorit des Originals beybehalten, welches bey solchen malerischen Gedichten doch beynahe die Hauptsache ist. Dieß ist auch der Grund, warum der Uebersetzer die letzte gewählet.[1]

> [a free rendering or a more literal one? The first has the advantage that it captures the author's thoughts more harmoniously and does less violence to his mother tongue; yet the second allows one to retain more of the colour and poetic atmosphere of the original, which after all is almost the most important thing with picturesque poems of this kind. This, then, is the reason why the translator chose the latter.]

What makes this case so peculiar is that the translation itself shows that Weiße's understanding of the dichotomy between 'free' and 'literal' remains limited to the level of language only. Saint-Lambert's poem is written in rhyming verse. In what may be the most significant shift in form between original and translation across his whole oeuvre, Weiße translates it in prose. Once the reader moves past this major difference, however, the 'literal' faithfulness to the style of the original is obvious. The anonymous review for the *Allgemeine deutsche Bibliothek* perfectly captures both the strengths and drawbacks of this approach:

> Der Uebersetzer, (der einer von unsern besten Dichtern seyn soll,) hat die Verse des Franzosen in eine Prose ausgelöset, die leicht

1 Jean-François de Saint-Lambert, *Jahreszeiten*, trans. by C. F. Weiße (Leipzig: Dyck, 1771), pp. vi–vii.

und fliessend und worinn größtentheils das Kolorit des Originals beybehalten ist. Aber warum übersetzte er einige gar zu sonderbare Ausdrücke und Beywörter des Originals, wie er sie fand?[2]

[The translator (who is said to be one of our foremost poets) has recast the French verse in a prose that is light and fluent, and in which the atmosphere of the original for the most part has been preserved. But why did he translate some all too peculiar expressions and adjectives in the original exactly as he found them?]

Similar complaints can be found in many reviews of Weiße's translations and they are by no means always products of the anxieties of the age about the purity of the German literary language. The review alludes to Weiße's translation of a number of metaphors that cluster together in the text; their juxtaposition with the original may serve as an illustration here:

La groseille pendante en grappes d'incarnat, S'y présente à mes yeux, charmés de son éclat; Ces rubis émaillés qu'arrondit la nature Sur ces arbres touffus sortent de la verdure.[3]	Die Erdbeere, die in incarnatenen Trauben herab-hängt, zeiget sich meinen, von ihrem Glanze ent-zückten Augen; diese emaillirten Rubinen, die die Natur auf diesen dicht belaubten Bäumen ründet, steiget aus dem Grünen hervor.[4]

While, in this passage, Weiße makes the dubious decision to translate 'groseille' [currant] as 'Erdbeere' [strawberry], his lexical choices are, if nothing else, consistent: 'Ces rubis émaillés' in the French original is no less extravagant an expression than 'diese emaillirten Rubinen' in the translation (and strawberries are about as plausibly ruby-like as redcurrants). Overall, Weiße's commitment to Saint-Lambert's style is reminiscent of the demand for equivalency of effect which

2 Anon., review of Jean-François de Saint-Lambert, *Jahreszeiten*, trans. by C. F. Weiße, *Allgemeine deutsche Bibliothek*, 1 (1777), Appx. 13–24, 431–32 (p. 432). Cf. Wilkie, 'Christian Felix Weisze', pp. 35–36.

3 Cited after Jean-François de Saint-Lambert, *Les Saisons* (Amsterdam: n. pub., 1769), p. 56.

4 Saint-Lambert, *Jahreszeiten*, p. 74.

several theorists of translation in the eighteenth century, Bodmer and Breitinger among them, had developed.[5]

Weiße also takes a consistent approach to the controversial problem of neologisms, loanwords and borrowed expressions. More than most translators of his day, he embraces the possibilities they offer to enrich the German literary language. He regularly employs loanwords that have become lexicalized in German, as, for instance, in the characteristic translation of the following passage from George Keate's sentimental *Sketches from Nature*:

> And yet, mighty deep! 'tis thy *surface* alone we view – Who can penetrate the secrets of thy wide domain? – What eye can visit thy immense rocks and caverns, that teem with life and vegetation? – or search out the myriads of objects, whose beauties lie scattered over thy dread abimes?[6]

> Und doch, mächtige Tiefe! sehen wir nichts von dir, als deine Oberfläche. – Wer vermag in die Geheimnisse deines allweiten Gebiets einzudringen? – Welches Auge kann deine unermeßlichen Felsen und Höhlen, schwanger von Leben und Vegetation, besuchen? – oder die Myriaden von Gegenständen ausforschen, deren Schönheit über deinen furchtbaren Abgründen zerstreut liegt?[7]

Weiße's use of 'Vegetation' in the German translation is just another instance of his predilection for Latinisms. More significantly, the word 'Myriaden' is an Anglicism which, as Peter Ganz explains, had entered the German language via early translations of Milton's *Paradise Lost* and quickly became a favourite among Bodmer's circle, thus attracting criticism from the hardliners.[8] By the time this translation was published in 1780, the word would have been less controversial (certainly, unlike with Saint-Lambert, no contemporary critic seems to have picked up on it). However, Weiße was also ready to introduce entirely foreign neologisms into his translations. Ganz lists Weiße's use of the adjective 'shandeisch', which appears twice in his translation of Laurence Sterne's letters, as the first use of the word

5 As discussed in Chapter 1.

6 George Keate, *Sketches from Nature; Taken, and Coloured, in a Journey to Margate*, 2nd edn (London: Dodsley, 1779), pp. 72–73.

7 George Keate, *Skizzen aus der Natur, auf einer Reise nach Margate entworfen und ausgemalt*, trans. by C. F. Weiße (Leipzig: Weidmanns Erben und Reich, 1780), pp. 62–63.

8 Ganz, *Der Einfluss des Englischen*, pp. 148–49.

in German.[9] It is the counterpart to Sterne's coinage, 'shandean', which can mean anything referring to his exceedingly popular novel, *The Life and Opinions of Tristram Shandy, Gentleman* (1759–67), as well as, in a narrower sense, anything exemplifying the latter's peculiar narrative style. Whether or not Weiße was aware of both shades of meaning, the decision to introduce the German term is a bold one. The case study which follows below contains more examples of this kind.

All this notwithstanding, Weiße did believe there were limits to the introduction of foreign vocabulary into German. The deciding factor seems to have been whether a word had been given a German shape or whether it was used as a foreign word proper. The latter case (once more with the exception of Latin) generally seems to have been unacceptable to him, as were uses of foreign vocabulary which he regarded as gratuitous. On the whole he also seems more hospitable to loanwords from the English than those imported from France. In a letter to Friedrich Justin Bertuch in 1772, he remonstrates with the latter about the quality of his translation of an unnamed Spanish text:

> Dass Ihre Übersetzung getreu ist, zweifle ich nicht: hin und wieder scheint mir aber die Sprache vernachläßiget und eine Weitläuftigkeit im Stil zu sein: Sie bedienen sich auch oft französischer Wörter, als *Personage, Illusion* u.a.m. wo wir recht gute deutsche Ausdrücke haben. Ich wünsche nicht, daß dieser Misbrauch unserer itzigen Schriftsteller überhand nähme: sonst machen wir aus unserer Sprache eine bigarrure.[10]

9 Ganz, *Der Einfluss des Englischen*, p. 31. Cf. Laurence Sterne, *Briefe an seine vertrautesten Freunde, nebst einem Fragment im Geschmacke des Rabelais und einer von ihm selbst verfaßten Nachricht von seinem Leben und seiner Familie*, trans. by C. F. Weiße (Weidmanns Erben und Reich, 1776), pp. 60, 248.

10 C. F. Weiße, Letter to Friedrich Justin Bertuch, 7 April 1772 (GSA06/2093 (7)). Often Weiße's own programmatic decisions in this regard did not bear the fruit for which he had hoped: see, e.g., his preface to the translation of Stéphanie-Félicité de Genlis, *Erziehungstheater für junge Frauenzimmer*, 4 vols (Leipzig: Crusius, 1780–82). In it he spends much time explaining how, in his rendering of the style, he has aimed for idiomatic German: 'Der Dialog, der in jeder Sprache seinen eignen Ton und Gang hat, schien es zu fodern, wofern er nicht steif und fremd klingen sollte' [The dialogue, which has its own tone and pace in each language, seemed to demand it lest it sound ceremonious and foreign] (pp. xv–xvi). However, the anonymous reviewer for the *Allgemeine deutsche Bibliothek* criticized the remaining Gallicisms in the text and the way in which the French 'shines through' the German (Anon., review of Stéphanie-Félicité Ducrest de Saint-Aubin, Comtesse de Genlis, *Erziehungstheater für junge Frauenzimmer* [1780], trans. by C. F. Weiße, *Allgemeine deutsche Bibliothek*, 46.2 (1781), 579–81).

> [I do not doubt that your translation is faithful: yet here and there it seems to me the language was neglected and there was a circuitousness about the style. You also often employ French words, such as *Personage, Illusion,* etc. for which we have good German expressions. I do not wish that this misuse among our current writers should prevail, otherwise, our language will become a *bigarrure.*]

Like many intellectuals of his period, Weiße read and was fascinated by the English moral weeklies, periodicals which more than any other genre provided a mirror for the development of the English language. The major ones passed by his oeuvre as a translator, though while translating William Hayley's aforementioned *Essay on Old Maids* ([29]) Weiße took the opportunity of Hayley's passing reference to a story in Steele's *Tatler* to append a lengthy footnote over nine pages containing the translation of the passage to which Hayley referred.[11] In 1782 Weiße had the opportunity to translate in its entirety a minor, but by no means insignificant, periodical, Henry Mackenzie's *The Mirror* (*Der Spiegel* [36]), 'das neuerlich in Schottland herausgekommen und zu den besten Schriften dieser Art gehöret' [which has recently been published in Scotland and is among the best works of its kind].[12] Mackenzie, who shared a professional commonality with Weiße inasmuch as he combined a literary career with the post of Comptroller of Taxes for Scotland, would publish another periodical a few years later, *The Lounger,* which Weiße also translated (*Der beobachtende Müßiggänger* [37]).

In his preface to the translation of the *Mirror* Weiße praises the moral content of the periodical and mentions the praise it had received in Britain (despite another reference to the editor's being Scottish, the translation mostly follows prevailing practice and uses the German 'England' for 'Britain'). Once more, the preface also serves as an apology for the literal translation of cultural specificities. Weiße hopes that the adage '*c'est tout comme chez nous*' applies in most cases and that a comparison with foreign customs will be advantageous to the German reader.[13] But the cultural gap is never

11 See Hayley, *Ein philosophischer Versuch,* pp. 91–99; cf. Richard Steele (ed.), *The Tatler* [1709] (Philadelphia: Woodward, 1831), no. 32.

12 C. F. Weiße, Letter to Lorenz Westenrieder, 22 September 1782, in 'Briefe von Christian Felix Weiße und Friedrich Jacobi an Lorenz Westenrieder aus den Jahren 1781–83', ed. by A. Kluckhohn, *Sitzungsberichte der philosophisch-philologischen und historischen Classe der K.B. Akademie der Wissenschaften zu München* (1889), 2 vols., I, 237–70 (p. 264).

13 'Vorbericht des Uebersetzers', in Henry Mackenzie, *Der Spiegel. Ein periodisches Blatt,* 3 vols (Leipzig: Crusius, 1782–83), I (1782), iii–vi (p. iv).

completely unmitigated, of course. Weiße's footnotes are economical, but generally appear where they are most needed. On this level, the difference between England and Scotland apparently does play a role. While, for instance, the schools of Eton and 'Westmünster' do not necessitate commentary,[14] a mention of the River Forth has the footnote, 'Einer der größten Flüsse in Schottland. Uebersetzer' [One of the biggest rivers in Scotland. Translator] (unlike some of his colleagues, Weiße is always conscientious about marking his own notes as such).[15] In the story of a journey from Edinburgh to Carron, the system of shareholders' participating in the lockage duty at the canal obviously requires an explanation for the German audience, especially as the passage is riddled with economic vocabulary:

> There was much the same difference in their sentiments with regard to the *Great Canal*; Mr. *Blubber* took out a bit of paper, on which he had marked down the *lockage duty* received in a week there; he shook his head, however, and said, he was sorry to find the shares were *below par*.[16]

> Eben so verschieden waren sie in ihren Meynungen über den großen Kanal. Herr Blubber zog ein Stückchen Papier heraus, auf dem er sich aufgesetzt, was der Schleußenzinns eine Woche lang hier betrüge, schüttelte den Kopf und sagte: das Interesse käme hier nicht für* die Theilnehmer heraus.

> *Privatpersonen bauen hier auf ihre Kosten Schleußen, wovon sie sich einen gewissen Zins bezahlen lassen. Anmerk. des Uebersetzers.[17]

Where Weiße has to concede his inability to find a genuine German equivalent for an English word, his explanatory footnotes are usually very short, but the *Mirror* translation contains a notable exception, one which shows us Weiße wrestling with a term, as it were – translating the original 'man of spirit' as 'Mann vom Kopfe', he explains:

14 *Der Spiegel*, I, no. 4, p. 27.

15 *Der Spiegel*, I, no. 8, p. 59; cf. Henry Mackenzie (ed.), *The Mirror: A Periodical Paper*, 9th edn, 2 vols (London and Edinburgh: Strahan, Cadell and Creech, 1792–93), I (1792), no. 8, p. 46.

16 *The Mirror*, I, no. 41, p. 281.

17 'Here private citizens build locks at their own expense and charge a certain interest on them' (*Der Spiegel*, II, no. 41, p. 39). In the period, the term 'Interesse' was still in use as an equivalent of the English word 'interest' in the financial sense.

> Im Englischen ein *Man of Spirit*. Im Deutschen erschöpft das Wort Kopf freylich nicht die ganze Bedeutung desselben, zumal da es der Verfasser hier auch auf das sittliche Verhalten anwendet; am wenigsten paßt es auf die *Ladies of Spirit*: aber ich kenne auch kein Deutsches, das dem Wortgebrauche des engl. Verfassers näher käme, oder bey uns üblicher wäre. Uebers.[18]

> [A *Man of Spirit* in the English. The German word *Kopf* obviously does not fully encompass the meaning of this term, especially since, in this instance, the author applies it to moral conduct as well; it is least appropriate for the *Ladies of Spirit*, yet I also know of no German word which was closer to the author's use of the term, or more common among us. Transl.]

Weiße's translations of prose fiction, especially popular novels, usually have fewer translator's footnotes than those of the essayistic texts. He only rarely relies on them to explain vocabulary for which he has not found a satisfactory German match, as in the abovementioned case of the 'man of spirit'. Two instances from his translation of Henry Brooke's sentimental novel *Juliet Grenville* in 1774 illustrate the two main forms of explanatory footnote which occur in the novels.[19] Both words are from a legal context. Faced with the English Latinism, 'quorum', Weiße decides to retain the word in the German text, but appends a footnote to explain it.[20] The term 'Coroner', which would have been fully opaque to even an educated German reader (even more so than 'Mann vom Kopfe'), is translated as 'Mordrichter' in the main text, with a footnote that reads, '*Coroner*. Ein Richter, der nebst zwölf andern bey einem gefundenen todten Menschen untersuchen muß, ob er gewaltthätiger, oder natürlicher Weise gestorben' [*Coroner*. A judge who, when a dead person is found, must investigate, together with twelve others, whether they died in a violent or natural way].[21] Ganz's dictionary of Anglicisms mentions that the word was occasionally to be found in German travel accounts, but the first example he cites was published no earlier than 1770.[22]

18 *Der Spiegel*, III, no. 102, pp. 288–89.

19 Charlotte Brooke, the daughter of Henry Brooke, would become involved in the discourse discussed in the previous chapter when, in 1789, she published a collection of *Reliques of Irish Poetry* (Dublin: Bonham) as a response to Macpherson and with a title obviously inspired by Percy's *Reliques*.

20 Henry Brooke, *Julie Grenville oder die Geschichte des menschlichen Herzens*, trans. by C. F. Weiße, 3 vols (Leipzig: Schwickert, 1774), I, 101.

21 Brooke, *Julie Grenville*, I, 60.

22 Ganz, *Der Einfluss des Englischen*, p. 53.

Even where the opacity of a foreign word prevented him from germanizing it all too easily, Weiße still liked to use the opportunity to educate his readers about foreign customs, a recurring motif in translators' notes more generally. Longer notes detailing further reading, the kind we have found in the non-fiction, are extremely rare in the novels. Weiße's translation of Phebe Gibbes's *Hartly House, Calcutta* (1789) (*Hartlyhaus* [20]), possibly the most obscure novel he ever translated, but one that has recently attracted attention for its depiction of Anglo-Indian colonial encounters, contains a few footnotes suggesting further reading on Indian history and culture.[23] On the whole, however, this practice marks an exception to his usual editorial reticence when it comes to translations of popular fiction.

Unlike his translations of essays and other non-fiction, the novels usually do not have a translator's preface affixed to them. One of the exceptions to this rule is his translation of Mercier's famous utopian novel *L'An 2440*, which was published by Schwickert in 1772 (*Das Jahr zwey tausend vier hundert und vierzig. Ein Traum aller Träume* [74]).[24] It was one of the most highbrow novels Weiße ever translated and he found it a difficult text, especially given that he had originally translated it 'not for honour':

> [Mercier] war zum Übersetzen ein schweres Buch: und ich hätte es gewiß nicht unternommen, wenn ich es erst fleißiger geprüft hätte, da es nicht der Ehre wegen, sondern, wie ich Ihnen schon gestanden, aus einer etwas unedlern Absicht von mir übersezt worden.[25]
>
> [[Mercier] was a difficult book to translate; and I am sure I would not have taken it on if I had examined it more thoroughly beforehand, since, as I have already confessed to you, I did not translate it for honour, but with a somewhat baser motive.]

23 As an illustration of the increasing interest in Gibbes, see Michael J. Franklin's introduction to his recent edition of *Hartly House* (Manchester: Manchester University Press, 2019).

24 Among all Weiße's translations of novels, this one has the distinction of having been reprinted most recently (Frankfurt am Main: Insel, 1989).

25 C. F. Weiße, Letter to Christian Ludwig von Hagedorn, 3 March 1772 (UBL Ms.0670u). In a letter to Friedrich Justin Bertuch a month later Weiße mentions that he translated this 'infamous' book following the urgent request of one of his closest friends ('habe binnen dieser Zeit außer meinen Berufsarbeiten auf das dringende Ansuchen eines meiner vornehmen Freunde das berüchtigte Buch das 2040. [*sic*] Jahr übersezt') (C. F. Weiße, Letter to Friedrich Justin Bertuch, 7 April 1772 (GSA06/2093 (7)).

Nevertheless, Mercier marks the rare case of a novel Weiße genuinely admired, which – in combination with the success of the original – presumably motivated his choice to preface the translation with his own thoughts on Mercier's utopian vision and style. He lauds the overall work – 'Dieses sonderbare Buch gehöret unstreitig unter die besten Schriften, die wir seit einiger Zeit aus Frankreich erhalten haben' [This strange book doubtlessly counts among the best works which have come out of France in some time] – but finds Mercier's social and political imagination a little too bold. Nevertheless:

> Bey dem allen bleiben des Verfassers Träume immer vortreffliche philosophische Träume, denen man größtentheils schon die Wirklichkeit zum Besten des menschlichen Geschlechts wünschen könnte. Was Wahrheit ist oder doch sein könnte, läßt sich leicht von dem, was Traum ist und es immer zu sein verdienet, unterscheiden.
>
> [At the same time, the author's dreams are always admirable, philosophical dreams. For the benefit of mankind, one could wish for the realization of the better part of them. It is easy to distinguish between what is, or at least could be, reality and that which is dream and deserves to remain dream forever.][26]

One of the few regards in which Weiße finds fault with Mercier is that the latter had not presented a Christian utopia. This might be the reason why *Das Jahr 2440* became the unusual case of the translator's expurgating a footnote contained in the original rather than adding one. This particular note by Mercier had suggested that theologists such as Calvin, Luther, Bossuet and others might have benefited humanity more if they had employed their genius to improve the world rather than fighting or propounding 'ridiculous dogmas'.[27] Aside from this, however, the translation is complete as always; and the expurgation of this note marks only a minor deviation from Weiße's usual editorial reserve. Despite his very measured enthusiasm about Mercier's utopia, and the fact that he generally preferred evolutionary over revolutionary change, Weiße's thoughts

26 Weiße, unpag. preface. For a broader discussion of Weiße's translation within the utopian discourse, cf. Andreas Dittrich, 'Traduire la pensée utopique: le transfert des paradigmes de L'An 2440', in *Cultural Transfer through Translation*, ed. by Stockhorst, pp. 121–39. Dittrich finds that Weiße's preface expresses, in a typical way, the position that the French utopian discourse of Mercier is characterized by exaggerated complaints and impracticable propositions (p. 139).

27 Cf. Wilkie, 'Christian Felix Weisze', p. 38. The only translator's footnote added by Weiße explains the geographical divisions of Paris, with which many of his readers would have been unfamiliar.

returned to *L'An 2440* during the French Revolution.[28] As he wrote to Herzog Friedrich Christian von Holstein-Augustenburg (another alumnus of the Alma Mater Lipsiensis) in 1793:

> Ich denke oft, daß die Zeitungen, die sich Mercier in seinem 2240. Jahre [*sic*!] erträumt hat, buchstäblich können in Erfüllung gehn: denn der Anfang ist in America dazu gemacht. So sehr der Despotismus noch hin und wieder sein eisern Zeptro führet, so wird er Vernunft und Freiheit doch nicht austilgen können: Der größte Druck veranlaßt den größten Widerstand, und ein eingesperrtes Feuer bricht mit destomehr Gewalt aus.[29]
>
> [I often think that the developments which Mercier imagines in his *Year 2240* [*sic*] could literally come true, for in America a start has been made. As much as despotism may now and again rule with a rod of iron, it will nevertheless not be able to extinguish reason and freedom: the strongest pressure creates the strongest resistance and a fire confined will erupt with all the greater a force.]

For all the care he expended on the language of his prose translations, Weiße was well aware that especially the popular novels were but ephemeral goods on the literary market, quickly to be replaced by more recent fiction and soon to be outdated as a result of the rapid evolution of the literary language in Germany. Unlike with his poems and plays, therefore, he never revised his translations of novels for republication – as he confessed to Ramler in 1787, fourteen years after the publication of *Julie Grenville*:

> Der Himmel bewahre mich, daß ich beÿ meinen alten Übersetzungen zumal von Romanen, die längst durch neue verdrängt sind, an eine Ausbesserung wieder denken sollte! Nein, (im Vertrauen zu Ihnen!) diese sehe ich beÿ mir immer als leichte Waare an, wo, wann sie verthan ist, die Mode sie durch etwas anders ersetzen muß, wenn sie Abgang finden soll: denn zu einer zwoten Auflage kömmt es nicht leicht, u. geschäh es ja, so sind die Buchhändler

28 Some of Weiße's few surviving sentiments on the events in France are published in Hans Schulz, 'Leipziger Stimmen von 1793 über Deutschland und die Revolution', *Euphorion*, 17 (1910), 48–55.

29 Conversely, during that period Weiße himself spent ever more time in his own utopia, his estate in Stötteritz, a practice he called 'stötterisiren', probably a dark pun on the French Revolutionary 'septembriser', which referred to the practice of executing political opponents *en masse*, as in September 1792 (C. F. Weiße, Letter to Friedrich Christian von Holstein-Augustenburg, 18 June 1793, in Schulz, 'Leipziger Stimmen', pp. 50–51 (p. 50)); alternatively, Weiße may have taken inspiration from Fanny Burney's coinage, 'Londonize' (see below).

> solche etc. dass sie lieber heimlich nachschießen, als dem Verfasser davon etwas entdecken, weil sie fürchten, daß, wenn er ja das Werk wieder übergehen wollte, sie Ehrenthalber ihm etwas für seine Mühe anbieten müßten. Julie Grenville ist also von dem Übersetzer, so wie von den Lesern vergessen.[30]

> [Heaven forfend I should ever think of revising my old translations, especially of novels which have long since been replaced by new ones. No, (between you and me!) I regard these as easy commodities which fashion, when they have been used, has to replace with something else if they are to be sold: for a second edition rarely comes to pass and, if it did, the publishers are such – that they prefer secretly to reprint rather than tell the author about it, for fear that, since he would then wish to revise the text, they would, as a matter of honour, have to pay him for his trouble. Julie Grenville is, therefore, forgotten, both by the translator and the readers.]

For all this exasperation and disdain, literary history has not only revalued many of the novelists translated by Weiße, but has also come to regard the novel as the most characteristic literary genre of the eighteenth century. For these reasons, and because novels made up at least a quarter of Weiße's published translations, a closer look at a particularly remarkable example is not out of place.

Weiße's Translation of Burney's *Evelina*: A Case Study

Weiße's translation of Fanny Burney's epistolary novel *Evelina* epitomizes his practice and abilities as a translator from the English in many ways, from the procurement of the original text for translation to the decisions involved in finding German matches for various minutiae of its idiom. It is also among the most ambitious and stylistically challenging long works of prose he translated in his life, which makes it particularly suitable as the object of an extended case study.[31]

30 C. F. Weiße, Letter to Karl Wilhelm Ramler, 18 May 1787 (GSA 75/229,4 (103)).

31 A few years later, Weiße also translated Burney's *Cecilia* (*Cecilia oder Die Geschichte einer reichen Waise* [7]). In a review of a later retranslation of the same novel by Wilhelm Heinrich Brömel, the anonymous reviewer for the *Allgemeine Literatur-Zeitung* looks back at Weiße's *Cecilia* as a 'nach dem gewöhnlichen Fabrikenschlendrian gemachte Uebersetzung' [a translation done in the common, sloppy, factory style]. This would certainly have been at odds with

Evelina, or, A young Lady's Entrance into the World was published anonymously in three volumes in January 1778 by the London publisher Thomas Lowndes. Later that same year Schwickert in Leipzig advertised the translation, *Evelina oder Eines jungen Frauenzimmers Eintritt in die Welt*, in the catalogue for the Leipzig fair.[32] The title pages of all three volumes of the translation give 1779 as the date of publication, as does Weiße himself in his *Selbstbiographie*.[33] Whichever date is correct, Weiße's translation followed the original so quickly that it must have been based not on the printed English first edition but on print sheets or printers' proofs which he had obtained through one of his or Reich's contacts in England. Conclusive evidence for this is provided by the errata sheet which came with the English first edition and to which Weiße clearly had no access: where the printed text reads, 'her daughter is under a thousand obligations to follow her', the errata page states, 'for *follow*, read *'attend'*.[34] Weiße's translation of this phrase, however, is, 'ihre Tochter hat tausend Verbindlichkeiten auf sich, ihr zu folgen'.[35] While this might still be coincidence, the following proves that Weiße did not know of the errata: where the original reads, 'When, at last, we stopped, at a *Glover's* in *High Holborn*', this is emended to 'for *a glover's*, read *an hosier's*'.[36] Weiße, unaware of the correction (as well as, apparently, of the meaning of the word 'glover'), translates: 'Als wir endlich bey Glovers in High Holborn stille hielten'.[37]

---

the impression left by his German *Evelina* (Anon., review of Frances Burney, *Cecilie Beverly*, I [1789], trans. by Wilhelm Heinrich Brömel, *Allgemeine Literatur-Zeitung*, 1.52 (1790), 415). Unfortunately, the author of the present volume did not have access to a surviving complete copy of Weiße's *Cecilia*, which is why a comparison between Weiße's and Brömel's translations remains impossible.

32 Anon., *Allgemeines Verzeichniß derer Bücher, welche in der Frankfurter und Leipziger Michaelmesse des 1778 Jahres entweder ganz neu gedruckt, oder sonst verbessert, wieder aufgeleget worden sind, auch inskünftige noch herauskommen sollen* (Leipzig: Weidmanns Erben und Reich, 1778), p. 545. Cf. Bibliography of Translations [6].

33 Weiße, *Selbstbiographie*, p. 240.

34 Frances Burney, *Evelina, or, A Young Lady's Entrance into the World*, 3 vols (London: Lowndes, 1778), I, 22. Original emphases here and in the following quotations.

35 Frances Burney, *Evelina, oder Eines jungen Frauenzimmers Eintritt in die Welt*, 3 vols (Leipzig: Schwickert, 1779), I, 27.

36 Burney, *Evelina*, II, 142–43.

37 Burney, *Evelina*, II, 435.

If Weiße produced his translation on the basis of uncorrected print sheets, then, he could not have been aware of the immediate success in England of Burney's debut novel. As was relatively common for popular novels, no translator's preface appeared at the beginning; and as far as the usual paratext is concerned, Weiße's 880-page translation of *Evelina* is sparse: unlike in the case of the above-mentioned *Julie Grenville* there are no explanatory footnotes, for example. Unlike the original, the German publication is paginated continuously over the three volumes and the numbering of the letters follows the same practice. Presumably with his German audience in mind, Weiße chooses to omit both the dedicatory poem prefaced to the English edition and Burney's note 'To the Authors of the Monthly and Critical Reviews'. The author's preface, however, is translated. Apart from these editorial interventions Weiße's translation foregoes abbreviation and summary, thus presenting the German reader with the complete text of the original, something which in the period could by no means be taken for granted.[38]

As far as lexical choices involved in the translation are concerned, one of the most basic challenges was the translation of forms of address, salutations and titles, which occur perhaps more frequently in an epistolary novel such as *Evelina* than in other forms of narrative prose. For the German translator, the specific differences between the social classes which they indicate also posed a challenge. Since the society in which Burney's protagonist moves had no precise social counterpart in eighteenth-century Germany, and no established convention regarding the translation of titles and forms of address existed yet, the translator, as always, had to balance faithfulness with comprehensibility. The very first letter in the novel, for instance, is written by '*Lady Howard to the Rev. Mr. Villars*'.[39] This is translated

38 As a matter of fact, the above-mentioned review of Brömel's translation of *Cecilia* commends him for freely cutting the 'longueurs' of the novel, thus making it more enjoyable 'particularly for the female audience', a widely accepted practice (Anon., review of *Cecilie Beverly*, p. 415). By contrast, Weiße's prose translations were often attacked for being complete or too conscientious: e.g., the reviewer of his translation of Guys's *Voyage littéraire de la Grèce* complained that the German version could be shorter if only Weiße had left the quotations from Racine untranslated, 'den, zur Ehre Deutschlands hoffe ichs, niemand in einer Uebersetzung lesen will' [whom, I hope for the honour of Germany, nobody wants to read in translation] (J. v. Müller, review of Pierre Augustin Guys, *Litterarische Reise nach Griechenland* [1772], trans. by C. F. Weiße, I and II, *Allgemeine deutsche Bibliothek*, 21 (1774), 605–07 (p. 607)).

39 All further quotations from the original version will be taken from the following edition: Frances Burney, *Evelina, or The History of a Young Lady's*

as, 'Lady Howard an den ehrw. Hrn. Villars'.[40] While there is no exact German equivalent of 'Reverend', the use of 'Lady' as a title would no longer have been regarded as a major exoticism by the time Weiße's translation appeared: Ganz cites examples of its usage in earlier works, including Lessing's *Miß Sara Sampson* (1755) and a German translation of Fielding's *Joseph Andrews* from 1765.[41] In the same manner, 'Lady Belmont' remains the same in German as in the English original. The translation of Mr. Villars's title is less felicitous: after the first letter, even the prefatory 'ehrw.' is dropped and he is subsequently referred to only as 'Herr Villars'.

The address 'Miss' is retained as 'Miß' throughout the translation and used in its original meaning. This is a less conventional choice than in the case of 'Lady': as Ganz notes, translations introduced the word into German, but it remained 'exotic'.[42] Remembering *Miß Sara Sampson* and Weiße's friendship with Lessing, it might seem less than exotic in the former's work; and Weiße had used these Anglicisms earlier, for example, in *Julie Grenville* (1774). He also generally maintains the original distinction between 'Miss' and 'Mrs' (the latter being translated as 'Frau'), despite the occasional slip.[43] 'Madam', as a salutation in the letters, appropriately becomes 'Madame' in the German version; yet while the original uses this very form of address to draw attention to Madame Duval's French origins whenever her character is mentioned, the distinction is necessarily lost in the translation. With Monsieur du Bois, on the other hand, Weiße alternates between the French title and 'Herr', something which seems a reasonably successful choice.

As far as class distinctions are concerned, Weiße does not always manage fully to convey the social stratification symbolized by the original titles. While he uses 'Lord' and 'Lady' throughout, his inability to find a German match for the title 'Sir' somewhat mars

---

Entrance into the World, ed. by Edward A. Bloom (London: Oxford University Press, 1968), which reproduces the text of the first edition of 1778. Quotations will appear in brackets and will give the number of the volume and that of the letter in roman numerals, as well as the page number in arabic numerals. The passage quoted above is I.i.11.

40 Burney, *Evelina, oder Eines jungen Frauenzimmers Eintritt in die Welt*, I.i.3.

41 Ganz, *Der Einfluss des Englischen*, p. 126.

42 Ganz, *Der Einfluss des Englischen*, p. 145.

43 Cf. the following: 'I dare not hesitate at a request from Mrs. Mirvan' (Burney, *Evelina*, ed. by Bloom, I.ii.13) becomes 'Ich unterstehe mich nicht, das Verlangen der Miß Mirvan abzuschlagen' (Burney, *Evelina, oder Eines jungen Frauenzimmers Eintritt in die Welt*, I.ii.8).

the representation of English society. In contrast to the above, he chooses not to retain the English word but indiscriminately translates both 'Mr.' and 'Sir' as 'Herr'. Thus, Sir John Belmont becomes 'Herr Johann [sometimes 'John'] Belmont', while Sir Clement Willoughby, rather inadequately, is addressed as 'Herr Clemens'. Since in the case of Willoughby his holding the title of Baronet is strongly emphasized by the author in order to highlight the contrast between his lofty title and dubious personality, the far more egalitarian choice, 'Herr', obscures a facet of the original. While the German offers no lexical equivalent of the English 'Sir', Weiße could have used the original title in his translation. It would, admittedly, have been an unusual choice, as the word was far from being an established Anglicism in the way 'Lady' was.[44] Nevertheless, given the distortion of the word's original compass, Weiße's choice to translate it as 'Herr' appears a serious blunder among his otherwise sound translations of titles and forms of address.

Beyond these fairly generic problems, which would have faced any translator of an English novel, *Evelina* poses two specific linguistic challenges. First, the vividness of Burney's account of metropolitan life and social intercourse depends to a great extent on neologisms and recent additions to colloquial vocabulary that had not yet been recorded in dictionaries. While the German language proved well-suited to accommodating Burney's many newly coined nominal compounds, some of the other words she invented or appropriated, employing them in different senses from the established ones, put Weiße's creative abilities to the test. Second, due to the particular social and cultural environment in which Evelina moves, a considerable amount of jargon from the world of fashion and related areas is employed in the novel, a set of expressions which were short-lived almost by definition and had rarely found their way into the dictionaries available to the translator.[45]

In most of these cases Weiße successfully extrapolated the meaning of new or unusual vocabulary, even though his German matches sometimes fail to capture certain nuances of the original semantics and he rarely matches English neologisms with German ones. In the case of the word 'dowdy' for a 'woman's cap' (as in, 'do you think I'd wear one of her dowdies?'), his rather felicitous match,

44 Ganz, *Der Einfluss des Englischen*, p. 207.

45 The choice of words and phrases examined here is based upon records provided by the *Oxford English Dictionary Online*, March 2015 (Oxford: Oxford University Press, 2015) <http://www.oed.com> [accessed 1 June 2015].

'Nest' ('denkst du denn, ich würde eins von ihren Nestern aufsetzen mögen?'), not only conveys the meaning of the word, but in addition emphasizes the contempt with which Madame Duval utters it.[46] Burney's wonderful and enduring coinage 'grumpy' is translated as 'widerwärtig', a decent choice considering the range of meanings which this word had at the time.[47] The 'violence of this [Captain Mirvan's] boobyish humour' is translated as 'die Heftigkeit seines wilden Gemüthes', which, while it fails to convey the connotation of silliness which Burney's neologism 'boobyish' carries, nevertheless adequately describes the troubling unruliness of the character in question.[48] Burney is the first to use 'make up' as a transitive verb in its modern meaning – 'powder, and daub, and make myself up'; this is translated by Weiße as 'mich pudern, und schmieren, und aufkrönen'.[49] Given the many references to hairstyles in the novel, it seems hardly surprising that he misconstrues 'make up' as referring to yet another one of these, yet while 'aufkrönen' certainly is not a lexical equivalent of the original expression, it works well in its German context.

Weiße is confident in translating the new, 'metropolitan' vocabulary employed by Burney, though here, as in the above, he rarely invents German words to match Burney's neologisms. The bold exception (considering the debates on translation which we have mentioned in preceding chapters) is 'londonisiren' for Burney's splendid 'Londonize'.[50] However, when the original, 'We have been *a shopping*, as Mrs. Mirvan calls it', is rendered as 'Wir sind [...] in den Galanterie-Läden gewesen, wie es Frau Mirvan nennet',

46 Burney, *Evelina,* ed. by Bloom, II.ii.151; *Evelina, oder Eines jungen Frauenzimmers Eintritt in die Welt,* II.xxxiii.313.

47 Cf. 'widerwärtig, adj., adv.', *Deutsches Wörterbuch von Jakob und Wilhelm Grimm,* online edn (Trier: Trier Center for Digital Humanities, 2011) <http://woerterbuchnetz.de/DWB/?sigle=DWB&mode=Vernetzung&lemid=GW19964#XGW19964> [accessed 3 June 2015].

48 Burney, *Evelina,* ed. by Bloom, II.iii.156; *Evelina, oder Eines jungen Frauenzimmers Eintritt in die Welt,* II.xxxiv.324.

49 Burney, *Evelina,* ed. by Bloom, I.xvi.61; *Evelina, oder Eines jungen Frauenzimmers Eintritt in die Welt,* I.xvi.116. For the range of meanings 'make up' took on after Burney, cf. section 10e in 'make, v.', *OED Online,* March 2015 (Oxford: Oxford University Press, 2015) <http://www.oed.com/view/Entry/112645> [accessed 1 June 2015].

50 Burney, *Evelina,* ed. by Bloom, I.x.25; *Evelina, oder Eines jungen Frauenzimmers Eintritt in die Welt,* I.x.35. Compare Weiße's own coinage 'stötterisiren', mentioned above.

the translator's inability to convey the novelty of the concept of 'shopping' makes the second half of the phrase seem rather pointless in the translation.[51]

While Weiße is never confounded by the compounds of Burney's own devising – 'tea-parties' become 'Thee-Gesellschaften'; 'window-seat' is translated simply as 'Fenster' – some of the more challenging ones inspire him to unusually creative choices which, in most cases, are highly successful.[52] Thus, for Burney's 'the women run skimper scamper', Weiße translates 'die Weibsen springen im Garten herum, hast du nicht gesehen!'.[53] Captain Mirvan's asking Mr. Lovel about his curious hairstyle, 'that frizzle-frize top of your own', in the German version entertainingly turns into '[das] Geschnörkel auf dem Gehirnkasten'.[54] 'Thing-em-bob' (as in, 'Pray, is one Miss Anville in any of them *thing-em-bobs*?' (in this case, carriages)) is not Burney's own invention – the *Oxford English Dictionary* cites an earlier use in Smollett's *Peregrine Pickle* (1751); and a colloquialism of this kind would in any case have been mainly in oral use – yet certainly the kind of nonsensical compound not defined by Weiße's dictionaries.[55] The first German translator of *Peregrine Pickle* had simply translated the phrase 'thingumbobs at the wrists' as 'was soll ich sagen für Angehänge an den Ermeln'.[56] Weiße, by contrast, misconstrued the word as having a meaning connected with the carriages to which it refers in the scene in *Evelina*, rather than recognizing it as a nonsensical expression for 'thing'. His translation as 'Purzelbude', however ('He! ist nicht eine gewisse Miß Anville in einer von den Purzelbuden da?') works perfectly well and the colloquial tone of the

51 Burney, *Evelina*, ed. by Bloom, i.x.27; *Evelina, oder Eines jungen Frauenzimmers Eintritt in die Welt*, i.x.38. Burney was not the first to use this term, yet it was a very recent addition to English vocabulary; the *OED* cites its first use in 1764 ('shopping, n.', *OED Online*, March 2015 (Oxford: Oxford University Press, 2015) <http://www.oed.com/view/Entry/178539> [accessed 1 June 2015]).

52 Burney, *Evelina*, ed. by Bloom, i.xvi.58; *Evelina, oder Eines jungen Frauenzimmers Eintritt in die Welt*, i.xvi.110; Burney, *Evelina*, ed. by Bloom, iii.xv.352; *Evelina, oder Eines jungen Frauenzimmers Eintritt in die Welt*, iii.lxxvi.760.

53 Burney, *Evelina*, ed. by Bloom, ii.xv.195; *Evelina, oder Eines jungen Frauenzimmers Eintritt in die Welt*, ii.xlvi.410.

54 Burney, *Evelina*, ed. by Bloom, iii.xxi.394; *Evelina, oder Eines jungen Frauenzimmers Eintritt in die Welt*, iii.lxxxii.853.

55 Burney, *Evelina*, ed. by Bloom, iii.xxi.390. Cf. 'thingamabob, n.', *OED Online*, March 2015 (Oxford: Oxford University Press, 2015) <http://www.oed.com/view/Entry/200791> [accessed 1 June 2015].

56 Cf. Tobias Smollett, *Begebenheiten des Peregrine Pickels*, 4 vols (Leipzig: Gleditsch, 1753), i, 19.

whole sentence is matched perfectly.[57] While some of these choices seem rather hit-and-miss, overall Weiße's translations of Burney's new and slang vocabulary are successful. Given the enormous time constraints under which this translation was produced, the first step towards comprehension would have been an educated guess rather than dedicated lexicological research, even if better dictionaries had been available. In any case, this vocabulary did not even pose the most significant challenge to a translator.

Perhaps the most enjoyable and recognizable feature of Burney's writing are the characteristic styles of speech which distinguish the main characters from one another, highly individual idioms on the reproduction of which the success of the translation hinges. The eponymous Evelina and the Branghtons, Madame Duval and Captain Mirvan, Lord Orville and Sir Clement Willoughby – more than by their actions, they are characterized by what they say and how they say it. Part of Weiße's task as a translator was to convey this stylistic variety to a German reader. We shall look at just two characteristic examples here.

Captain Mirvan's way of expressing himself is distinguished by his tactless exclamations, frenzied, broken-up syntax and frequent use of naval metaphors. The peculiarity of his style is especially noticeable when it is juxtaposed directly with the sober tones of Evelina, as in the following scene:

We had hardly proceeded half a mile, when a gentleman from a post-chaise, which came galloping after us, called out to the servants, 'Holla, my Lads, – pray is one Miss Anville in any of them *thing-em-bobs?*'	Wir waren kaum eine Viertelstunde fort, als eine Postschaise in vollem Galoppe hinter uns her kam, und ein Herr aus derselben den Bedienten zurief: Holla, Bursche, – He! ist nicht eine gewisse Miß Anville in einer von den Purzelbuden da?
I immediately recollected the voice of Captain Mirvan, and Lord Orville stopt the phaeton. He was out of the chaise, and with us in a moment. 'So, Miss Anville,' cried he, 'how do you do? so I hear you're Miss Belmont now; – pray how does old Madame French do?'	Ich erkannte sogleich die Stimme des Capitän Mirvan, und Lord Orville hielt mit seinem Phaeton stille. Er sprang mit uns zugleich aus dem Wagen. Nu, Miß Anville, schrie er, wie befinden sie sich? Nu, ich höre ja, sie sind jetzt Miß Belmont? –, Sagen sie mir doch was die alte französische Madame macht?

57 Burney, *Evelina, oder Eines jungen Frauenzimmers Eintritt in die Welt,* III. lxxxii.845.

'Madame Duval,' said I, 'is, I believe, very well.'	Frau Duval, sagte ich, befindet sich, wie ich glaube sehr wohl.
'I hope she's in *good case,*' said he, winking significantly, 'and won't flinch at seeing service: she has laid by long enough to refit and be made tight. And pray how does poor Monsieur Doleful do? is he as lank-jawed as ever?'[58]	Ich hoffe, antwortete er, sie wird sich in guten Umständen befinden, und einen Dienst nicht ausschlagen; sie hat lange genug auf der Rhede gelegen, und kann nun wohl einmahl wieder kalfatert werden. Und was macht denn der arme Monsieur Wimmerig? Ist er noch immer so dünnbäckig als sonst?[59]

On balance, Weiße's German rendering of Mirvan's characteristic idiom can be regarded as successful. There is only one small omission in the translation ('winking significantly' – perhaps because Weiße was justifiably unsure what sort of deplorable innuendo was hidden there), but Weiße's German matches for the Captain's striking naval imagery in the last paragraph are more than adequate. The translation of 'cried' as 'schrie' is, unfortunately, not indicative of Mirvan's tone of voice, but rather Weiße's standard translation of the word, which, at many points in the novel, gives a false impression of the emotional state in which conversations are being conducted; 'rufen' might have been the more appropriate choice there.

Apart from this, however, the translation fully conveys the many characteristic linguistic traits of the Captain. There is almost perfect congruity between the registers, most significantly with regard to the many colloquialisms: thus, 'Lads' becomes 'Bursche', 'So' is translated as 'Nu' and 'Monsieur Doleful' is aptly called 'Monsieur Wimmerig'. Weiße does not mitigate the skittish syntax of the Captain and retains the (certainly deliberate) stylistic contrast with Evelina's succinct, polite reply – all this to the effect that in the German version Captain Mirvan has as distinct an idiom as in the original and is as recognizable for it.

The second example is the French Madame Duval's speech. The idiom of a non-native speaker, in its original form it frequently features contractions and double (sometimes even triple) negatives. The style of an ignorant, boorish and emotional person withal, it is distinguished

58 Burney, *Evelina*, ed. by Bloom, III.xxi.390–91 (paragraph layout adjusted to aid comparison).

59 Burney, *Evelina, oder Eines jungen Frauenzimmers Eintritt in die Welt,* III. lxxxii.845.

by exclamations and outbursts on any occasion. Once more, the calm interpolations of Evelina often serve as a contrast to Madame Duval's breathless speeches. The scene below follows the two women's encounter with footpads on their journey to Justice Tyrell:

> 'Fright, child!' repeated she, 'why, that's not half; – I promise you, I wish it was; but here I'm bruised from top to toe, and it's well if ever I have the right use of my limbs again. [...]

> Schrecken, Kind? wiederhohlte sie; o, das ist noch das wenigste – wahrhaftig, ich wünschte es wäre das alles; aber da bin ich vom Kopf bis auf die Fäße ganz zerstoßen, und es wird viel seyn, wenn ich jemahls wieder den gesunden Gebrauch meiner Glieder bekommen werde. [...]

> But here the worst is to come, for I can't go out, because I've got no curls, and so he'll be escaped, before I can get to the Justice to stop him.

> Aber das schlimmste kommt noch, denn ich kann nicht ausgehen, weil ich keine Locken habe, und so wird er glücklich davon kommen, ehe ich zu dem Richter kommen kann, ihn setzen zu lassen.

> I'm resolved I'll tell Lady Howard how her man served me, for if he had n't made me fling 'em away, I dare say I could have pinned them up well enough for the country.'

> Ich habe mir vorgenommen, ich will es der Lady Howard erzählen, wie ihr Lakey mich bedient hat, denn hätt er nicht gemacht, daß ich sie weggeworfen hätte so hätte ich sie doch noch wieder zusammenstecken können, denn vor das Land wären sie noch gut gewesen.

> 'Perhaps Lady Howard may be able to lend you a cap that will wear without them.'

> Vielleicht kann ihnen Lady eine Haube borgen, die sie ohne Locken aufsetzen können.

> 'Lady Howard, indeed! why, do you think I'd wear one of her dowdies? No, I'll promise you, I sha'n't put on no such disguisement. It's the unluckiest thing in the world that I did not make the man

> Lady Howard? wahrhaftig! – denkst du denn, ich würde eins von ihren Nestern aufsetzen mögen? Nein, wahrhaftig nicht, so mag ich mich nicht verstellen. Es ist ein entsetzliches Unglück, daß ich den Menschen die

pick up the curls again; but he put me in such a passion, I could not think of nothing. I know I can't get none at Howard Grove for love nor money, for of all the stupid places ever I see, that Howard Grove is the worst! There's never no getting nothing one wants.'[60]	Locken nicht wieder aufklauben ließ; aber er brachte mich in solchen Zorn, daß ich nicht daran denken konnte. Ich weiß, ich kann weder für Geld noch für gute Worte welche zu Howard-Grove bekommen, denn von allen dummen[61] Orten, die ich nur gesehen habe, ist Howard-Grove der ärgste, da kann man nichts bekommen, was man braucht.[62]

This example illustrates the limits of how far Weiße is willing to go in his translation of linguistic idiosyncrasies. While in the German version Madame Duval's speech is still distinguishable from that of other characters, it does not include nearly as many of its original distinctive features as is the case with Captain Mirvan. The German syntax mirrors the English closely and while at times it feels rather alien, at least it works to the extent of conveying Madame Duval's breathless manner of speaking. Nonetheless, Weiße drastically smooths out her erratic grammar and pronunciation: there is no German counterpart for either her contractions (can't, 'em, 'sha'n't, etc.) or the multiple negatives ('there's never no getting nothing one wants'). Presumably, these features were beyond what Weiße felt was acceptable as literary language; his decision is typical for his time, yet it certainly makes Madame Duval's speech much less distinctive in his version.

Captain Mirvan and Madame Duval's characteristic idioms are representative of those of the whole set of characters. Weiße's ability to convey their linguistic mannerisms, a feature from which much of the novel's comedy derives, into the target language is decidedly uneven. Perhaps thanks to his experience in writing and translating comic plays, he acquits himself very well at creating a German equivalent for Sir Clement Willoughby's exaggerated rhetoric of

60 Burney, *Evelina*, ed. by Bloom, ii.ii.151 (layout adjusted to aid comparison).

61 A significant mistranslation; the *OED* cites from *Evelina* this very example of the use of 'stupid' in the sense of 'Void of interest, tiresome, boring, dull' ('stupid, adj. and n.', *OED Online*, March 2015 (Oxford: Oxford University Press, 2015) <http://www.oed.com/view/Entry/192218> [accessed 1 June 2015]).

62 Burney, *Evelina, oder Eines jungen Frauenzimmers Eintritt in die Welt*, ii.xxxiii.312–13.

love-making, but his attempt at translating Mrs. Selwyn's caustic wit is significantly less successful. Weiße seems most confident when approaching the sober styles of Arthur Villars or Evelina herself. The overall effect is that while the German translation is consistent in itself and still a readable literary text – including in the sense that the distinctions between characters are reflected in their way of speaking – the German *Evelina* offers only a toned-down version of the elaborate and highly effective system of idiolects and jargon which Burney uses to let her characters take shape.

As mentioned earlier in this sub-chapter, the absence of paratextual additions to the text by the translator is noteworthy. Considering that Weiße (like most translators of his age) employed explanatory footnotes in several of his translations, their complete absence from *Evelina* is particularly striking. In certain places the translator has made very slight alterations to the text in order to render it more comprehensible to his German readers, especially where cultural knowledge is needed. Such is the case of 'the birth-day' which Sir Clement Willoughby mentions as a defining event of the London season.[63] Unobtrusively, this becomes 'de[r] Geburtstag des Königes' in the translation, proof, incidentally, of how well acquainted Weiße was with London social customs (though, equally, at some points it is evident that he had not caught up with the very latest developments).[64] In most cases of this kind, however, he foregoes explanation altogether; and this in a novel which in any modern edition necessitates endnotes by the dozen. German readers either have to be already familiar with London entertainments, the culture of English resort towns and the customs of the gentry, or a good portion of the deeper layers of Burney's text will be lost on them.

While this does mark a deviation from Weiße's usual practice, it is, in less pronounced ways, a feature of his other translations of popular novels as well. Here, then, the combination of the enormous haste with which the book was translated and the attitude of the period regarding the literary value of popular fiction takes full effect. Since *Evelina* is not among those prose translations mentioned by Weiße in his letters, we can assume that for him it constituted mere bread-and-butter business. While the translation is very successful in some ways, it does not rise to the challenge of the original. The German version cannot be regarded as achieving a stature equal to Burney's original. The enormous success of the original eluded it completely; in fact,

63 Burney, *Evelina*, ed. by Bloom, ɪɪ.i.135.

64 *Evelina, oder Eines jungen Frauenzimmers Eintritt in die Welt*, ɪɪ.xxxii.278–79.

we could not find a single contemporary review of the translation. Aside from the translation's own deficiencies, the speed with which Schwickert inevitably had to publish the book may, ironically, have contributed to this. In time, the success enjoyed by *Evelina* in Britain would find a modest reflection among the German reading public, yet when Weiße's translation came out in 1779 it was just another novel among countless others published that year.[65]

Unlike some of his translations and adaptations of French and English plays and poetry, Weiße's translations of popular novels, while a key part of his oeuvre and characteristic of the developments in the book market during that period, remained of little literary significance. As his career as a translator reached its most productive stage, it was his ability to shape the work of others through his various literary networks which allowed him to have a much deeper impact.

65 The German reception of Burney has so far attracted little attention. For a brief enquiry into the German reception of *Evelina*, see Catherine M. Parisian, 'German Audiences for Frances Burney's *Evelina, or A Young Lady's Entrance into the World*', *The Center and Clark Newsletter*, 49 (2009), 2–4. No less than the present investigation, Parisian's survey of German translations of *Cecilia* is hampered by the lack of surviving copies (Catherine M. Parisian, *Frances Burney's 'Cecilia': A Publishing History*, Ashgate Studies in Publishing History (London/ New York: Routledge, 2016), pp. 67–92).

7. Networks: The 'Uebersetzungsentrepreneur'

It has already been mentioned that the 'flood' of translations, especially from the English, paired with a perceived decline in their quality, led to increasing criticism of commercial translators and the publishing industry in the second half of the century. With the growing market share of translated literature, the occupation which produced it had become highly differentiated. Friedrich Nicolai, in his novel *Das Leben und die Meinungen des Herrn Magister Sebaldus Nothanker* (1776), provided a comprehensive, and often satirical, description of the business.[1] After a post in Leipzig has been secured for the protagonist of the novel, the clergyman Nothanker, he learns about the commercial practices that prevail in the capital of the German book trade. The lesson includes the following typology of translators:

> Ein Uebersetzer aus dem engländischen ist vornehmer, als ein Uebersetzer aus dem französischen, weil er seltener ist. Ein Uebersetzer aus dem italiänischen läßt sich schon bitten, ehe er zu arbeiten anfängt [...]. Einen Uebersetzer aus dem spanischen aber, findet man fast gar nicht [...]. Uebersetzer aus dem lateinischen und griechischen sind häufig, werden aber gar nicht gesucht, daher bieten sie sich mehrentheils selbst an. Außerdem giebt es auch Uebersetzer, die zeitlebens gar nichts anders thun als übersetzen; Uebersetzer, die ihre Uebersetzungen in Nebenstunden zur Erholung machen [...]; Vornehme Uebersetzer, diese begleiten ihre Uebersetzungen mit einer Vorrede, und versichern die Welt, daß das Original sehr gut sey; Gelehrte Uebersetzer, diese verbessern ihre Uebersetzungen, begleiten sie mit Anmerkungen und versichern, daß es sehr schlecht sey, daß Sie es aber doch leidlich gemacht hätten; Uebersetzer, die durch Uebersetzungen Originalschriftsteller werden, diese nehmen ein französisches oder engländisches Buch, lassen Anfang und

1 Friedrich Nicolai, *Das Leben und die Meinungen des Herrn Magister Sebaldus Nothanker*, 3 vols (Berlin/Stettin: Nicolai, 1773–76) (*Verzeichniß der Bibliothek*, 1352).

> Ende weg, ändern und verbessern das übrige nach Gutdünken [...] und geben das Buch für ihre eigene Arbeit aus. Endlich giebt es Uebersetzer, die ihre Uebersetzungen selbst machen, und solche die sie von andern machen lassen.[2]
>
> [A translator from the English ranks higher than a translator from the French because he is rarer. A translator from the Italian will give himself airs before he sets to work [...]. Yet a translator from the Spanish can scarcely ever be found [...]. Translators from the Latin and Greek are common, but not wanted; therefore, they will usually advertise themselves. There are also translators who never do anything but translate; translators who do their translations in idle hours, for recreation [...]; elegant translators, who add a preface to their translations and assure the world that the original is very good; learned translators, who improve their translations, annotate them and affirm that they [the originals] are bad, but they made them passable after all; translators who through translations become original writers: these take a French or English book, leave out the beginning and end, revise and improve the rest at their discretion [...] and pass off the book as their own work. Lastly, there are translators who do their translations themselves and those who have them done by others.]

While presented in the form of fiction, this is one of the most elaborate contemporary accounts of the state of literary translation. Of course, many translators could have been classed under several of these types, Weiße included. The 'ranking' of languages, meanwhile, is certainly an accurate description of the state of affairs in the second half of the century. The need for publishers to acquire the necessary expertise to match original works with suitable translators from a vast, ever-growing pool gave rise to a new type of agent in the market, an 'entrepreneur' of translations, as Nicolai calls it:

> Sie müssen wissen, daß es berühmte Leute giebt, die die Uebersetzungen im Großen entrepreniren, wie ein irrländischer Lieferant das Pöckelfleisch für ein spanisches Geschwader, und sie hernach wieder an ihre Unterübersetzer austheilen. Diese Leute haben von allen neuen übersetzbaren Büchern in Frankreich, Italien und England die erste Nachricht, wie ein Mäckler in Amsterdam Nachricht von Ankunft der ostindischen Schiffe im Texel hat.[3] An diese wenden sich alle Buchhändler, die Uebersetzungen haben wollen, und sie kennen wieder jeden ihrer Arbeiter, wozu er zu gebrauchen ist, und wie hoch er im Preise stehet. Sie wenden ihnen Arbeit zu,

2 Nicolai, *Sebaldus Nothanker*, I, 100.

3 Dutch merchant ships would load and unload cargo in the Texel Roads.

bestrafen sie wenn sie säumig sind mit Entziehung ihrer Protection, merzen die Fehler ihrer Uebersetzungen aus, oder bemänteln sie mit ihrem vornehmen Namen, denn mehrentheils sind Entrepreneure von dieser Art stark im Vorredenschreiben. Sie wissen auch genau, wie viel Fleiß an jede Art der Uebersetzung zu wenden nöthig ist, und welche Mittel anzuwenden sind, damit ihre Uebersetzungen allenthalben angepriesen, und dem berühmten Manne öffentlich gedanket werde, der die deutsche gelehrte Welt damit beglückt hat.[4]

[You should know that there are famous people who do business in [lit. 'entrepreneer'] translations on a large scale, as an Irish merchant buys brawn for a Spanish fleet, and afterwards distribute them to their sub-translators. These people receive the first news of all new translatable books from France, Italy and England, as a broker in Amsterdam receives news of ships from the Indies arriving at Texel. All booksellers who want translations turn to them; and they in turn know every worker, what he can do and what prices he commands. They allocate work to them, punish them if they are tardy by withdrawing their protection; they correct their mistakes, or cloak them in their own famous names, for entrepreneurs of this kind are usually good at writing prefaces. They also know exactly how much diligence needs to be expended on each kind of translation and by which means they can ensure that their translations are universally applauded; and public thanks is given to the famous man for thus favouring the learned German world.]

This extraordinary passage has been quoted here at such length because it seems likely that Weiße was among the people whom Nicolai had in mind when he composed his satire. While there is no indication in the sources that Weiße ever put his name on a translation produced by another, and he had little financial gain from his role as an intermediary between publishers and translators (in fact, on more than one occasion he sacrificed his own time and money to obtain a commission for a struggling young practitioner), he nevertheless qualified as an 'entrepreneur' of translations.[5] His

4 Nicolai, *Sebaldus Nothanker*, I, 101–02.

5 In any case, Blankenburg's review of the novel in Weiße's *Bibliothek* did not comment on the passages quoted here (Christian Friedrich von Blankenburg, review of Friedrich Nicolai, *Das Leben und die Meinungen des Herrn Magister Sebaldus Nothanker*, I (1773), *NBSWFK*, 17.2 (1775), 257–84). At the same time, of course, Weiße exemplified not only the 'entrepreneur', but also a second type described by Nicolai: 'Unsere beste Schriftsteller haben zuweilen, die Muße, die sie zu ihren vortreflichsten eigenen Werken nöthig gehabt haben, durch fabrikenmäßige Uebersetzungen, kümmerlich verdienen müssen. Es ist leider fast gar kein anderes Mittel da, um einen Gelehrten der kein Amt hat und kein Amt bekommen kann, vor dem Hunger zu verwahren' [Our best writers have

role to this effect at Weidmann's has already been discussed, but over time Weiße came to fulfil a similar function for a range of mostly Leipzig-based publishers with a focus on translation, chief among them Crusius, Dyck and Schwickert, all of whom also published his own translations and original works.

An Intermediary between Publishers and Translators

After Weidmanns Erben und Reich, perhaps the second closest relationship Weiße had with a publisher-bookseller was the Dycksche Buchhandlung in Leipzig, which after the death of its founder Johann Gottfried Dyck in 1762 was managed by his widow, Regina Elisabeth Dyck (née Köhler). The firm published not only Weiße's *(Neue) Bibliothek der schönen Wissenschaften und der freyen Künste* but also his original and translated works for the stage. The most important professional relationship for Weiße in the 1760s must have been Reich at Weidmann's, but as far as his role as a facilitator or 'entrepreneur' of translations was concerned, he was similarly well-connected to the house of Dyck.[6] As an independent agent, Weiße himself determined which projects suited which publisher and then usually recommended a title along with a translator. In January of 1762, for example, he wrote to his new friend, Hagedorn:

> Wegen des Wright habe ich den Entschluß gefaßt: ihn der Weidmannischen Handl. vorzuschlagen, welche die Kosten des Verlags eher tragen kann: der rechtschaffenen [Dÿckin] will ich das ganz vortreffl. Buch, das vor kurzen erst in England erschienen ist, *Elements of Criticism by Henry Home* in 3 Vols. übersetzen laßen.[7]

sometimes wretchedly had to earn the leisure necessary for their own greatest works with factory-type translations. Unfortunately, there is hardly any other means of preserving a scholar from hunger when he has no official post, and no hope of obtaining one] (Nicolai, *Sebaldus Nothanker*, I, 107).

6 Not least because Reich himself was. During the 1760s, while Regina Elisabeth Dyck was at the helm of the business, Reich served as a trustee and Engelhard Benjamin Schwickert as the chief executive of the company. In 1770 Johann Gottried Dyck the Younger (1750–1813) took control of the firm ('Dycksche Buchhandlung', in Helmut Bähring and Kurt Rüddiger, *Lexikon Buchstadt Leipzig. Von den Anfängen bis zum Jahr 1990* (Taucha: Tauchaer Verlag, 2008), pp. 75–76 (p. 75)).

7 C. F. Weiße, Letter to Christian Ludwig von Hagedorn, 2 January 1762 (UBL Ms.0670u (10)).

> [Regarding the Wright, I have decided to offer it to Weidmann's, who are likelier to be able to afford the publishing costs; for the honest Mrs Dyck, I will have a most excellent book translated, which was only recently published in England, *Elements of Criticism* by Henry Home in 3 vols.]

The 'Wright' mentioned here was Edward Wright, author of a travel account which in the end Reich did not publish.[8] The Scottish Enlightenment thinker Henry Home's influential *Elements of Criticism*, on the other hand, was published by Dyck in three volumes between 1763 and 1766 as *Grundsätze der Critik*, a translation whose success

8 Nevertheless, and despite the fact that Weiße in all likelihood had little to do with the eventual translation of the book, the history of its publication deserves to be recounted, if only to illustrate the sometimes adventurous conditions under which translations were produced in this period. Edward Wright's *Some Observations Made in Travelling through France, Italy, etc. in the Years 1720, 1721, and 1722* had been published in two volumes in 1730 (London: Ward & Wickseed), with a second edition printed in 1764 (London: Millar). Eventually, the German translation of this book was published as a supplement to another travel account, [Joseph de?] Blainville's *Reisebeschreibung durch Holland, Oberdeutschland und die Schweiz besonders aber durch Italien*, in five volumes (Lemgo: Meyer, 1764–67), translated by Johann Tobias Köhler (1720–1768), a professor at Göttingen who probably had access to both editions of the English original. The supplement to Blainville was published as Wright's *Beobachtungen, die er auf seinen Reisen durch Frankreich und Italien in den Jahren 1720. 1721. 1722. gemacht* (the last two of the five volumes of the above, published in 1767). In his preface to the translation, Köhler explains that after Blainville wrote the original manuscript of his travel account in a variety of European languages, it had been translated into English by a triumvirate consisting of William Guthrie, George Turnbull and John Lockmann. During his work on the translation of the fourth volume, Lockmann, travelling by coach from his Salisbury estate to London with Blainville's original manuscript in his luggage, became the victim of footpads, who stole all his belongings including the manuscript, which they later burnt. Thus, the manuscript volume containing Blainville's account of his travels in Italy was lost. Köhler therefore decided to supplement his own translation of Blainville with Wright's travel accounts, which according to him were particularly valuable in their depiction of Italy. It is haphazard processes of reception such as these which make the attention paid by cultural transfer theory to nonlinear engagements so rewarding. As a another side note, the very John Lockmann mentioned here, who Köhler claims was a German-born immigrant to Britain, was the same who provided the English translation of Voltaire's *Letters Concerning the English Nation*, an instrumental text in the discourse on European Anglophilia in the eighteenth century (J. Patrick Lee, 'The Unexamined Premise: Voltaire, John Lockman and the Myth of the English Letters', in *From Letter to Publication*, ed. by Robert V. McNamee, Studies on Voltaire and the Eighteenth Century 2001:10 (Oxford: Voltaire Foundation, 2001), pp. 240–70).

mirrored that of the original.[9] The translator was Johann Nicolaus Meinhard (1727–1767), a regular contributor to Weiße's *Bibliothek* for whom he sometimes obtained commissions.

The opposite case, examples of which have already been cited in connection with Weidmann's, was a (usually struggling) translator's approaching Weiße to ask either for intercession with a publisher or a recommendation for a book to translate as well. In many of these instances, Weiße readily mobilized his networks to come to their aid, in a manner that makes him stand apart from the 'entrepreneurs' so harshly satirized by Nicolai. One such translator was Karl August Kütner (1748–1800), who studied at the University of Leipzig between 1767 and 1772 and later became Professor of Greek at the Academia Petrina in Mitau. Translating seems to have been an important way of providing for himself when a student. The first time Weiße refers to him is in a letter to Hagedorn in March 1770, where he mentions that he 'had' Kütner's translation of the *Iliad*, 'die nicht übel gerathen ist' [which is not badly done], printed 'in der Mad. Dÿckin Verlage', where the first of two volumes came out the following year.[10]

As soon as the *Iliad* had gone to print, Kütner told Weiße that he had also translated 'den ganzen Horatz' [the whole of Horace] in the original metre. Appropriately enough, Weiße forwarded a selection of the translated odes to his friend the 'German Horace', Ramler, asking him for comment and mentioning in passing the *Iliad* translation which he had had printed 'um ihm zu ein paar Thln zu helfen' [to help him to a few Thalers], thus emphasizing Kütner's financial need.[11] The Horatian odes would be published only the following year by Schwickert.[12] Despite his readiness to intercede on behalf of the likes of Kütner, always remembering his own dependence on commissions early in his career, Weiße takes his next reference to Kütner in a letter to Ramler as an opportunity to complain about the onslaught of supplicants that invade his office every day. While the

9 Norbert Bachleitner, 'Die Rezeption von Henry Homes "Elements of Criticism" in Deutschland 1763–1793', *Arcadia*, 20 (1985), 113–33. Weiße owned two editions of the translation (*Verzeichniß der Bibliothek*, 1506 and 1508–10).

10 C. F. Weiße, Letter to Christian Ludwig von Hagedorn, 26 March 1770 (UBL Ms.0670u (26)). Cf. Homer, *Iliade*, 2 vols, trans. by Karl August Kütner (Leipzig: Dyck, 1771–73).

11 C. F. Weiße, Letter to Karl Wilhelm Ramler, 8 May 1771 (GSA 75/229,2 (42)).

12 Cf. also Weiße's letter to Benedict Maria von Werkmeister, 27 May 1777 (Weiße, 'Briefe an Werkmeister', p. 284).

complaint is a recurring one throughout his letters, this particular passage is especially poetic:

> Ich habe eine große Plage mit den hiesigen jungen Witzlingen. Täglich kömmt eine Heerde mit Embryonen ihrer Musen und raubt mir meine schönste Zeit, die Zeit, die mir nur in kleinen Tröpfchen zu Autorgeschäften zugezählet ist, u. ich bin so ein guter Narre, daß ich mir auch diese von andern weghaschen lasse: aber ich denke immer, was hat dein Rammler an Dir gethan.[13]

> [The local young wits are a great plague to me. Every day, a herd of them come with embryos of their muses and consume my best time, that time which, for the business of writing, is allocated to me only in the smallest portions; and I am such a kind fool as to allow others to snatch it from me: yet I always think of what my Ramler has done for me.]

It was by no means only for the big publisher-booksellers or those who published his own works that Weiße brokered translations. His wide-ranging networks allowed him to place translations (as well as original publications) with all sorts of publishers, though the great majority of them were based in Leipzig. Even when he did not facilitate the translation, Weiße frequently revised and copy-edited the translations of friends and colleagues (often, and once more in deviation from Nicolai's satire, without financial reward). This was the case, for instance, with the translation of Beaumont and Fletcher's *The Maid's Tragedy* (1619) which Heinrich Wilhelm von Gerstenberg, another frequent contributor to the *Bibliothek*, had completed. The book, which in addition to the play contained translated dissertations on various Early Modern poets, was published by a publisher-bookseller (who attended the book fair in Leipzig every year) in Gerstenberg's then home town of Copenhagen and the translator dedicated the volume to Weiße.[14]

Thanks to his role as a go-between in the publishing industry, Weiße's networks always included the youngest generation of fledgling writers and translators, something which contributed much to his image as the genial old man presiding over the literary

13 C. F. Weiße, Letter to Karl Wilhelm Ramler, 24 September 1771 (GSA 75/229,2 (46)).

14 Francis Beaumont and John Fletcher, *Die Braut: eine Tragödie; Nebst kritischen und biographischen Abhandlungen über die 4 größten Dichter des ältern brittischen Theaters und einem Schreiben an den Kreis-Steuer-Einnehmer Weiße in Leipzig*, trans. and ed. by Heinrich Wilhelm von Gerstenberg (Kopenhagen/Leipzig: Rothens Wittwe & Profft, 1765); cf. Weiße, *Selbstbiographie*, pp. 61–62.

establishment in Leipzig.[15] In his relations with publishers, Weiße's ties were mainly to members of his own generation; among his 'regular' publishers, Schwickert was the only one to have been born after 1740 and had had his start in Leipzig as chief executive at Dyck's (1763–70).[16] Nevertheless, there is occasional evidence that Weiße's networks stretched into the next generation of publisher-booksellers as well. For the writer Johann Gottfried Seume (1763–1810), now best known for his *Spaziergang nach Syrakus im Jahre 1802*, who had been released on bail by a Prussian press gang, Weiße obtained a commission to translate Robert Bage's sentimental novel *The Fair Syrian*, thus enabling him to repay his bail money.[17] The translation, entitled *Honorie Warren*, was published by Göschen in 1788. Georg Joachim Göschen (1752–1828) had established his own business only in 1785 but would soon win fame as Goethe and Schiller's publisher. He had worked at Crusius's bookshop in the 1770s and thus had become part of the same circles.[18] On the whole, however, most of Weiße's connections in the publishing industry seem to have been made in the 1760s and 1770s. He was able to draw on many of them to the end of his life, but it is possible that the gradual reduction in his networking activities in the 1790s was not exclusively due to the effects of old age, but partly the result of a generational gap that was beginning to make itself felt.

15 Walter Pape has suggested that Weiße's infamous reticence in public literary debates and his refusal to enter into conflict also predestined him to become a literary broker because they suggested disinterestedness (Walter Pape, '"Ein Billetdoux an die ganze Menschheit". Christian Felix Weiße und die Aufklärung', in *Zentren der Aufklärung III*, ed. by Martens, pp. 267–95 (p. 273).

16 Bähring and Rüddiger, 'Dycksche Buchhandlung', p. 75.

17 See, e.g., Stephan Füssel (ed.), *Georg Joachim Göschen. Ein Verleger der Spätaufklärung und der Deutschen Klassik*, Studien zur Verlagsgeschichte und zur Verlegertypologie der Goethe-Zeit, 1 (Berlin: de Gruyter, 1999), pp. 219–21.

18 The professional connection does not seem to have been a particularly close one, however. Between his years at Crusius's and his return to Leipzig, Göschen had worked for the Dessau 'Buchhandlung der Gelehrten'. During his time there he was approached in 1784 by Weiße, who misremembered Göschen's name as 'Jäschke' and who wrote to him to recommend Karl Gottfried Schreiter (1756–1809), a young philosopher and translator in Leipzig and frequent contributor to Weiße's *Bibliothek*, as a translator for Hugh Blair's *Lectures on Rhetoric and Belles Lettres*, which the 'Buchhandlung' should publish. However, the 'Buchhandlung' went out of business only a year later, prompting Göschen's return to Leipzig (Mark Lehmstedt, 'Ein Empfehlungsschreiben an "Herrn Jäschke" in Dessau', *Börsenblatt*, 157.9 (1990), 156–58).

Our Man in Leipzig

Even more than for the aspiring young writers and translators in Leipzig, a well-connected manager such as Weiße was important for those who lived far from the centres of the trade. Even the most accomplished of them often experienced difficulties obtaining commissions because of the speed with which negotiations had to be conducted. One such provincial translator was the philosopher Christian Garve.[19] In the mid-1760s he had briefly lived in Leipzig and made friends with Weiße, to whose *Bibliothek* he would be a lifelong contributor. As a translator, he made a name for himself with translations of key works of the Scottish Enlightenment, such as Adam Ferguson's *Institutes of Moral Philosophy* and Adam Smith's *Wealth of Nations*, as well as of Edmund Burke's *Enquiry into the Origin of our Ideas of the Sublime and Beautiful*.[20]

Despite the significance of these works, Garve, for whom the translations were an important means of augmenting his income, always found it difficult to obtain commissions from the big publishers in Leipzig. His correspondence with Weiße, which spans three decades, is full of enquiries about the latest foreign publications and exhortations to intercede with publishers on his behalf. For all the developments in the European book trade of the period, physical proximity to its centres remained an important factor in a translator's career. As Garve complains in an early letter from Breslau, 'Hier kann man Französische oder Englische Bücher fast gar nicht finden' [It is almost impossible to find English or French books here].[21] One of the main lines of enquiry across the correspondence, therefore, concerns new publications in French and English, always with a view towards what might be suitable for translation. 'Ist denn kein guter Roman erschienen?' [Has there not been a good new novel?], he asks Weiße; and in his next letter he demands information on new English books about which he has read in the journals.[22] A recurring request is that Weiße send him new issues or volumes of the *Reviews* which

19 For Garve's biography, see Kurt Wölfel, 'Garve, Christian', in *Neue deutsche Biographie*, VI (1964), 77–78.

20 See also Norbert Waszek, 'Übersetzungspraxis und Popularphilosophie am Beispiel Christian Garves', *Das achtzehnte Jahrhundert*, 31 (2007), 42–64.

21 Christian Garve, Letter to C. F. Weiße, 4/7 November 1772 (Garve, *Briefe an Christian Felix Weiße*, I, 8–9).

22 Christian Garve, Letter to C. F. Weiße, 10 January 1773 (Garve, *Briefe an Christian Felix Weiße*, I, 12–13) and 28 April 1773 (I, 23).

Weiße used for his *Bibliothek*.[23] The book fair in Leipzig could be used as an opportunity to transport books between the cities: 'Wenn von den englischen Büchern mir einige können zum Durchlesen erlaubt werden: so würden die Breslauer Buchhändler sie bequem mitnehmen' [If some of the English books can be spared for me to read, the Breslau booksellers could easily take them with them], Garve wrote in a letter to Weiße dated 27 April 1774, three days after the Easter Fair in Leipzig had begun.[24]

The correspondence between Garve and Weiße also illustrates the limits of the latter's influence, particularly with regard to the problems Garve faced because of his provincial abode. In numerous letters he complains about how commissions for translations were snatched away from him because he did not have information about the translatable book in time.[25] Many times Garve asks Weiße whether a certain title is still available for translation, only to learn that the commission has already been given to someone else.[26] On numerous occasions he proposes titles for translation which he asks Weiße to forward to Reich at Weidmann's and which the latter does not decide to pick up in the first place.

A particularly revealing case in this regard was the translation and publication of the Scottish historian William Robertson's highly successful *History of America* (1777–96). Three years before the book was first published in London, the network around Weiße and Reich already knew about the upcoming title. In March 1774 Garve announced to Weiße that 'Wenn Robertsons Geschichte von Amerika herauskommen wird, das wäre etwas für mich zu übersetzen' [When Robertson's *History of America* is published, that would be something for me to translate].[27] Aside from the fact that he felt suited to the

23 Cf. Christian Garve, Letter to C. F. Weiße, 22 April 1784, in which Garve asks Weiße to press Schwickert to respond to Garve, who had asked him whether his channels would enable him to provide English journals even faster (Garve, *Briefe an Christian Felix Weiße*, I, 179).

24 Garve, *Briefe an Christian Felix Weiße*, I, 67.

25 See, e.g., Garve, *Briefe an Christian Felix Weiße*, II, 12–13 and 35.

26 See, e.g., Garve's letter to Weiße, 14 December 1781, in which he enquires whether there might be an opportunity to translate Johnson's *Lives of the Poets*, which he had read about in the *Reviews* (Garve, *Briefe an Christian Felix Weiße*, I, 164). At that point, however, the translation by Blankenburg was already underway.

27 Christian Garve, Letter to C. F. Weiße, 12 March 1774 (Garve, *Briefe an Christian Felix Weiße*, I, 59).

task, there soon was a certain urgency in Garve's requests regarding the book:

> Ueberdies würde es mir eine Einnahme verschaffen, die mir nicht unlieb wäre. Haben Sie also die Güte, sich zu erkundigen, wer die Uebersetzung ankündigt, ob das Werk im Englischen schon heraus, ob die Uebersetzung schon angefangen sey. Wenn es einen Buchhändler giebt, der warten kann und mich nicht treibt, und das Buch nicht zu ungeheuer groß ist; so möchte ich es gerne übernehmen.[28]
>
> [In addition, it would provide some income for me, which would not be unwelcome. Would you, therefore, be so kind as to enquire who will publish the translation, whether the book has come out in English yet and whether the translation has already been started. If there is a bookseller who can wait and who will not push me, and if the book is not too big, then I would like to undertake it.]

Given the market pressure under which titles as eagerly anticipated as the *History of America* had to be translated, Garve's condition that the publisher not 'push' him seems downright naïve. In response to Weiße's letter indicating that the book had to be translated rather quickly, Garve complained:

> [S]o bitte ich Sie doch um des Himmels willen, was wird denn aus unsrer Litteratur werden, wenn sich die Autoren so nach dem Willen der Buchhändler bequemen sollen? [...] Ich kann das nicht, wenn ich auch wollte; und ich will es auch nicht.[29]
>
> [I ask you, for heaven's sake, what will become of our literature if the authors should thus conform to the will of booksellers? [...] I could not do it even if I wanted to; and I do not want to.]

Despite Garve's eagerness to translate the Robertson, Reich gave the commission directly to his London agent, Johann Friedrich Schiller, an indication of the special urgency with which the title was to be brought to print.[30]

28 Christian Garve, Letter to C. F. Weiße, 19 October 1774 (Garve, *Briefe an Christian Felix Weiße*, I, 85).

29 Christian Garve, Letter to C. F. Weiße, 22 November 1774 (Garve, *Briefe an Christian Felix Weiße*, I, 91–92).

30 William Robertson, *Geschichte von Amerika*, trans. by Johann Friedrich Schiller, 3 vols, I and II (Leipzig: Weidmanns Erben und Reich, 1777). For the full history of the title's publication in German, see Mark Lehmstedt, 'Die Geschichte einer Übersetzung. William Robertsons "Geschichte von Amerika" (1777)', *Leipziger Jahrbuch zur Buchgeschichte*, 1 (1991), 265–97.

As Mark Lehmstedt observes, Garve's hope that the authority of Weiße could alleviate or even abolish these conditions was misdirected: both as Reich's advisor and a translator constantly at work, Weiße was himself subject to the constraints of the system of the 'translation factory'.[31] As compensation of sorts, Reich and Weiße offered Garve the translation of a text by another representative of the Scottish Enlightenment, Alexander Gerard's *Essay on Genius*, a task Garve took on with a mixture of resignation and enthusiasm; the book was published by Weidmann's in 1776, ironically still prior to the publication of the Robertson translation.[32] Motivated perhaps by the depressing lesson he had just learnt, Garve explained to Weiße that he had developed a new approach to translating non-fiction: 'Man sollte aus jedem Absatze bloß den Sinn, die Hauptidee fassen, und diese kurz und rund ausdrücken' [One should grasp only the sense, the general idea of each paragraph, and express it succinctly and coherently].[33] Garve had finished the translation of Gerard by September 1775 and, following Weiße's recommendation, sent the manuscript to Zollikofer for revision before it was published the following year.[34] Nevertheless, the experience left its mark and a number of subsequent letters feature complaints about the state of translation and its effect on literature: 'Es ist unglaublich, wie viel der allgemeine Geschmack durch die häufige Lesung schlecht übersetzter Bücher leidet. Man weiß bald nicht mehr, was gutes oder was schlechtes Deutsch [...] ist' [It is incredible how much popular taste suffers from repeatedly reading bad translations. Soon one will be unable to tell good from bad German].[35]

Garve had even worse luck with Weidmann's when it came to his retranslation of Adam Smith's *Wealth of Nations* (1776). He first mentioned his intention to retranslate the book, which suited his profile as a translator of the Scottish Enlightenment, to Weiße in the summer of 1791. An earlier translation, that by the aforementioned Johann

31 Lehmstedt, 'Struktur und Arbeitsweise', p. 122.

32 Alexander Gerard, *Versuch über das Genie*, trans. by Christian Garve (Leipzig: Weidmanns Erben und Reich, 1776). Cf. Christian Garve, Letter to C. F. Weiße, 1 April 1775 (Garve, *Briefe an Christian Felix Weiße*, I, 125).

33 Christian Garve, Letter to C. F. Weiße, 5 May 1775 (Garve, *Briefe an Christian Felix Weiße*, I, 130).

34 Christian Garve, Letter to C. F. Weiße, September 1775 (Garve, *Briefe an Christian Felix Weiße*, I, 138).

35 Christian Garve, Letter to C. F. Weiße, 1 March 1785 (Garve, *Briefe an Christian Felix Weiße*, I, 197).

Friedrich Schiller, had been published by Weidmann's since 1776. The fact that Garve felt this translation was already outdated once more illustrates how quickly the literary idiom of the period evolved, though Garve also simply regarded Schiller's as a bad translation. In August he asked Weiße whether the latter knew anything of other attempts at retranslating Smith.[36] For once, Weiße's networking activities in Leipzig backfired. He told Weidmann's (now, after Reich's death, with Marie Louise Weidmann at the helm) about the project and they immediately took steps to protect their own product, having Garve attacked in the press just as the latter signed a contract for the translation with the Breslau-based publisher-bookseller Korn. Garve complained to Weiße:

> Zuerst sind die Verleger so übereilt mit der Uibersetzung neuer ausländischer Producte; sie ziehen den schnellen Uibersetzer dem guten so sehr vor, daß sich kein Mensch, der nicht des Brotes wegen arbeitet, darauf einlassen kann. Daraus entsteht dann aber auch, daß der größte Theil unsrer Uibersetzungen schlecht, oder doch im Styl höchst mittelmäßige Arbeiten sind. – Und durch eine solche übereilte Fabrikübersetzung eines guten Werks, sollten auf so lange, bis diese völlig verkauft ist, alle andern Gelehrten abgehalten werden, eine bessere zu machen?[37]
>
> [First, the publishers rush the translation of the latest foreign product; they prefer the quick translator over the good one, to such an extent that nobody who does not work for bread alone can accept it. This is the reason the greater part of our translations are bad or, at least, highly mediocre works in terms of their style. And for such a rushed factory translation of a good book, all other learned men should be prevented from providing a better one until the first is completely sold out?]

After briefly hesitating for fear of harmful action from Weidmann's, Garve and his publisher nevertheless went ahead with the retranslation.[38] In his work on the book Garve was assisted by August Gottlob Dörrien (1746–1813), a public servant in Leipzig and Göttingen. Weiße was kept in the loop all the while, not least as an informant on the current mood at Weidmann's, but also to comment

36 Christian Garve, Letter to C. F. Weiße, 26 August 1791 (Garve, *Briefe an Christian Felix Weiße*, II, 30).

37 Christian Garve, Letter to C. F. Weiße, 11 December 1791 (Garve, *Briefe an Christian Felix Weiße*, II, 34–35).

38 See, e.g., Christian Garve, Letter to C. F. Weiße, 11 December 1791 (Garve, *Briefe an Christian Felix Weiße*, II, 43).

on the translation itself.[39] He could occasionally utilize his networks to make up for the earlier *faux pas* – for instance, when Garve grappled with translation problems. In a letter in 1794, for example, he asks Weiße what he thought the term 'tallies' meant in the context of Adam Smith's thoughts on the Bank of England.[40] Weiße, whose own knowledge of English would have been equally baffled by advanced economic terminology, was able to obtain an explanation for Garve from a certain 'Marsh'. This was probably Herbert Marsh (1757–1839), a Cambridge-educated theologian with an interest in fiscal politics, who was well-connected among the German literati.[41] As so often, his connection to Weiße depended on Leipzig's role as an international intellectual centre: in the late 1780s Marsh had studied in Leipzig and at the time of Garve's enquiry had just returned there.[42]

The *Neue Bibliothek* as a Launchpad for Translators and Translations

As the preceding chapters have already shown, Weiße's position as editor of the *Neue Bibliothek* allowed him to launch and promote translations of various kinds. His translations of poetry, such as George Wither's 'The Shepherd's Resolution' ('Der entschloßne Schäfer' [64]) and Sappho's fragment of an ode ([89]), which he first published as part of extended reviews in the *Bibliothek* and later reprinted in his collections of poetry, have already been mentioned. However, there were also longer texts which, once they had been translated for publication in the *Bibliothek*, either outgrew the journal or became the nucleus of book publications in other ways. For a start, these could be Weiße's own translations, of course. In a letter to Hagedorn written in 1770 he explains the origin of the volume, *Von den Barden*, printed by Dyck that year:[43]

39 See, e.g., Christian Garve, Letter to C. F. Weiße, 7 January 1794 (Garve, *Briefe an Christian Felix Weiße*, II, 113).

40 Christian Garve, Letter to C. F. Weiße, 2 February 1794 (Garve, *Briefe an Christian Felix Weiße*, II, 122–23).

41 Christian Garve, Letter to C. F. Weiße, March/April 1794 (Garve, *Briefe an Christian Felix Weiße*, II, 126–31 (pp. 128–29).

42 See also Edmund Venables, 'Marsh, Herbert', in *Dictionary of National Biography*, ed. by Leslie Stephen and Sidney Lee, 63 vols (London: Smith, Elder & Co., 1885–1900), XXXVI (1893), 211–15.

43 Bibliography of Translations [38]. Cf. Chapter 5.

> Die Übersetzung von den Barden ist von mir. Ich hatte sie vorm Jahre für die Bibliothek übersezt: sie war mir aber dennoch zu lang und zu seichte, und da die Mad. Dÿckin gern so was kleines zum Umsatz haben wollte, gab ich sie ihr doch unter der Bedingung den Übersetzer nicht zu nennen.[44]
>
> [The translation of the Bards is mine. I did it a year ago for the *Bibliothek*, but I nevertheless thought it too long and too trivial, and since Mrs. Dyck wanted something short to sell, I gave it to her on condition that the translator would not be named.]

As we shall see, this practice of 'recycling' a translation would become more important later in Weiße's career, especially as he came to publish across various media, including multiple periodicals.[45] In this instance it was his working relationship with the firm of Dyck that allowed him to change the venue of the publication. On other occasions the *Bibliothek* became the venue for serialized advance publication of translations which would afterwards be printed by regular publishers. One such instance, again a cooperation with Dyck, was Giovanni Battista Casanova's essay on the art collections of the Saxon Elector in Dresden. The Italian-born painter Casanova (1730–1795) had been living in Dresden since 1764, where he taught at Hagedorn's Academy.[46] In 1770 Dyck published the Italian original of the essay.[47] Even at that stage Weiße seems to have been an intermediary, but even more so as the *Bibliothek* became involved. A few months prior to the publication of the original he wrote to Hagedorn:

> Wenn ich des Hn. *Casanuova* Aufsatz bald erhielt, so könnte doch die Übersetzung davon wenigstens ganz im einem Band kommen, wenn ich in das 1te Stück die eine u. in das 2te die andere Hälfte nehme. Italiänisch könnte es zusammen und sehr bald beÿ der Mad. Dÿck abgedruckt werden: nur ist die Frage, was Cas. dafür verlangen wird. Man hat mir immer vor des Mannes Charakter ein wenig Angst gemacht.[48]

44 C. F. Weiße, Letter to Christian Ludwig von Hagedorn, 12 January 1770 (UBL Ms.0670u).

45 Cf. Chapter 9.

46 Werner Teupser, 'Casanova, Giovanni Battista', in *Neue deutsche Biographie*, III (1957), 163–64. For a comprehensive biography, see Roland Kanz, *Giovanni Battista Casanova (1730–1795). Eine Künstlerkarriere in Rom und Dresden*, Phantasos, 7 (Paderborn: Fink, 2007).

47 Giovanni Casanova, *Discorso sopra gl'antichi e varj monumenti loro per uso degl'alunni dell'Elettoral' Accademia delle bell' arti di Dresda* (Leipzig: Dyck, 1770).

48 C. F. Weiße, Letter to Christian Ludwig von Hagedorn, 26 July 1770 (UBL Ms.0670u).

> [If I received Mr. Casanuova's essay soon, its translation could be published all in one volume, if I put one half in the first issue and the other in the second. The complete Italian version could very soon be printed for Mrs. Dyck: the only question is what Cas. will ask for it. What people say has made me slightly afraid of the man's character.]

Apparently, Casanova's demands were not out of proportion, for this is exactly what happened. After the Italian version had been printed, Weiße's *Bibliothek* published a German translation of the essay in two consecutive issues, each (as was the journal's wont) at the very beginning of the respective issue.[49] Immediately afterwards the complete German translation was published by Dyck as well.[50] This example perfectly illustrates how effective Weiße's networks could be under the right circumstances: his role as a freelance advisor to Dyck's, his friendship with Hagedorn (the author's employer) and his editorship of the *Bibliothek* here came together to enable him to facilitate three publications in two venues.

During Weiße's whole career as a translator, the journal and its contributors remained at the heart of his professional network. At the same time, and more so than his translations, Weiße often felt the *Bibliothek* took time away from literary activities nearer and dearer to his heart. The letters are full of complaints about the great amount of work it entailed in return for scant reward. As he confessed to Ramler in 1772, 'die Bibliothek aber ist mir so zum Eckel, daß ich nur gezwungen eine Feder ansetze und so bald ich nur noch ein paar Bände heraus gewürget habe, soll das Lied ein Ende haben' [but the *Bibliothek* is so loathsome to me that I put pen to paper only under compulsion and once I have disgorged a few more volumes, it shall

49 Giovanni Casanova, 'Abhandlung über verschiedene alte Denkmäler der Kunst, besonders aus der churfürstl. Antiquitätensammlung zu Dresden', *NBSWFK*, 11.1 (1770), 1–42; contd. in 11.2 (1771), 205–54. Perhaps as part of the agreement with Dyck, the advance publication came with a note declaring that the translation was based only on the original and no changes or revisions had been made (p. 254), a comment that once more illustrates how prevalent editorial interference in translated texts was. The translator could not be identified.

50 Giovanni Casanova, *Abhandlung über verschiedene alte Denkmäler der Kunst, besonders aus der churfürstl. Antiquitätensammlung zu Dreßden* (Leipzig: Dyck, 1771).

be the end of the story].[51] Such drastic plaints notwithstanding, he would remain the active editor of the journal for another decade before relinquishing his position. Among other functions, it served as one of the main venues in which Weiße promoted foreign literature, an activity examined in the following chapter.

51 C. F. Weiße, Letter to Karl Wilhelm Ramler, 2 November 1772 (GSA 75/ 229,2 (52)).

8. Networks: Facilitating Cultural Transfer

So far, our investigation of Weiße's networks has only examined the ways in which he facilitated translations from languages with which he himself was familiar, translations which, therefore, intersected closely with his own practice as a translator from the English, French and classical languages. However, as an 'entrepreneur' of translations and editor of a journal devoted to European literature and art, Weiße's role as agent, broker and advisor extended to works in other languages as well. More than with his usual exploits, it was often his personal friendships with influential popularizers of foreign culture that led to his employing his networks in their service. As a summary of his most significant activities in this respect, this chapter will provide a brief survey of Weiße's contribution to the reception of Spanish and Italian literature and art in Germany.[1]

While Italian art and literature had exerted a broad influence on German culture since the Renaissance, Spain remained something of a *terra incognita* up until the eighteenth century. Since the sixteenth century a negative image of Spain, the so-called 'Spanish Black

1 In recent years Weiße's interest, and especially that of his *Bibliothek*, in Russian literature have also received some attention (Christiane Schulz, 'Eine nützliche und angenehme Lektüre. Christian Felix Weiße und die russische Literatur', in *Christian Felix Weiße und die Leipziger Aufklärung*, ed. by Löffler and Stockinger, pp. 31–70). The seventh volume of the *Neue Bibliothek* contained an anonymous essay on Russian theatre (*NBSWFK*, 7.1 (1768), 188–200), which was later reprinted and translated into French (Schulz, 'Eine nützliche und angenehme Lektüre', pp. 39, 42–43). The actor and writer Ivan Afanassievic Dmitrevskij (1734–1821), who came to Leipzig as a traveller, had written a history of Russian theatre which a student in the university translated into German for Weiße's private use (p. 39). Nevertheless, because the source material on Weiße's engagement with Russian culture is scarce, and his interest in Italian and Spanish art and literature was certainly greater, this chapter limits its investigation to the Romance languages.

Legend', had been well established in Germany.[2] A destination for few German travellers, during the early Enlightenment the country had been described as backward and superstitious, governed by political and clerical despotism.[3] This changed over the course of the eighteenth century for a variety of reasons, including the fact that Enlightened thinkers increasingly viewed cultural alterity as a positive feature, but also because writers in the German states could interpret Spanish patriotism and civic *Freisinn* as a model for their own nation.[4] Nevertheless, because direct observation of the country remained a rarity, the idea of Spain that replaced the 'Black Legend' in the second half of the century would be a heavily romanticized one.[5] The reception of Spanish literature, in which Weiße had a share, therefore has to be seen not least in the context of German intellectuals' desire to 'discover' native, unspoilt literary traditions of the kind Ossian had offered them. At the same time, in Weiße's engagement with Spanish literature we see an enthusiastic editor and literary go-between at work who is perfectly ready to defer to the established experts on the culture of this exotic nation.

One of Weiße's most regular correspondents during his most productive period in the 1770s was Friedrich Justin Bertuch; and many of their letters revolve around the translation and popularization of Spanish literature in Germany.[6] Over twenty years Weiße's junior,

2 Dietrich Briesemeister, '"Die spanische Verwirrung" (J. W. von Goethe). Zur Geschichte des Spanienbildes in Deutschland', in Dietrich Briesemeister, *Spanien aus deutscher Sicht. Deutsch-spanische Kulturbeziehungen gestern und heute*, ed. by Harald Wentzlaff-Eggebert, Beihefte zur Iberomania, 20 (Tübingen: Niemeyer, 2004), pp. 97–112 (pp. 99–101).

3 Ulrike Hönsch, 'Das deutsche Spanienbild in literarhistorischen Abhandlungen des 18. Jahrhunderts: Christian Heinrich Schmids *Theorie der Poesie* (1767) und Johann Friedrich Butenschoens *Versuch über die spanische schöne Litteratur* (1789)', in *Spanien und Portugal im Zeitalter der Aufklärung*, ed. by Christoph Frank and Sylvaine Hänsel (Frankfurt am Main: Vervuert, 2002), pp. 147–162 (p. 147). Cf., in the same volume, Christian von Zimmermann, '"Fast fremder als Japan und manche entfernte Reiche ...". Die Aufklärung in Spanien und Portugal im Blick der deutschen Reisenden', pp. 123–136 (pp. 123–27).

4 Hönsch, 'Das deutsche Spanienbild', p. 161.

5 Cf. Briesemeister, '"Die spanische Verwirrung"', pp. 104–05.

6 Parts of this correspondence have been published by Ludwig Geiger, 'Christian Felix Weisses Briefe an F. J. Bertuch', *Zeitschrift für vergleichende Litteraturgeschichte*, 9th ser., 10 (1896), 235–51; passages referring to translation rarely feature in these, however, which is why the passages cited below have all been transcribed from the original letters in the Goethe- und Schiller-Archiv, Weimar.

Bertuch (1747–1822) was not only an important literary figure in his own right but one of the few colleagues whose activities were as manifold as Weiße's own.[7] At the time their correspondence sets in, Bertuch was still learning Spanish while working as a private tutor on the estate near Altenburg of Ludwig Heinrich Bachoff von Echt, a former Ambassador to Madrid (his 'Principal', as he is called in the letters). Even though Bertuch was only just embarking on a career as a translator, his most influential translation from the Spanish, *Don Quixote* (published by Fritsch in Leipzig between 1775 and 1777), was only a few years away.[8] An early letter of Weiße's to Bertuch discusses various projects related to Spanish literature. Because it illustrates the extent of both men's activities, it will be quoted here at length:

> Von der Spanischen Bibliothek Ihres Hrn. Principals hat mir schon vormals der Hr. Graf v. Moltke [...] viel gesagt. Aber ich, ich muß Ihnen gestehen, daß ich ziemlich ein Fremdling dieser Sprache bin und daß die Schätze dieses Volks gänzlich für mich verschlossen sind: und wo hätte ich sie lernen sollen, als in ganz Leipzig kein spanischer Dichter aufzutreiben ist und also Zeit und Mühe, die ich darauf verwenden wollen, wären verloren gewesen. Sie werden hieraus leicht mutmaßen, daß ich weder der Verf. der kleinen Abhandl. über die Sp. Litteratur, noch der Beurtheilung des Velazqvez. in meiner Bibl. gewesen bin. Die erste schrieb sich vom D. Schiebeler, der vor Kurzen in Hamburg gestorben, die andre von meinem Freund, dem Hofr. Kästner aus Göttingen her. Der Pr. Dieze darselbst, ist, wie er mich nur noch vor Kurzem schriftlich versichert, immer noch Willens, uns mit dem Witze dieses Volkes näher bekannt zu machen, so bald er mit der Spanischen Geschichte, wovon er die Ausfertigung zur allgem. Geschichte des Guthrie und Graÿ übernommen, zu Stande ist: aber er ist ein Trödler und wir können noch Jahre lang warten: er schmält inzwischen so arg, als Sie auf den *Linguet*. Ich

7 For background on Bertuch and his networks, cf. *Friedrich Justin Bertuch (1747–1822). Verleger, Schriftsteller und Unternehmer im klassischen Weimar*, ed. by Gerhard R. Kaiser and Siegfried Seifert (Tübingen: Niemeyer, 2000); *Friedrich Justin Bertuch. Ein Leben im klassischen Weimar zwischen Kultur und Kommerz*, ed. by Walter Steiner and Uta Kühn-Stillmark (Cologne/Weimar/Vienna: Böhlau, 2001); and Katharina Middell, *'Die Bertuchs müssen doch in dieser Welt überall Glück haben'. Der Verleger Friedrich Justin Bertuch und sein Landes-Industrie-Comptoir um 1800* (Leipzig: Leipziger Universitätsverlag, 2002). For an overview of Bertuch's role in the literary transfer between Spain and Germany, cf. Briesemeister, 'Bertuchs Bedeutung für die Aufnahme der spanischen und portugiesischen Literatur in Deutschland', in *Spanien aus deutscher Sicht*, ed. by Wentzlaff-Eggebert, pp. 256–67.

8 This makes Bertuch's complaint about fledgling translators taking on great literary masterpieces, quoted on p. 31 above, seem rather hypocritical.

hätte ihn um ein [*sic*] Recension für die Bibliothek dießfalls gebeten, wenn ich nicht gefürchtet hätte, dem deutschen Übersetzer, dem Prof. Gärtner in Brschw. dadurch einigen Verdruß zu verursachen [...].[9] Aber Sie fragen, m. T. Fr., ob, bey dem Mangel spanischer Bücher eine *Recopilacion* auserlesner Stücke nicht ein Dienst für die Deutschen seyn würde? Ich zweifle. Meine Gründe sind die Ihrigen. Die Nation muß nothwendig erst hinlänglich gereizet werden, Spanisch zu lernen: sie wird sie aber nicht eher lernen, als bis sie Beweise genug in Händen hat, daß ihre Mühe nicht vergebens gewesen ist. Diese kann sie aber nicht anders erhalten, als durch Übersetzungen wichtiger Schriften. Die Kleinigkeiten des Gongora von Jacobi sind dazu nicht hinreichend:[10] aber so wenig die allgemeinen Anpreisungen des sel. Cronegks und auch Diezens: man hält die jenigen immer für partheyisch, die uns etwas loben, wovon wir selbst nichts verstehen.[11] Wohlan! Thun Sie es! übersetzen Sie uns einige vortreffliche Werke dieser Nation und sie werden uns eine Begierde einflößen, sie näher kennen zu lernen. Vielleicht wäre kein besserer Weg hierzu, als [...] einen Versuch von Spanischen Dichtern zu machen, worinnen nach einer kritischen Beleuchtung ihrer vorzüglichsten Tugenden und Fehler, ein Auszug aus ihren wichtigsten Schriftstellern nebst einer Übersetzung der vorzüglichsten und schönsten Stellen, die man im Originale darunter setzen könnte: so erhielten die Leser zugleich eine kleine spanische Bibliothek.

Die Übersetzung der Cantilenas des Villegas wird mir so angenehm seyn, als es das nußbraune Mägd. des Prior gewesen ist.[12]

[I have already heard much about your Principal's Spanish library from the Graf von Moltke. Yet I have to confess that I am rather a stranger to that language and that the treasures of that nation are sealed to me completely: and where should I have learnt it, since there is not a single Spanish poet to be found in Leipzig and therefore all the time and energy I would have been willing to spend would have been wasted. From this, you will easily conclude that I was neither the author of the little treatise on Spanish literature nor of

9 Karl Christian Gärtner (1712–1791), Professor of Ethics and Rhetoric at Braunschweig.

10 Luis de Góngora y Argote, *Romanzen,* trans. by J. G. Jacobi (Halle: Gebauer, 1767).

11 As early as the mid-1750s Johann Friedrich von Cronegk had written an essay, 'Über die spanische Bühne', which was eagerly received by German Hispanophiles (Hönsch, 'Das deutsche Spanienbild', p. 152).

12 C. F. Weiße, Letter to Friedrich Justin Bertuch, 28 January 1772 (GSA06/ 2093 (3)). In 1772 Bertuch had published *Heinrich und Emma, ein Gedicht nach dem Modell des Nußbraunen Mädchens* (Altenburg: Richter), a translation of Prior's *Henry and Emma.*

the appraisal of Velazquez in my *Bibliothek*. The first was written by Dr Schiebeler, who recently died in Hamburg; the other by my friend Hofrat Kästner in Göttingen. In that very place Prof. Dieze, as he assured me in a recent letter, is still willing to acquaint us with that nation's wit as soon as he has finished the Spanish history which he is contributing to Guthrie and Gray's *Allgemeine Geschichte*, but he is a dawdler and it may be a long time in the coming; at this point, he reviles it as much as you do the *Linguet*. I would have asked him to write a review for the *Bibliothek*, had I not been afraid of offending the German translator, Prof. Gärtner in Braunschweig. [...] But you, my dear friend, are asking whether, considering the lack of Spanish books, a *Recopilacion* of selected plays would not be a service to the Germans? I have doubts. My reasons are yours: the nation must needs be sufficiently enticed to learn Spanish first, yet they will not learn it until they have proof in their hands that it will be worthwhile. This they cannot receive but in the form of translations of important works. Gongora's trifles by Jacobi will not suffice, no more the general advertisements by the late Cronegk and Dieze himself: we always regard those as biased who praise something we do not understand. Well, then! Do it! Translate some excellent works of this nation and you will instil a desire into us to know them better. Perhaps the best way would be [...] to compile a selection from the Spanish poets in an essay which, following a critical assessment of their most prominent virtues and vices, would contain excerpts from their most important poets along with a translation of the most remarkable and beautiful passages, the original of which could be printed alongside: in this way the readers would also receive a little Spanish library.

I shall like the translation of Villegas's *Cantilenas* as much as I did the *Nußbraunes Mädchen* by Prior.]

Despite the fact that Weiße opens this passage with the confession that he is a 'stranger to that language', the letter demonstrates how well-connected he was among the translators and editors responsible for the popularization of Spanish literature and culture in Germany.[13] While the treatises he mentions in the beginning were published in the *Neue Bibliothek*, the authors had been friends of Weiße's since his (in Kästner's case) or their (in Schiebeler's) student days and, once more, many of these connections had originated in Leipzig. Daniel Schiebeler (1741–1771) studied in Leipzig between 1765 and 1768 and quickly developed an interest in Spanish and

13 The difficulties of finding 'a single Spanish poet' in Leipzig mentioned by Weiße once more point to the limited availability of foreign literature; even in the capital of the German book trade, the focus continued to be on French and English publications, often to the exclusion of other languages. Cf. Nicolai's comments cited at the beginning of the previous chapter.

Italian literature.[14] His own poetry and librettos were often based on Spanish models. Following Weiße's invitation, Schiebeler had provided the anonymous essay on Spanish literature which was published in the *Neue Bibliothek* in 1766 and which Weiße mentions in the letter.[15] It discusses Spanish poetry, drama and prose at some length, with special attention given to Lope de Vega and Cervantes. Schiebeler's survey of Spanish literature was practically unique in the German-speaking realm until Luis Velázquez's *Geschichte der spanischen Dichtkunst* appeared.[16] The review of this work by the poet and polymath Abraham Gotthelf Kästner is the other contribution highlighted by Weiße in the letter; it was printed in the *Neue Bibliothek* three years after Schiebeler's essay.[17] Velázquez's treatise had been translated into German with comments by Johann Andreas Dieze (1729–1785), custodian of the University Library and Professor of Philosophy at Göttingen. It is this Dieze whom Weiße mentions as a slovenly worker on the Spanish history he produced as part of the translation of Guthrie and Gray's abovementioned *General History of the World* which Reich published at Weidmann's. The deplorably low speed with which Dieze worked was a source of concern for Reich and his agent Weiße, both of whom regularly corresponded with him. The translation would finally be published in 1774 under the title *Mittlere und neuere Geschichte von Spanien und Portugal*.[18] Finally, the translator whom Weiße does not wish to offend by allowing Dieze to review his translation of Linguet's *Théâtre Espagnol*, Karl Christian Gärtner (1712–1791), was another Leipzig alumnus who had become

14 Erich Schmidt, 'Schiebeler, Daniel', in *Allgemeine deutsche Biographie*, ed. by Historische Commission bei der Bayerischen Akademie der Wissenschaften, 56 vols (Leipzig: Duncker & Humblot, 1875–1912), xxxi (1890), 176–78.

15 Daniel Schiebeler, 'Einige Nachrichten, den Zustand der spanischen Poesie betreffend', *NBSWFK*, 1.2 (1766), 209–34.

16 Jens Häseler, 'Spanische Literatur in der Neuen Bibliothek der schönen Wissenschaften und der freyen Künste', in *Spanien und Portugal*, ed. by Frank and Hänsel, pp. 137–46 (pp. 139–43).

17 Abraham Gotthelf Kästner, review of Luis José Velázquez, *Geschichte der spanischen Dichtkunst*, trans. by Johann Andreas Dieze, *NBSWFK*, 8.2 (1769), 240–60. See this review for the image of Spanish literature among German intellectuals.

18 Cf. Buchner, *Aus dem Verkehr*, p. 14. The editor of the *Geschichte*, the aforementioned Heyne, repeatedly complained to Reich about how he was pressing Dieze for speed, but to no avail (Lehmstedt, 'Struktur und Arbeitsweise', p. 120).

Professor of Ethics and Rhetoric at the Collegium Carolinum in Braunschweig and who seems to have been a member of Weiße's circles as well, even though no letters between the two appear to have survived.[19] In all of this, the first half of this passage from the letter reads like a *Who's Who* of Weiße's contacts and collaborators among the German Hispanophiles. It is evident that the authors published in the *Neue Bibliothek* were aware that knowledge of Spain and its literature was sorely lacking in Germany.[20]

The second half of Weiße's letter to Bertuch marks the beginning of a fruitful co-operation in which Weiße acted as a reviewer and, once more, 'entrepreneur' of Bertuch's translations of Spanish literature. Even though Weiße did not have a working knowledge of the Spanish language, Bertuch regularly sent him his translations for review. To name but one example, the translation of Villegas's *Cantilenas* mentioned at the end of the extract quoted above was sent to Weiße a full two years before its publication and Weiße commented upon it extensively.[21] Among Bertuch's translations of Spanish literature brokered by Weiße, the most significant one was of José Francisco de Isla's *Historia del famoso Predicador Fray Gerundio de Campazas, aliás Zotes*. Weiße first mentions the title to Bertuch in July 1772:

> Haben Sie in Ihres verehrungswürdigsten Hn. Principals Spanischer Bibliothek den bekannten *Frey Gerundio*? Man hat ihn itzt in englischen übersetzt: nach einigen Auszügen, die ich in *Critical and Monthly Review* gefunden, muß ungemein viel Laune in diesem Buche seÿn und verdiente also wohl auch [...] Übersetzung. Es ist zwar eine bloße Satÿre auf die Unwissenheit der Spanischen Geistlichkeit: aber giebt es nicht auch unter uns höchst unwissende Geistlichen, hauptsächlich in katholischen Ländern? Wenn Sie, mein Freund zur Übersetzung Lust hätten, so wollte ich Ihnen für einen Verleger gleich die Gewähr leisten.[22]

19 The translation was published as Simon Nicolas Henri Linguet, *Spanisches Theater*, 3 vols (Braunschweig: Waisenhaus, 1770–71).

20 Häseler, 'Spanische Literatur', p. 139.

21 C. F. Weiße, Letter to Friedrich Justin Bertuch, 7 April 1772 (GSA06/2093 (7)). The translation of the *Cantilenas* can be found in Bertuch's anonymously published essay, 'Versuch über Don Estevan Manuel de Villegas, einen lyrischen Dichter der Spanier', *Der teutsche Merkur*, 5 (1774), 237–58.

22 C. F. Weiße, Letter to Friedrich Justin Bertuch, 7 July 1772 (GSA06/2093 (8)).

> [Do you have the well-known *Frey Gerundio* in your venerable Principal's Spanish library? He has just been translated into English; from several extracts which I found in the *Critical and Monthly Review* the book seems to be full of spirit and deserving of [...] translation. It may merely be a satire on the ignorance of the Spanish clergy – but do we not also have highly ignorant clergymen, mainly in Catholic states? If you, my friend, would like to translate it, I should guarantee you a publisher.]

In this case, Weiße's knowledge of the book derives from the same periodicals he mined for reviews of English books to use in his *Bibliothek* and, in fact, the translation of this Spanish title would take a detour via the English. The reason for this practice, which by this point had become rather unusual in the publishing industry, was Spanish censorship, as Weiße explains to Bertuch several weeks later when he sends him the English translation, *Friar Gerund de Campazas*, which had just been published:

> Ich schicke Ihnen hier den engl. *Frey Gerundio*. Haben Sie Lust ihn zu übersetzen, so steht es beÿ Ihnen. Ich habe schon deswegen mit dem Buchhändler Schwickert geredet, der mir die Sorge für die Übersetzung überlassen will. [...] Nach den englischen Schriften hat der Spanier dem englischen Übersetzer die Fortsetzung seines Buches anvertrauet, weil sie in Spanien nicht gedruckt werden dürfen.[23]

23 C. F. Weiße, Letter to Friedrich Justin Bertuch, 18 August 1772 (GSA06/ 2093 (9)). Thus, the case of *Frey Gerundio* in more ways than one exemplifies Enlightenment clichés about Spain as a backward nation under the rule of narrow-minded clergymen and England, conversely, as the home of freedom. It should be noted that of the various Enlightenment ideological battlegrounds, religious toleration was one that Weiße considered particularly important. Nowhere does this become more apparent than in his final *Trauerspiel,* entitled *Der Fanatismus, oder: Jean Calas,* written in 1774 and published in 1780. Its subject is a contemporary historical event: the judicial murder of the Toulouse Protestant Jean Calas, who had been sentenced to death in 1762 following a sham trial for the murder of his son, whom he was accused of having killed to prevent the latter's impending conversion to Catholicism. The case sparked outrage among Enlightenment writers and philosophers and became a frequent point of reference in discussions of religious tolerance. As Weiße complained to Ramler, the play could not be performed even in Leipzig and Dresden because the Catholic actors feared a negative reaction from their father confessors and the Catholic-dominated court in Dresden (Katrin Löffler, 'Aufklärung und Konfessionspolitik. Weißes Trauerspiel "Der Fanatismus, oder: Jean Calas"', in *Christian Felix Weiße und die Leipziger Aufklärung*, ed. by Löffler and Stockinger, pp. 95–127 (p. 100)). See also Albert R. Schmitt, 'Christian Felix Weißes *Jean Calas* – Dokumentarisches Theater im 18. Jahrhundert', in *Aufnahme – Weitergabe: Literarische Impulse um Lessing und Goethe*, ed. by John A. McCarthy and others (Hamburg: Buske, 1982), pp. 2–30.

[Enclosed, you will find the Engl. *Frey Gerundio*. It is yours if you would like to translate it. I have spoken to the bookseller Schwickert about this, who will leave the translation to my care. [...] According to the English journals, the Spanish author entrusted the English translator with the continuation of his book because in Spain it was not allowed to be printed.]

Bertuch therefore translated the *Gerundio* straight from the English, as he would point out in his preface to the published translation, which also mentions the Spanish ban on the original.[24] As the two letters quoted above already show, at this stage in his career Weiße could, with some degree of self-assurance, vouch for a publisher's interest before negotiations about the translation had even begun; and it took him only a conversation with Schwickert for the latter to place responsibility for the project in Weiße's hands. In the year leading up to the publication of Bertuch's German *Gerundio*, Weiße provided numerous editorial suggestions to the translator, all of which Bertuch followed:

Wie erfreulich ist es mir, daß Ihnen die Übersetzung des Freÿ Gerundio kein unangenehmer Auftrag gewesen. Allerdings wird eine Vorrede des deutschen Übersetzers von nöthen seÿn. Da Sie mit der spanischen Litteratur so bekannt sind, werden Sie auch vielleicht gute Nachrichten von dem Zustande derselbigen mit einzustreuen [*sic*]: auch wird wohl selbst in dem Buch hin und wieder eine kleine Anmerkung für den deutschen Leser nöthig seyn, wo auf eine Spanische Sitte oder Geschichte Anspielung geschieht. Ich habe mit H. Schwickerten auf den gedruckten deutschen Bogen zu Ihrem besten gehandelt [...]. Er kann vor der Messe in keiner Druckerpresse unterkommen: Sie brauchen daher mit Übersendung einzelner Bogen sich nicht zu übereilen und es hat Zeit zu Überschickung des Manuscripts wenn Sie mit der Hälfte des ersten Theils fertig sind. Ob ich es vor dem Drucke werde überlesen können, das wird von meiner Zeit abhängen. O daß ich nur der Zerstreuungen nicht so viel hätte! ich bin aber im Voraus überzeugt, daß man der Übersetzung nicht die Übersetzung ansehen wird.[25]

[I am so glad that you did not find the translation of the *Friar Gerund* an unpleasant task. A preface by the German translator will certainly be necessary. Since you are so well acquainted with Spanish literature, you might be able to intersperse it with good information

24 See his preface to José Francisco de Isla, *Geschichte des berühmten Predigers Bruder Gerundio von Campazas*, trans. by Friedrich Justin Bertuch, 2 vols (Leipzig: Schwickert, 1773), I, III–VII.

25 C. F. Weiße, Letter to Friedrich Justin Bertuch, 9 September/[November?] 1772 (GSA06/2093 (10)).

> about its present state; additionally, in the book itself, a little note for the German reader here and there will perhaps be necessary, in places where reference is made to Spanish customs or history. I have negotiated to your advantage with M. Schwickert about the printed German sheets [...]. He is unable to place it with a printer before the Fair: therefore, you need not rush to send us the individual sheets and you can send over the manuscript when you are finished with half of the first part. Whether or not I will be able to read it before the printing will depend on how much time I have. Oh, if I had not all these distractions! yet I am already certain that the translation will not betray its status as a translation.]

Despite Weiße's guardedness about his own role in possible revisions of the manuscript, when Bertuch complained that the first print sheets of the German *Gerundio* were marred by misprints, he was not above offering to copy-edit the remaining ones himself, as well as promising to ensure that the publisher paid his translator promptly.[26] Beyond the fact that he never put his own name on other translators' work, this level of editorial care lets Weiße appear a very different kind of 'entrepreneur' of translations from the type Nicolai described in his *Sebaldus Nothanker*. What his work for the *Gerundio* translation also illustrates is how, as a facilitator of cultural transfer, Weiße was involved on all levels – from the broad survey of Spanish literature and its German reception down to the copy-editing of individual print sheets of a translation.

Weiße and Bertuch continued to plan and execute various projects together; and when Bertuch launched his *Magazin der spanischen und portugiesischen Literatur* (1780–82), Weiße had his call for contributors printed in the *Neue Bibliothek*.[27] More than with Spanish literature, this journal also served as an important venue for the German reception of Italian art and literature.[28] Not only did it help to popularize the most important contemporary Italian publications, the *Bibliothek* was, in turn, well known among the Italian *cognoscenti* of German literature.[29] The journal's practice of opening new volumes with

26 See C. F. Weiße, Letter to Friedrich Justin Bertuch, 18 December 1772 (?) (GSA06/2093 (11)).

27 *NBSWFK*, 23.2 (1779), 325–26.

28 See, e.g., Dietrich Scholler, 'Die Rezeption der romanischen Literaturen in der (*Neue*[n]) *Bibliothek* und im *Journal étranger*, dargestellt am Beispiel Algarotti', in *Sächsische Aufklärung*, ed. by Klingenberg and others, pp. 211–29.

29 See Giulia Cantarutti, '"La biblioteca di belle lettere del Sig. Weisse". Eine neue Quelle für den italienisch-deutschen Kulturtransfer', in *Sächsische Aufklärung*, ed. by Klingenberg and others, pp. 251–66.

translated treatises on art and literature extended to the Italian realm. For instance, a regular contributor, Johann Nicolaus Meinhard (who has already been mentioned as the translator of Henry Home's *Elements of Criticism*, a translation brokered by Weiße), translated the writer and translator (of Ossian, among others) Melchiorre Cesarotti's literary-historical essay *Sopra l'origine ed i progressi dell'arte poetica* for the *Neue Bibliothek* in 1766.[30]

The *Bibliothek* may also have had a role in bringing about Weiße's only apparent translation from the Italian. While there is practically no evidence that he possessed a more than superficial knowledge of the Italian language, the anonymous German translation of Pietro Metastasio's libretto *La passione di Gesù Cristo* (1730), which first appeared in the Hamburg-based journal *Unterhaltungen* in 1767, was subsequently attributed to Weiße when it was reprinted in Schmid's *Anthologie der Deutschen* in 1771.[31] The translation (entitled *Das Leiden Jesu Christi, ein Singstück*) is ably done, free from fundamental errors and major omissions. The most striking difference between original and translation is the way in which the latter stylistically heightens the pathos of the text, especially where the vocabulary of emotion and Christian conscience is concerned. To name but a few examples from among the first few lines: 'il mio fallo' [my error] becomes 'die schwärzeste der Sünden' [the blackest of all sins]; 'Non ritrovo più pace' [I no longer find peace] is translated as 'geht, wo ich geh, das wilde Schrecken mit' [where I go, wild terror goes with me]; and 'Sento i rimorsi, | Ascolto la pietade' [I feel remorse, | I hearken to pity] rather dramatically turns into 'Mich quälen Grausame Leiden im Gewissen, | Vom Mitlied wird mein Herz zerrissen' [My conscience is plagued by horrible anguish | My heart is torn by pity].[32] Nevertheless, here, as on other levels, the formal choices seem quite deliberate and the final product is a fluent and stylistically homogenous translation.[33]

30 Melchiorre Cesarotti, 'Abhandlung über den Ursprung und Fortgang der Poesie', trans. by Johann Nicolaus Meinhard, *NBSWFK*, 2.1 (1766), 1–54.

31 See Bibliography of Translations [76].

32 Pietro Metastasio, *La Passione di Gesù Christo* (Florence: Viviani, 1736), p. 3; and *Das Leiden Jesu Christi, ein Singstück*, in *Anthologie der Deutschen*, ed. by Heinrich Christian Schmid (Frankfurt und Leipzig: Schwickert, 1771), II, 314–31 (p. 315).

33 The author is grateful to Claudia Cippitelli (Venice) for help in assessing the quality of this translation.

Nonetheless, a number of factors cast doubt at least on Weiße's exclusive authorship of this translation. Leaving aside the fact that the attributions in the *Anthologie der Deutschen* were anything but reliable, the lack of evidence of any extensive knowledge of Italian on Weiße's part is, of course, the most striking one. The venue of the first publication, the Hamburg *Unterhaltungen*, was also a highly unusual choice for Weiße. It therefore seems probable that another translator had a hand in this project. The likeliest candidate is Daniel Schiebeler, the student in Leipzig who has been mentioned above as the author of an essay on Spanish literature in the *Neue Bibliothek* which was printed in 1766, a year before the Metastasio translation appeared. Schiebeler was a native of Hamburg and during his time in Leipzig regularly contributed to the *Unterhaltungen*. He was also developing a passion for Metastasio right around the time the translation was published.[34] For these reasons, it seems most likely that Schiebeler and Weiße collaborated on a translation which may well have benefited from the latter's talent for libretti and which they published anonymously (as was either man's wont) in the *Unterhaltungen*. As in many other cases, the anonymity did not last, but in this case Weiße, as the more celebrated of the two poet-translators, benefited from a mechanism which, earlier in his career, had often obscured his role in the collaboration with Lessing. When the *Deutsche Bibliothek der schönen Wissenschaften* reviewed *Das Leiden Jesu Christi*, the reviewer simply found it 'vortrefflich übersetzt vom Herrn Weisse. Welche schöne Versification, welche musikalische Wortfügung!' [excellently translated by M. Weisse. How beautiful the versification, how musical the phrasing!].[35] It is difficult to determine, meanwhile, what prompted the stylistic choices that characterize the German translation: both Schiebeler's and Weiße's own original libretti were often equally floral in their descriptions of emotion, yet the style of the translation may also reflect a closer adaptation to the sentimental style of the period.

In any case, what this chapter once more demonstrates is that Weiße's role in the cultural transfer between European literatures

34 Schmidt, 'Schiebeler, Daniel', pp. 176–78.

35 Anon., review of Heinrich Christian Schmid (ed.), *Anthologie der Deutschen*, II, *Deutsche Bibliothek der schönen Wissenschaften*, 5.19 (1770), 509–26 (p. 522).

was not always tied to his work as a literary translator. As we have seen, his extensive networking activities allowed him to shape the German reception of Spanish and Italian literature despite his direct engagement with the works in question being at times limited. His curiosity extended far beyond the cultures with which he was familiar and his belief in the value of intercultural exploration for the benefit of his native culture was typical of the Enlightenment.

9. Translations of Children's Literature

Among all the parts of Weiße's wide-ranging oeuvre his writing for children is probably the best researched.[1] He had become a children's writer not, as he himself claimed in his autobiography, upon becoming a father, but because the Danish composer Johann Adolf Scheibe invited him to write songs for children in 1765.[2] Weiße joined a broad and influential reform movement which, in the second half of the eighteenth century, implemented the values of the Enlightenment in pedagogy and whose best-known representatives in the German-speaking states were Johann Bernhard Basedow, Joachim Heinrich Campe, Johann Heinrich Pestalozzi, Christian Gotthilf Salzmann and Ernst Christian Trapp.[3] Prior to, and well into, the eighteenth century the books read by children had often been either of religious origin – catechisms, primers and conduct books written by clergymen – or popular reading not specifically aimed at them – such as certain *Volksbücher*, that is, chapbooks containing popular prose narratives.[4] The eighteenth century sees not only the birth of German children's literature, but also the rise of secular children's writing specifically, which was a product of the wider process of secularization in the period.[5] Weiße's works and translations for young readers exemplify this trend.

1 For an overview, cf. Sebastian Schmideler, 'Christian Felix Weiße (1726–1804). Ein Kinderbuchautor und Jugendschriftsteller der Leipziger Spätaufklärung', in *Kinder- und Jugendliteratur in Leipzig*, ed. by Susanne Riegler and Sebastian Schmideler (Leipzig: Leipziger Universitätsverlag, 2016), pp. 221–52.

2 Walter Pape, *Das literarische Kinderbuch. Studien zur Entstehung und Typologie* (Berlin/New York: de Gruyter, 1981), p. 159.

3 Maurer, *Aufklärung und Anglophilie*, p. 439.

4 Pape, *Das literarische Kinderbuch*, p. 56.

5 Pape, *Das literarische Kinderbuch*, p. 68, see also pp. 69–76.

More particularly, as a children's writer Weiße became an ally (if not quite a member) of the largely Leipzig-born 'philanthropist' movement in pedagogy, which, inaugurated by Basedow, aimed to focus on children's individuality, to encourage independent thinking and religious tolerance.[6] The publishing house of Crusius in Leipzig, the largest pedagogical publisher in Germany at the time, became a favourite place of publication for the philanthropist writers.[7] Following a suggestion from Basedow, Weiße published a primer (*Kleines A, B, C Buch*) with Crusius in 1772, establishing a connection with a publisher who would soon after publish Weiße's hugely innovative children's journal *Der Kinderfreund* (1776–82). Begun as a continuation of Adelung's *Leipziger Wochenblatt für Kinder* (1772–74), the *Kinderfreund* quickly gained huge popularity, changing Weiße's life in the process. As he put it in a letter to Ramler:

> Der Kinderfreund hat mir mehr Beÿfall verschaft, als Alles was ich in der Welt geschrieben habe: Doch erkenne ich auch hier, so eitel es aus dem Munde eines Autors klingt: *magna fama, magnum malum*! Ich werde von Aufträgen, Hofmeister u. Kinderlehrer zu verschaffen u. von Briefen von Aeltern u. Kindern bald überschüttet, u. diese Messe bin ich von Besuchen so bestürmt worden, daß sie die beschwerlichste für mich gewesen, die ich jemals gehabt habe.[8]
>
> [The *Kinderfreund* has garnered more praise than anything else I have ever written; yet I also realize, as conceited as it may sound from the mouth of an author: *magna fama, magnum malum*! I am being showered with requests to provide tutors and teachers and with letters from parents and children; and during this past Fair I was so besieged by visitors that it was the most exhausting one I have ever experienced.]

The overstatement is not an enormous one, therefore, when Jakob Minor says that after Gellert's death (in 1769) Weiße, through his writing for children, became the most popular man in Germany.[9] Walter Pape has estimated that each of Weiße's children's books

6 For the emergence of the philanthropist movement, see Jürgen Overhoff, *Die Frühgeschichte des Philanthropismus 1715–1771. Konstitutionsbedingungen, Praxisfelder und Wirkung eines pädagogischen Reformprogramms im Zeitalter der Aufklärung* (Tübingen: Niemeyer, 2004).

7 Günter Mühlpfordt, 'Gelehrtenrepublik Leipzig', in *Zentren der Aufklärung III*, ed. by Martens, pp. 39–101 (p. 54).

8 C. F. Weiße, Letter to Karl Wilhelm Ramler, 18 May 1784 (GSA 75/229,4 (92)).

9 Jakob Minor (ed.), 'Einleitung', in *Lessings Jugendfreunde*, Deutsche National-Litteratur, 72 (Berlin/Stuttgart: Spemann, [1883]), pp. V–XXV (p. XI).

potentially had between 100,000 and 150,000 readers.[10] Between 1784 and 1792 Weiße continued the *Kinderfreund* with an – ultimately less successful – sequel aimed at a juvenile audience, the *Briefwechsel der Familie des Kinderfreundes*. Together the journals attracted readers all over Europe. Even though the periodicals were aimed at the offspring of the educated middle classes, Weiße received news that crowned heads read them with their children as well. Marie-Elisabeth de la Fite, who served the German-born British Queen Charlotte, translated parts of the *Kinderfreund* and sent them to Weiße.[11] Both the *Kinderfreund* and its successor were read by the children of George III and Queen Charlotte.[12] Similarly, the Queen of Naples read the *Briefwechsel* with her children even after publication had ceased.[13]

As the author of the *Kinderfreund*, Weiße provided much inspiration to the philanthropist pedagogues; and the journal of the leading philanthropist Gotthilf Salzmann, *Unterhaltungen für Kinder und Kinderfreunde* (published by Crusius between 1778 and 1787) was modelled directly on Weiße's periodical. Next to Campe, Weiße was the most popular German children's writer of his day.[14] His own inspiration for establishing the *Kinderfreund*, which combines songs and plays for children with didactic conversations, all within the framework of a fictional family whose children are thereby educated, has been debated. For instance, Weiße himself professed that he modelled the journal on the English moral weeklies, but Bettina Hurrelmann has suggested that Adelung's *Wochenblatt für Kinder* may have provided much more direct inspiration.[15] In any case, the journal quickly developed its own dynamic and became the cornerstone of Weiße's reputation as a children's writer. Given this reputation and the unceasing interest in this area of his activities, it is

10 Pape, *Das literarische Kinderbuch*, p. 168.

11 Weiße, *Selbstbiographie*, p. 193.

12 Cf. Weiße, *Selbstbiographie*, p. 196; and C. F. Weiße, Letter to Karl Wilhelm Ramler, 5 February 1785 (GSA 75/229,4 (95)).

13 E.g., C. F. Weiße, Letter to Karl Wilhelm Ramler, 27 April 1793 (GSA 75/229,4 (104)).

14 Mühlpfordt, 'Gelehrtenrepublik Leipzig', p. 56.

15 Bettina Hurrelmann, *Jugendliteratur und Bürgerlichkeit. Soziale Erziehung in der Jugendliteratur der Aufklärung am Beispiel von Christian Felix Weißes 'Kinderfreund' 1776–1782*, Informationen zur Sprach- und Literaturdidaktik, 5 (Paderborn: Schöningh, 1974), p. 73; Carola Cardi, *Das Kinderschauspiel der Aufklärungszeit*, Europäische Hochschulschriften I/693 (Frankfurt am Main: Lang, 1983), p. 107.

more surprising here than anywhere else that Weiße's translations of literature for children and young adults have so far attracted scarcely any scholarly attention. However, it is not for this reason alone that they deserve their own chapter in this study, but also because they stand apart from the rest of Weiße's oeuvre as a translator in a number of significant ways.

As a group, the translations of literature for children and young adults make up a large fraction of Weiße's output as a translator. They are almost all translations from the English, a reflection not merely of the flourishing of anglophone writing in this genre, but also of an Anglophile prejudice towards British pedagogy: from John Aikin and Anna Laetitia Barbauld, John Burton, Hester Chapone, Thomas Day, James Fordyce and Hannah More to Lucy Peacock, Elizabeth Pinchard and Wetenhall Wilkes, the list includes many of the leading British children's writers of the period. Well over a quarter of Weiße's translations from the English belong to the children's/young adult genre. He only translated the works of a single French writer, but Madame de Genlis was among the most influential pedagogical writers of her age.[16]

If we divide these translations into two groups – conduct books for young adults and literature aimed at children and young teenagers respectively – they can be seen to belong to roughly two different stages in Weiße's career. During the 1760s and 1770s, when he mainly worked for and with Weidmanns Erben und Reich, Weiße chiefly translated titles from the first group, most of them aimed at young women approaching marriageable age. These included, for example, Wetenhall Wilkes's *Letter of Genteel and Moral Advice to a Young Lady* (*Erinnerungen an ein junges Frauenzimmer*, 1763 [63]); James Fordyce's *Sermons to Young Women* (*Predigten für junge Frauenzimmer*, 1767 [18]); and a volume of essays and letters by Hannah More, Hester Chapone and 'Mrs Cartwright' (*Versuche mancherley Inhalts für junge Frauenzimmer*, 1778 [41]).[17]

More than half of Weiße's translations of children's and young adult literature, however, were published after 1785, in the last phase of his career, when practically all his other literary activities

16 Weiße translated both Genlis's *Théâtre à l'usage des jeunes personnes* (*Erziehungstheater für junge Frauenzimmer*, 1780–82 [69]) and *Les Veillées du Château* (*Abendstunden auf dem Lande*, 1784–86 [70]), published in a total of eight volumes by Crusius.

17 The titles were by no means limited to the education of girls and women: e.g., Weiße also translated Fordyce's *Addresses to Young Men* (*Reden an Jünglinge*, 1778 [19]).

were in decline.[18] He unfolded his greatest productivity in this area only in the 1790s, after his original children's writing had all but ceased, and in the last decade of his life almost exclusively translated books aimed at younger children. This included the popular series of 'Weihnachtsgeschenke für die Jugend' [Christmas Presents for Young People] published by Gräff in Leipzig between 1792 and 1803, in which were published Weiße's translations of works by Aikin and Barbauld, Thomas Day, George Keate, Lucy Peacock, Elizabeth Pinchard and Charlotte Smith.

As we have seen in the previous chapters, one of Weiße's guiding principles as a translator was to provide German renderings of the complete source text, usually without abridgement, extensive commentary, or expurgation and including all the culturally specific references, a practice which distinguished him from many practitioners in the period. For the most part he follows this principle with the works for children as well, even if this occasionally damages their didactic effect. In the preface to his translation in 1787 of John Aikin's *Calendar of Nature* (1784), a popular book intended to educate children about the seasonal changes in nature and agriculture, Weiße explains:

> Der Uebersetzer war Anfangs Willens, gewisse kleine Umstände, die bloß auf England passen, durch andere aus unsern Gegenden zu ersetzen: er sah aber bald, daß dann die Stellen aus den englischen Dichtern [characteristically, Aikin's book is full of quotations from English poets] hin und wieder auch eine Veränderung leiden müßten, und daß das Ganze vielleicht dadurch ein schiefes Ansehen gewinnen würde. Er glaubte also besser zu thun, dem englischen Produkte, durch Verpflanzung auf deutschen Boden, nicht sein eigenthümliches Ansehen zu benehmen, da überdieß der größte Theil der Naturerscheinungen und Behandlungen daselbst völlig mit denen in unserer Himmelsgegend übereinstimmt. Besser also, wenn sich Jemand fände, der einen solchen ganz einheimischen Naturkalender abfaßte, und ihn mit Stellen aus unsern besten Dichtern [...] ausschmückte![19]

18 This, in many ways, suits both the period's and Weiße's own assessment of translating as an 'easy' occupation fit for idle hours or, in this case, retirement.

19 C. F. Weiße, Preface to John Aikin, *Naturkalender zum Unterrichte und Vergnügen junger Leute* (Weidmanns Erben und Reich, 1787), pp. v–vii. Weiße's hope that a German writer would undertake a similar, original project was fulfilled not long after: in 1789, inspired by Aikin's *Calendar* and apparently unaware of Weiße's translation, the Berlin-based writer Friederike Helene Unger published an original *Naturkalender zur Unterhaltung der heranwachsenden Jugend* (Berlin: Unger).

> [The translator had originally intended to replace certain minor facts which only apply to England with those pertaining to our own region; yet he soon realized that the selections from the English poets would then also have to suffer a change here and there and that the whole work might thus take on a skewed appearance. He therefore believed it was better not to rob the English product of its characteristic appearance by transplanting it onto German soil, especially since the greater part of the natural phenomena and actions it describes correspond to those of our own region. It would be better, therefore, if someone were to compose an entirely native calendar of nature of this kind and embellish it […] with selections from the best of our poets.]

The preface also contains Weiße's idea of the target group, since he mentions that the book is aimed at 'young people' between the ages of ten and fourteen.[20] However, it seems doubtful whether, for instance, the distinction Aikin makes between the fine wool produced by Dorsetshire sheep and the coarser wool from Yorkshire sheep would not have eluded young readers, or indeed puzzled them needlessly.[21] On such occasions Weiße's principled stance may be considered to have backfired; and contemporary reviews regularly criticized his way of maintaining foreign cultural specificity, as, for example, in a review of his translation *Dramen zur Belehrung junger Frauenzimmer nach ihrer ersten Erziehung, von einer englischen Dame* (possibly by Elizabeth Pinchard [45]) in the *Allgemeine deutsche Bibliothek*, in which the reviewer suggests that Weiße would have done better to replace the foreign customs with native ones and to produce more than a 'mere' translation.[22]

20 Weiße, Preface to Aikin, *Naturkalender*, p. iii.

21 Akin, *Naturkalender*, p. 78.

22 Anon., review of Elizabeth Pinchard [?], *Dramen zur Belehrung junger Frauenzimmer nach ihrer ersten Erziehung, von einer englischen Dame*, trans. by C. F. Weiße, I and II, *Allgemeine deutsche Bibliothek*, 81 (1788), 245–47. In his preface to this translation, Weiße explains: 'Gern hätte der Uebersetzer mit dem deutschen Gewande auch den handelnden Personen deutsche Sitten gegeben; aber bey einiger Prüfung fand er, daß die englische Gewohnheit, die jungen Frauenzimmer in öffentliche Schulen oder Pensionen zu schicken, wo sie ihre ganze erste Erziehung […] erhalten, so wie andere eigenthümliche Volkssitten zu sehr darein verwebt waren, als daß sie schicklich eine andere Gestalt annehmen konnten. Da sich aber der Mensch unter ähnlichen Situationen immer gleich bleibt, und die Charaktere mit so viel Natur und Wahrheit gezeichnet sind; so wird die Moral derselben in Gleichen Fällen nicht weniger anwendbar seyn' [Along with the German shape, the translator would have liked to give the characters German habits as well; yet after some consideration he realized that the English custom of sending young females to public schools or finishing schools, where they

In what ways, then, do the translations of literature for children and young adults differ from the rest of Weiße's oeuvre examined in this study? There are two significant distinctions and both are connected to the intersection between Weiße's original writing for children and his translations. First of all, the editorial approach is often a very distinct one. Weiße's translations of adult fiction are usually very linear German renderings of a certain work in a similar form and shape, rarely accompanied by translators' prefaces or other paratexts. Where the translations of literature for children and young adults are concerned, however, Weiße feels much less bound by the textual shape of the original and often very overtly serves as editor as well as translator. His own writing for children in various media, particularly the *Kinderfreund* and its successor, allows him to 'recycle' and reassemble translations. In the process of recycling, he sometimes even has recourse to the translations of others.

A good example of this last kind of editorial practice is George Keate's *Interessante und rührende Geschichte des Prinzen Li-Bu, eines Eingeborenen der Pelew-Inseln*, published by Gräff in 1792 as the inaugural 'Weihnachtsgeschenk für die Jugend'.[23] This was Weiße's translation of *The Interesting and Affecting History of Prince Lee Boo, a Native of the Pelew Islands*, which had been published in London in 1789.[24] The English original was based on an episode in Keate's far more substantial *Account of the Pelew Islands* (1788), which Georg Forster had translated into German the same year as the shorter *History of Prince Lee Boo* was printed.[25] Weiße reproduces this pattern of abridgement by basing his German version of the shorter work directly on Forster's translation of the longer one. As a footnote to the preface explains, '[w]ir haben von diesem Werke eine vortrefliche deutsche Uebersetzung von Herrn Hofrath Forster [...]. Wenn man bey gegenwärtiger Abkürzung jene Uebersetzung benutzt, so wird es ihr unfehlbar mehr zum Vortheile, als Nachtheil gereichen' [we have

[...] receive their entire early education, as well as other characteristic national customs, were too much a part of the whole for them appropriately to be given a different shape. Yet since people in similar circumstances will always be alike, and since the characters have been drawn with so much truth and nature, their morals will be no less applicable to similar cases] (p. iv).

23 Bibliography of Translations [31]. Weiße's earlier translation of Keate's sentimental *Sketches from Nature* has already been discussed (pp. 68, 98 above).

24 *Verzeichnis der Bibliothek*, 3836.

25 George Keate, *Nachrichten von den Pelew-Inseln in der Westgegend des stillen Oceans*, trans. by Georg Forster, Neuere Geschichte der See- und Land-Reisen, 1 (Hamburg: Hoffmann, 1789).

an excellent German translation of this book by the Hofrat Forster [...]. If, for the present abridged version one uses that translation, it will certainly be to its benefit rather than its detriment].[26]

Like many of Weiße's translations for children, this one also comes with a preface ('An die deutschen jungen Leser' [To the Young German Readers]) in which he expounds the educational value of the book. In the case of *Li-Bu* this means drawing his readers' attention to the many ways in which this noble savage, 'der ohne alle jene gekünstelte und gelehrte Erziehung, deren wir unter tausenderley Hülfsmitteln der Aufklärung genießen, so viel herrliche Eigenschaften des Geistes und des Herzens vereiniget' [who, without any of the artificial and learned education which we enjoy thanks to a thousand resources for enlightenment, unites in himself so many glorious qualities of the heart and mind], can serve as an example for them to emulate.[27] The preface also establishes a contrast between this book and the more entertaining novels which the same young readers might otherwise enjoy. In this respect the book certainly suits Weiße's own educational outlook; and, as we shall see throughout this chapter, the prefaces he adds to these translations often serve to integrate the latter into his programme of education. It also exemplifies two features which Walter Pape has highlighted as typical of philanthropism: first, the causal relation between reason based in nature (here represented by the ostensibly unspoilt *Li-Bu*), which then leads to virtue, which in turn is the basis of felicity; and, second, the 'obsession' with utility vis-à-vis mere entertainment that led the philanthropists to take the *prodesse* part of their writing further than many other educational writers of the Enlightenment.[28]

A second translation which exemplifies both this editorial practice and the recycling of previous translations – this time, Weiße's own – is the aforementioned *Naturkalender zum Unterrichte und Vergnügen junger Leute* by John Aikin. Before we have a closer look at it, however, we need to examine the sources of the translations which

26 George Keate, *Interessante und rührende Geschichte des Prinzen Li-Bu, eines Eingeborenen der Pelew-Inseln*, trans. by C. F. Weiße, Weihnachtsgeschenk für die Jugend, 1 (Gräff, [1792]), unpag. preface.

27 C. F. Weiße, 'An die deutschen jungen Leser!', in Keate, *Interessante und rührende Geschichte*, unpag.

28 Pape, *Das literarische Kinderbuch*, pp. 132–38; Gertrud Fankhauser, '"Der Kinderfreund" (1775–84): die Kinderzeitschrift von Christian Felix Weiße als Spiegelbild der Erziehungs- und Gesellschaftsideale des deutschen Bürgertums am Ende des Aufklärungszeitalters' (unpublished doctoral thesis, New York University, 1975; abstract in *Dissertation Abstracts*, 36 (1975–76), 11, 7451–A).

Weiße reused for this title. The fourth volume of Weiße's *Briefwechsel der Familie des Kinderfreundes* (1785) contains a lengthy passage in which Herr Spirit, the author's fictional alter ego, instructs young Karl regarding the importance of aesthetics in education, a regular concern of Weiße's that is as characteristic of his work as it is rare in the educational writing of the period.[29] In the context of literature, specifically, Herr Spirit talks about the importance of models in aesthetic education:

> Man muß die allerbesten in jeder Art wählen, und nur bedenken, daß sich unser Geschmack eben so gut an das Mittelmäßige und Schlechte, als an das Beste gewöhnen kann, und daß sich ein verwöhnter Geschmack so wenig als gewisse üble Falten aus einem Zeuge heraus bringen lassen.[30]
>
> [One has to choose the best of each kind, remembering that our taste can be accustomed to the mediocre and the bad as easily as to the best; and that a spoilt taste is as impossible to remove as bad creases from certain fabrics.]

Aside from the fact that this is reminiscent of some of the comments we have heard about the ostensibly declining quality of literary translation in the second half of the century and the effects it had on the German language, it also stresses the supreme importance of early aesthetic education. As Herr Spirit explains, many people who have not had the benefit of having such sensibilities instilled in them never learn to recognize beauty. As an example, he cites a certain 'Herr Percival':

> Der wilde Indianer, bloß mit den Bedürfnissen seines Lebens beschäftiget, durchstreicht die Wüste, so wie die blumenreiche Flur, mit derselben Gleichgültigkeit. Gierig auf seine Jagd, kehrt er auf seinem Wege kaum ein Auge auf die Seite, die goldnen Strahlen der

29 C. F. Weiße, 'Herr Spirit an Karln', *Briefwechsel der Familie des Kinderfreundes*, 4 (1785), 259–82. As Pape points out, the focus Weiße places on aesthetics is what really sets him apart from other children's writers of the period. With his idea of education producing good taste, Weiße represents a broader tendency of the time, but he is the only one whose writing aims to make this 'aesthetic-social education' a reality. Specifically, the way in which poets and poetry feature in Weiße's *Kinderfreund* is almost singular in contemporary literary production for children (*Das literarische Kinderbuch*, pp. 138–50). Pape also aptly describes the *Briefwechsel* as a 'Fundgrube' [treasure trove] of the otherwise so very reticent Weiße's views on art (Pape, '"Ein Billetdoux an die ganze Menschheit"', p. 268).

30 Weiße, 'Herr Spirit an Karln', p. 266.

> untergehenden Sonne, die von dem See zurück gegeben werden, zu betrachten.[31]

'Herr Percival' turns out to be Thomas Percival, from whose *Moral and Literary Dissertations* (1784) this passage is taken – specifically from the dissertation 'On the Advantages of a Taste for the General Beauties of Nature, and of Art':[32]

> The savage Indian, wholly occupied in providing for the necessities of life, traverses the desert, and the flowery lawn, with equal indifference. Eager in the chase, he scarcely turns his eye, as he passes along, to contemplate the golden beams of the setting sun, reflected from the lake of Erie.[33]

Another passage in the same dissertation by Percival, this time in a section devoted to 'the Beauties of Nature', contains the brief quotation of a single stanza of a poem by William Shenstone, an inscription from his estate The Leasowes.[34] Weiße somehow obtained the full text of the poem and included a free German rendering of it in the next volume of the *Briefwechsel der Familie des Kinderfreundes* in 1786.[35]

Now for the recycling: Percival reappears in Weiße's preface to his translation of Aikin's *Calendar of Nature*, the abovementioned *Naturkalender*, in 1787. The preface, as usual, stresses the usefulness of the book, particularly with reference to the agricultural knowledge it imparts.[36] However, it also places the *Naturkalender* in the context of an aesthetic contemplation of nature. This is largely achieved by

31 Weiße, 'Herr Spirit an Karln', p. 261. This, incidentally, furnishes an example of how, even in Enlightenment writing, the paradigm of the noble savage always coexisted with clichés that were reductive in the opposite way.

32 Thomas Percival, 'On the Advantages of a Taste for the General Beauties of Nature, and of Art; Section II: On a General Taste for the Fine Arts', in Thomas Percival, *Moral and Literary Dissertations* (Dublin: Graisberry, 1786), pp. 229–37.

33 Percival, 'On the Advantages, Section II', pp. 229–30. The fact that Weiße in his translation omits the specific reference to Lake Erie marks an exception to the rule, but is probably motivated by the function of this brief isolated quotation within Herr Spirit's speech.

34 Thomas Percival, 'On the Advantages of a Taste for the general Beauties of Nature, and of Art; Section I: On the Beauties of Nature', in *Moral and Literary Dissertations*, pp. 219–28 (pp. 222–23).

35 William Shenstone, 'In den moosbewachsnen Zellen', *Briefwechsel der Familie des Kinderfreundes*, 6 (1786), 164–65 (Bibliography of Translations [53]).

36 Weiße, Preface to Aikin, *Naturkalender*, p. v.

Weiße's quoting the entire section 'On the Beauties of Nature' from Percival's *Dissertations*, complete with the Shenstone poem, again in its entirety as previously printed in his *Briefwechsel*.[37] Aside from the fact that Weiße thus recycles translations across media (in this case, from periodical to book), by having recourse to Percival he also makes Aikin part of a nature-aesthetic programme of education which, while it is not in conflict with the translated text, is also by no means inherent in it.[38]

As this brief examination of Weiße's habit of recycling translations of children's and educational literature has already shown, the editorial freedom he allows himself in these genres exceeds that which we find in his other translations. The remainder of this chapter is devoted specifically to those textual and editorial interventions which appear to be the product of his own involvement in educational writing. On the most inconspicuous level, his identity as an 'expert' often leads Weiße to add bibliographical information and context in the form of prefaces or footnotes in a way we rarely find in his translations of adult fiction, for instance. A good example of this practice is his translation in 1795 of John Burton's *Lectures on Female Education and Manners* (*Vorlesungen über die weibliche Erziehung und Sitten* [8]), which also exemplifies the highly gendered nature of many of these texts.[39] The translator's preface includes a list of (male) English 'moralists' who have (ostensibly) made a significant contribution to the education of women – Weiße names Joseph Addison, Richard Steele, John Locke, Samuel Richardson, James Fordyce, John Gregory, John Wilkes, William Enfield, Joseph Priestley and John Aikin – as well as the women writers themselves – Hester Chapone, Elizabeth Griffiths, Hannah Cowley, Anna Laetitia Barbauld, Hannah More, Susannah Dobson, Charlotte Smith, Elizabeth Robinson, Elizabeth Inchbald, Anna Seward, Helen Maria Williams, Harriet Lee and Frances Burney – asserting that many of them were already known in Germany through translation.[40] In fact, out of the twenty-three representatives he names,

37 Weiße, Preface to Aikin, *Naturkalender*, pp. ix–xxvi.

38 While Aikin's book is largely practical in its content, it contains frequent quotations from English poets, mainly Thomson (whom Weiße rather successfully translates, not in the original iambic pentameter but in free verse), which provide an aesthetic reflection of nature outside the main text.

39 This translation has been the subject of an extended study in Christine Mayer's article, 'Female Education and the Cultural Transfer of Pedagogical Knowledge in the Eighteenth Century', *Paedagogica Historica*, 48 (2012), 511–26 (pp. 515–26).

40 C. F. Weiße, Preface to Burton, *Vorlesungen*, p. v; cf. I, 204.

Weiße himself translated no fewer than ten. This bibliographical vein extends into the text of the book: for instance, in a passage in which Burton discusses the question of whether men and women possess equal intellectual capabilities, Weiße appends a footnote pointing to Mary Wollstonecraft's 'excellent' (vortrefflich) *Vindication of the Rights of Women*, which had been published three years earlier and which Weiße recommends as proof of the detrimental effects of the intellectual discrimination against women.[41]

While most editorial interventions remain limited to recommendations of further readings and the like, sometimes Weiße's own views on education are challenged by the translated text in such a way as to elicit a more extensive, critical comment from him. The most pronounced example of this can be found in his translation of the Irish writer and poet Wetenhall Wilkes's *Letter of Genteel and Moral Advice to a Young Lady* (*Erinnerungen an ein junges Frauenzimmer*, 1763 [63]). At one point in his essay Wilkes proposes that women who choose to remain unmarried in order to devote their lives 'to the spiritual Bride-groom' in a monastery (or at least, this is what one takes Wilkes's reference to 'Superannuated Virginity' to mean) lead what may 'properly be call'd a Life of Angels'.[42] This much piety seems to have been too much for Weiße: the otherwise so reticent translator appends a footnote which, by his standards, is inordinately long:

> Treibt der Verfasser die Lobsprüche auf den ehelosen Stand [...] nicht zu hoch? sollte eine fromme Mutter, die der Welt rechtschaffne Kinder giebt und sie zur Gottseeligkeit und Tugend erzieht, nicht eben so viel, wo nicht mehr Verdienste haben, als eine, die in einer speculativischen Einsamkeit ihre Zeit mit lauter Uebungen der Gottseligkeit anfüllt? Das letztere ist gewiß der Absicht des Schöpfers weit weniger gemäß und mit so viel Gefahren verbunden, daß man fast niemals einer jungen Person darzu rathen sollte, wenn sie sich auch in allem Ernste einfallen ließ, ein solches Leben der Engel zu leben.[43]
>
> [Does the author not take his praise of unmarried life [...] too far? Should not a devout mother who gives honest children to the world and raises them to be virtuous and godly receive the same, if not more credit than one who, in speculative solitude, fills her time with so

41 Burton, *Vorlesungen*, I, 200; cf. Mayer, 'Female Education', p. 523.

42 Wetenhall Wilkes, *A Letter of Genteel and Moral Advice to a Young Lady*, 2nd edn (Dublin: Nelson, 1741 [1740]), pp. 122–23.

43 Wilkes, *Erinnerungen*, p. 177, n.

> many exercises of godliness? Surely the latter is less in accord with the intentions of the Creator and involves so many dangers that one should hardly ever recommend it to a young person, even if she seriously intended to live such a Life of Angels.]

The critics certainly appreciated such candour. As the anonymous reviewer for the *Göttingische Anzeigen* put it rather vividly: 'Vielleicht war bey dieser Stelle eben sein Gegengift nöthig' [Perhaps his antidote was necessary at this very point].[44] What we can see here, however, is Weiße's identity as an educator overriding his usually unobtrusive translator persona. Especially the reference to the mother 'who gives honest children to the world and raises them to be virtuous and godly' can be understood as a description of the type of young woman Weiße himself was attempting to help produce – through both his original writing and his translations.[45] The intersection between the two was hardly ever more obvious and productive in his oeuvre than in the genre of educational writing. At the close, therefore, Weiße's alter ego in the *Briefwechsel der Familie des Kinderfreundes*, Herr Spirit, will make one more appearance. In a passage which follows closely upon the one quoted above from his speech on aesthetic education, he explains to Karl:

> So lange man noch nicht selbst reich genug an Gedanken ist, oder diese hin und her schwanken, oder noch nicht an Anstrengung gewöhnt ist; so würde ich es für sehr dienlich halten aus fremden guten Schriften, sie mögen in Prosa oder in Versen geschrieben seyn, zu übersetzen, hauptsächlich aber solche zu wählen, die unserer Hauptneigung zusagen. Man erwirbt sich dadurch einen Reichthum an Gedanken, so wie an Sprache: denn, indem ich einen fremden Gedanken in der meinigen mit eben der Richtigkeit und Bestimmtheit ausdrücken will, muß ich ihn auch von manchen Seiten betrachten und auf mancherley Art wenden und drehen, ehe ich gerade den

44 Anon., review of Wetenhall Wilkes, *Erinnerungen an ein junges Frauenzimmer*, trans. by C. F. Weiße, *Göttingische Anzeigen von gelehrten Sachen*, 1.8 (1764), 64.

45 The reference is also notable in that it seems to place educational responsibility with the mother rather than the father, a rather unusual idea in the period and certainly different from the model presented in the *Kinderfreund* and *Briefwechsel*, where the typical male authorities fulfil this role. Weiße's reaction to Wilkes's suggestion is also probably a result of Lutheran prejudice against too much otherworldliness, whereas Wilkes, though Protestant, may simply have shared the Irish acceptance of monasticism.

> Ausdruck finde, der den Sinn des Verfassers ganz umfaßt, und ihm vollkommen angemessen ist.[46]
>
> [As long as one is not sufficiently abundant in thought oneself, or the thoughts fluctuate, or one is not yet used to exertion: then, I believe, it would be most helpful to translate good foreign writings, whether they be in prose or verse, but to choose mainly such as agree with our main inclination. In this way one purchases a wealth of thoughts and language alike: for if I want to express a foreign thought in my own language accurately and precisely, I have to consider it from all aspects and look at it this way and that before I can find exactly that expression which wholly matches the purport of the author and is entirely appropriate to it.]

The act of literary translation itself thus becomes part of the didactic programme of the *Briefwechsel*. Rather than simply providing an element of an education in modern languages, however, in Weiße's view it enriches the young mind with a 'wealth of thoughts'. In this way the act of cultural transfer becomes a regular part of the education of a young person and, as so often in this journal, Weiße speaks from his own experience. Never do his activities as a translator and educator combine more neatly than in this passage. Weiße, whose own translating all too often follows the vagaries of commercial pressure, publishers' whims and the demands of a fickle readership, suggests a loftier ideal to the younger generation: an education in which the literate engagement with modern 'foreign thought' is instrumental in the formation of an enlightened mind.

46 Weiße, 'Herr Spirit an Karln', pp. 274–75. Gottsched had made a similar observation in the definition of translation included in his *Handlexicon*, though in this case obviously aimed at the adult writer. Nevertheless, the priority of the autodidactic element in the following is remarkable: 'Uebersetzung, heißt die Ueberbringung einer Schrift in eine andre Sprache. Diese ist eine sehr nützliche Uebung in der Schreibart. Denn ein Uebersetzer giebt auf alle Worte, Redensarten, Sätze und Glieder der ganzen Rede weit mehr Achtung, als ein bloßer Leser' [Translation is the transfer from one language into another. This is a very useful exercise of one's writing style: for a translator pays much more attention to all words, expressions, sentences and parts of the whole speech than a mere reader does] (Johann Christoph Gottsched, *Handlexicon oder kurzgefaßtes Wörterbuch der schönen Wissenschaften und der freyen Künste* (Leipzig: Fritsch, 1760), col. 1584).

10. *Nulla Dies Sine Linea*: Conclusion

'Christian Felix Weiße gehört unter die unbeliebten Erscheinungen, welche durch die Masse ihrer Produktionen eine größere Beachtung zu erzwingen scheinen, als ihnen der Beurteiler ihrem inneren Werte nach zuerkennen will' [Christian Felix Weiße is one of those unpopular figures who by virtue of the sheer volume of their production seem to compel more attention than the critic would bestow on them based on their intrinsic merit alone].[1] Thus wrote the Germanist Jakob Minor in 1883. Born half a century after Weiße's death, Minor devoted more time than anyone else to researching Weiße's life and works – and treating both with unconcealed contempt. For a long time German Studies have exhibited scant regard for Weiße's works; the reasons for this have, in the wake of his rediscovery, been examined elsewhere.[2] Perhaps overshooting the mark in the opposite direction, Weiße's contemporaries certainly accorded him the highest rank among the German writers of his day. The elegy written by the Leipzig philologist Johann Georg Eck after Weiße's death in 1804 expresses widespread sentiments:

> Vergebens fragt ihr nun, da Er vollendet,
> wo ist der Deutsche Dichter, der gleich ihm
> des B r i t t e n Funken zu der hellsten Gluth
> Entflammte? Der weit glücklicher
> Als C o r n e i l l e und R a c i n e vom Kothurn
> Zum Sokkus griff? – Ihr fragt und sucht vergebens. –

1 Minor, 'Einleitung', p. v.

2 See Krätzer, 'Christian Felix Weiße in der deutschen Germanistik', who focuses on Weiße's role as a supposed 'precursor' to later developments and a figure in the shadow of Lessing even in his own lifetime as reasons for his marginalization. Cf. also Pape, '"Ein Billetdoux an die ganze Menschheit"', pp. 268–69 as well as Schmideler, 'Christian Felix Weiße'.

Die Grazien lehrten Ihm der Unschuld Lieder,
Die Er so wahr und kindlich sang;
Die Mütter lehrten sie den zarten Kindern wieder,
In deren Herz des Dichters Tugend drang.[3]

[In vain you ask, now that He's gone to his reward,
where is the German poet who, like him,
ignites the British spark, kindles its fire,
Who more felicitously than C o r n e i l l e and R a c i n e
Exchanged the cothurnus for the soccus?[4]
– You ask and seek in vain. –

The Graces taught him songs of Innocence
Which he sang childlike, full of truth;
And mothers taught them to their children sweet,
Into whose hearts the poet's virtue sank.]

The points of reference in this summary of Weiße's achievements are telling: he was among the leading lights of a transitional period in which German literature assimilated British and French influences alike, eventually to gain a new confidence in its own forms and language. Weiße only reached that latter stage in his children's writing; as a translator and facilitator of cultural transfer, however, he helped to drive this larger development. Compared to Weiße's original writing, the translations are in some ways a special case. Not all of them have been examined critically in the present study – to do so would be an exhausting effort in more senses than one – and it would certainly be a stretch to say that more than a handful of them deserved a reprint. Regardless of their quality, translations are rarely ever canonized and the fact that most of the contemporary works translated by Weiße were not canonized either certainly did not help.[5] This is partly because the list of his translations in many ways exemplifies social, literary and intellectual developments typical of the period: for instance, a quarter of the books he translated were the work of women writers. Especially the latter have only relatively recently begun to attract scholarly attention. The fact that, in addition to all this, Weiße took his habit of authorial anonymity further than most of his colleagues (almost all of

3 Johann Georg Eck, *Elegie auf Christian Felix Weisse* (Leipzig: Gräff, 1805), ll. 35–44.

4 The cothurnus or buskin, a boot worn by tragic actors in ancient Greece; the soccus, a flat slipper worn by their comic counterparts.

5 Conversely, his translation of Mercier's *L'An 2440*, perhaps the most canonical of the eighteenth-century works translated by Weiße, has been reprinted until quite recently.

his translations were published without mention of his name) seems almost negligible next to these other factors.

Nonetheless, what the present study has attempted to show is that Weiße's supreme quality was, so to speak, quantity. In his work both as a translator and as an 'entrepreneur' of translations, Weiße was more prolific than any of his German colleagues. As a matter of fact, he himself, in a rather modern way, frequently took pride in how busy he was:

> Rechnet man zur Weitläufigkeit dieses Briefwechsels und seiner übrigen beschriebnen litterärischen Thätigkeit noch die Menge von Uebersetzungen, welche er geliefert hat, so wird man ihm wohl auch das Selbstlob verzeihen und zugestehen, daß bey ihm wirklich *nulla dies sine linea* war.[6]
>
> [If, in addition to the vast extent of this correspondence and his other aforementioned literary activities, one considers the number of translations he has provided, one may excuse his self-praise and concede that with him there was indeed *nulla dies sine linea*.]

The quantity of his output, negligible though this category may seem to literary historians, not only made him the most prolific German translator of English literature in the eighteenth century; it was also a precondition of all the ways in which Weiße exemplifies the emergence of the professional translator. As we have seen, his connections to publishers – as their translator, author, agent and copy-editor; to other writers and translators – as their advocate, counsellor and promoter; his status as an intermediary between both groups; and his position as the long-time editor of the (*Neue*) *Bibliothek der schönen Wissenschaften und der freyen Künste* all intersected, creating the vast professional and private network that allowed Weiße to become such an influential facilitator of cultural transfer between the European literatures, a writer who enjoyed the 'interkulturelle[] Karriere[]' [intercultural career] which Matthias Middell has highlighted as a key characteristic of the agents in this transfer.[7] It has also been shown to what extent this role depended on his living in Leipzig, a city where so many of his connections were formed early in his life, a place that enabled Weiße's networks and, in turn, was made more of a literary centre by his being based there.

What Weiße's activities also exemplify is that the culture of the Enlightenment was never a purely intellectual one. In his *Saggio sulla*

6 Weiße, *Selbstbiographie*, p. 238.

7 Middell, 'Kulturtransfer, Transferts Culturels', unpag.

filosofia delle lingue [*Essay on the Philosophy of Languages*], first published in 1785, the aforementioned Italian writer and philologist Melchiorre Cesarotti characterizes the European intellectuals as 'one great family' of like-minded thinkers, in a style which has come to be regarded as typical of the Enlightenment: '[L]'Europa tutta nella sua parte intellettuale è ormai divenuta una gran famiglia, i di cui membri distinti hanno un patrimonio commune di ragionamento, e fanno tra loro un commercio d'idee, di cui niuno ha la proprietà, tutti l'uso' [The whole of Europe in its intellectual part has now become one great family, whose individual members have the common heritage of argumentative reason and among themselves trade in ideas which nobody owns, but everybody has the use of].[8] Weiße certainly participated in this 'trade in ideas', yet his professional practice rarely featured intellectual property without an owner: aside from being 'one great family', the European 'Republic of Letters' was also one big market for ideas, entertainment and preferment in which intellectual interests were always inextricably bound up with commercial ones. This also relates to the role of letter-writing in these exchanges: as we have seen, despite his being conveniently located in Leipzig, Weiße's networks depended to a great extent on written communication. Through a reading of Nicolai's *Sebaldus Nothanker*, Nacim Ghanbari has proposed that in contrast to earlier forms of patronage, eighteenth-century networks relied on new forms of support and interpersonal connection, exemplified by the letter of recommendation, a genre of writing on which Weiße spent a considerable amount of his time. Its aim was to secure professional employment rather than (the traditional) stipends and annuities; and it could be exchanged between individuals who were connected by friendship as much as by patronage or professional relationships.[9] Thus, 'career management' became one of the functions of these forms of correspondence and exchange.[10] This book has demonstrated that one would be hard pressed to find a contemporary of Weiße's who exemplified such developments better than he did. Nevertheless, while

8 Melchiorre Cesarotti, *Saggio sulla filosofia delle lingue* (Naples: Bonis, 1818), p. 124.

9 Nacim Ghanbari, 'Netzwerktheorie und Aufklärungsforschung', *Internationales Archiv für Sozialgeschichte der Deutschen Literatur*, 38 (2013), 315–35; Hannes Fischer and Erika Thomalla, 'Literaturwissenschaftliche Netzwerkforschung zum 18. Jahrhundert', *Zeitschrift für Germanistik*, n.s., 26 (2016), 110–17.

10 Erdmut Jost, 'Einführung: Das 18. Jahrhundert als Formierungsphase der Netzwerkgesellschaft', in *Briefwechsel. Zur Netzwerkbildung in der Aufklärung*, ed. by Erdmut Jost and Daniel Fulda, IZEA – Kleine Schriften, 4/2012 (Halle/Saale: Mitteldeutscher Verlag, 2012), pp. 7–14 (p. 9).

the intercultural literary activities examined in this volume were often driven by economic motives at least as much as by intellectual interest, Weiße, here as in every other aspect of his work, honestly believed in the improvement of humankind through art and literature – not least, as has been shown, in his writing for children. While always hesitant to embrace any kind of social or intellectual change that could appear radical, Weiße was deeply enthusiastic about the core values of the Enlightenment, which informed much of his view of himself. As he wrote to the Catholic theologian and Church reformer Benedict Maria von Werkmeister (1745–1823) in April 1774: 'Bey der Toleranz und Freyheit zu denken, die jetzt überall mehr überhand nimmt, kann man gewiss erwarten, dass der menschliche Geist sich immer mehr erweitert und licht um sich macht' [Considering the tolerance and liberty which now prevail everywhere, we can surely expect that the human spirit will expand ever more and create light around itself].[11] Weiße certainly regarded himself as part of this process. His doubts about the reformability of the German courts remained with him all his life, meanwhile, as part of his civic identity as a Leipzig *Bürger*. As he explained to Werkmeister in January 1789, shortly before the French Revolution: 'Nie sind unsern Monarchen wohl derbere Wahrheiten so laut gesagt worden, als jetzt, und ich sehe keinen, der sich desswegen bessert' [Never have our monarchs been told harsh truths as loudly as today and I see none who improves because of it].[12] Nonetheless, his overall optimism could not be dampened by the endurance of Absolutism in the German states and the American Republic seemed to Weiße a model of a better world.[13]

All this is not to say, however, that Weiße is of no interest as a literary translator in his own right. As this study has shown, his work is distinctive in more than one regard. The variety of his literary exploits allowed him to 'syndicate' and recycle translations across different media. We have seen how his work as an original writer intersected with his translations – from the plays early in his career, when adherence to convention and an often unbending idea of the ideal structure of plays led to his adapting and 'germanizing' French and English comedies; to the translations of educational works, in which Weiße's own interests as an educator and children's writer prompted textual and editorial intervention; and, not least, the

11 Weiße, 'Briefe an Werkmeister', p. 278.

12 Weiße, 'Briefe an Werkmeister', p. 297.

13 As described in the letter to Friedrich Christian von Holstein-Augustenburg (1793) cited above (Weiße, Letter to Holstein-Augustenburg, 18 June 1793, in Schulz, 'Leipziger Stimmen', p. 50).

absence of this intersection in his translations of popular fiction, especially of novels, in which an unobtrusive, extremely restrained translator Weiße emerges, whose choice to maintain the integrity of the original text is rarely applauded by the critics.

Nonetheless, the social side of Weiße's literary activities in the realm of translation emerges as the more significant aspect of this part of his oeuvre. Several chapters have demonstrated how wide-ranging his activities were. In particular, his co-operation with the congenial Philipp Erasmus Reich at Weidmann's and his editorship of the *Bibliothek* stand out among the ways in which he shaped the German reception of foreign literatures. As has been shown, even in areas where Weiße's own translations were relatively insignificant within the larger discourse – as, for instance, in the German reception of Ossian – his position as an entrepreneur of translations and a journal editor nevertheless allowed him to become an integral part of that discourse. In other areas, most notably with children's and young adult literature, the translations became part of Weiße's own important and lasting contribution to a field of literature. The eighteenth century is a period in which writers and critics eagerly looking for a national cultural identity appropriate foreign works of literature in German translation as part of the German literary canon in a way that is rare among European nations.[14] Even though Weiße himself did not translate any of the books that became a core part of that identity, his activities as a go-between in the literary industry helped the larger process in a singular way.

At many points the research for this book suggested a logical complement to the present study – an investigation of Weiße in foreign translation. Not only were his plays translated and adapted all over Europe, his *Kinderfreund* and other writings for children were translated into all major and a good many minor European languages. Among the translators of Weiße into French and English are also some writers whom he himself had translated, something which makes for a peculiar kind of connection, obscured only by the ever-prevalent anonymity.[15] And while it may take a long time for another scholar to undertake such a project, this already demonstrates that

14 Friedmar Apel and Annette Kopetzki, *Literarische Übersetzung*, 2nd edn (Stuttgart: Metzler, 2003), p. 71.

15 For instance, Mercier's play *Les Tombeaux de Vérone* (1782) was largely based on Weiße's *Romeo und Julie* (1767). For the various translations of the *Kinderfreund*, see, e.g., Göte Klingberg, *Das deutsche Kinder- und Jugendbuch im schwedischen Raum. Ein Beitrag zum Studium der Verbreitungswege der Kinder- und Jugendliteratur*, Internationale Untersuchungen zur Kinder- und Jugendliteratur, 3 (Weinheim/Basel: Beltz, 1973); Johann Wilhelm Lindner, 'Vollständiges Verzeichniß der

the topic of Weiße and translations has not quite been exhausted by the present study.

In the preface to his first *Magazin der spanischen und portugiesischen Literatur* Weiße's friend Bertuch wrote: 'Wir Teutschen waren von je her, und seitdem unsre Väter die Künste und sanfteren Musen aufnahmen, die Bienen fremder Literaturen. Keine Nation lernte allgemeiner und lieber die Sprachen aller andern, und durchsuchte ihre gelehrten Schätze so gern als wir' [We Germans have always, and since our forefathers adopted the Arts and the gentler Muses, been the bees of foreign literatures. No nation studied the languages of all the others more joyfully and in greater numbers, or examined their troves of knowledge as readily as we did].[16] Weiße would certainly have liked to regard himself as such a bee, industrious and useful in the service of the Muses. While the way in which Weiße frequently took pride in his industriousness was undoubtedly connected to his self-perceived lack of 'genius', it is also, in a broader sense, wholly consistent with the work ethic with which he and many other writers of the Enlightenment approached intercultural engagement – an industriousness which helped to create and sustain a new literary industry while at the same time being a product of its pressures. Of course, the present study offers only a glimpse of Weiße's versatility and productivity, since it has only been able to hint at his other activities, almost all of which in his own eyes ranked above translation. Nevertheless, at the end of this book it should be obvious that no engagement with Weiße the writer could ever be considered complete without a study of his translations. We hope it has also demonstrated that the history of literary translation in Germany in the period of the Enlightenment would be incomplete without a chapter dedicated to Christian Felix Weiße.

Schriften von und über Chr. F. Weiße', in Heinrich Curt Iphofen, *Lebensgeschichte Christian Felix Weißens*, ed. by G. F. Döhner (Freiberg: Craz & Gerlach, 1826), pp. 95–113; Schulz, 'Eine nützliche und angenehme Lektüre', p. 44 n. 36, p. 63; the anonymous review of a Hungarian translation, *A' jelesebb rendeken lévö nevendék gyermekek*, trans. by K. Seelmann, *Siebenbürgische Quartalschrift*, 4 (1795), 291–93; and Odin Wolff, *Nyttige Kundskaber for Ungdommen i et morende, fatteligt Foredrag* (Copenhagen: Poulsen, 1791). The most significant and influential foreign engagement with the *Kinderfreund* is probably Arnaud Berquin's *Ami des enfans* (1782–83), which draws heavily on Weiße's original (François Genton, 'Christian Felix Weiße et Arnaud Berquin ou l'influence de la littérature d'enfance et de jeunesse allemande en France au XVIIIe siècle et au-delà', in *Révolution, Restauration et les jeunes*, ed. by Gilbert Van de Louw and Elisabeth Genton (Paris: Didier Erudition, 1989), pp. 47–73).

16 Friedrich Justin Bertuch, *Magazin der spanischen und portugiesischen Literatur*, 1 (1780), iii.

Bibliography of Translations by Christian Felix Weiße

The following bibliography lists all the translations which could be attributed to Weiße with reasonable certainty. For the sake of brevity, only first editions have been listed, with the exception of titles that were substantially revised after their first publication and of cases in which a list of subsequent editions could clear up confusion in existing bibliographical sources. The 'borrowed' book reviews in the *Bibliothek der schönen Wissenschaften* are not featured in this list. The following bibliographies have been used in the process of attribution:

[Fromm] Hans Fromm, *Bibliographie deutscher Übersetzungen aus dem Französischen 1700–1948*, 6 vols (Baden-Baden: Verlag für Kunst und Wissenschaft, 1950–53)

[HB] Michael Holzmann and Hanns Bohatta, *Deutsches Anonymen-Lexikon 1501–1850*, 7 vols (Weimar: Gesellschaft der Bibliophilen, 1902–26)

[Lehmstedt] Mark Lehmstedt, 'Anhang I. Übersetzungen aus dem Englischen', in '"Uebersetzungsmanufactur" und "Proletarische Scribenten". Quellenstudie zur Sozialgeschichte der Deutschen Aufklärung' (unpublished diploma thesis, Humboldt University, Berlin, 1987)

[Lindner] Johann Wilhelm Sigismund Lindner, 'Vollständiges Verzeichnis der Schriften von und über Chr. F. Weiße', in Heinrich Curt Iphofen, *Lebensgeschichte Christian Felix Weißens* (Freiberg: Craz & Gerlach, 1826), pp. 95–113

[Price/Price] Mary Bell Price and Lawrence Marsden Price, *The Publication of English Literature in Germany in the Eighteenth Century*, University of California Publications in Modern Philology, 17 (Berkeley, CA: University of California Press, 1934)

[Weiße] Christian Felix Weiße, *Selbstbiographie*, ed. by Christian Ernst Weiße and Samuel Gottlob Frisch (Leipzig: Voß, 1806)

The bibliographical information given here is based on first-hand examination of the titles whenever possible since especially the older sources often contain errors. The checklist below is largely limited to translations in the narrow sense; to account for the fluid boundaries between translation and adaptation in the eighteenth century, however, adaptations are listed if they bear a close enough relation to the original to be reasonably understood as bordering on translations. Most of the titles listed below are long works; especially for translations of short prose and poetry, which Weiße often published in articles in periodicals or in the prefaces to other, longer works, the cut-off point in terms of length might seem somewhat arbitrary, but the main criterion for inclusion in this list was that they be translations of complete sections or units of original text, such as a chapter, an essay or several complete stanzas of a poem. The place of publication is Leipzig unless otherwise stated. The spelling of the publisher Dyck (sometimes 'Dyk' or 'Dÿck') has been standardized.

Translations from the English

[1] Anon., 'Romanze, Die Schöne Rosemunde', in [Rudolf Erich Raspe], review of *Reliques of Ancient English Poetry*, ed. by Thomas Percy, *NBSWFK*, 2 (1766), 54–89 (pp. 70–86)

Reprinted in *Anthologie der Deutschen*, ed. by H. C. Schmid (Frankfurt and Leipzig: Schwickert, 1771), II, 346–53 (translation attributed to Raspe, but see Minor, *Christian Felix Weiße*, p. 76, n. 1: 'rührt indes von Weiße her'; cf. also [64])

= 'Fair Rosamond' (trad., *Reliques of Ancient English Poetry* (1765))

[2] Aikin, John, *Naturkalender zum Unterrichte und Vergnügen junger Leute* (Weidmanns Erben und Reich, 1787)
(Lehmstedt I, 204; Lindner I, 75; Price/Price 14; Weiße 240)
Contains extensive poetic selections from Thomson's *Seasons*; contains [44]
= *The Calendar of Nature* (1784)

[3] Barbauld, Anna Laetitia, and John Aikin, *Das geöffnete Schreibepult zum Unterrichte und Vergnügen junger Personen*, 9 vols (Gräff, 1795–1803) (Lindner I, 91–93; Price/Price 62; Weiße 241)
Also as Weihnachtsgeschenk für die Jugend, 4–12
Vols 4–5 also as *Der Besuch von einer Woche* (see [42])
Vols 6–9 also as *Spaziergänge in Gesprächen* (see [55])
= *Evenings at Home; or, The Juvenile Budget Opened* (1792–96)

[4] Bonhote, Elizabeth, *Die Wanderungen des Herrn Frankly, von seiner Schwester Herausgegeben*, 4 vols (Weidmanns Erben und Reich, 1773–77)
(Lehmstedt I, 81; Lindner I, 60; Weiße 240)
= *The Rambles of Mr. Frankly* (1772–76)

[5] Brooke, Henry, *Julie Grenville oder Die Geschichte des menschlichen Herzens*, 3 vols (Schwickert, 1774)
(Lindner I, 55; Price/Price 135; Weiße 239)
= *Juliet Grenville or The History of the human Heart* (1774)

[6] Burney, Fanny, *Evelina oder eines jungen Frauenzimmers Eintritt in die Welt*, 3 vols (Schwickert, 1779)
(Lindner I, 63; Price/Price 148; Weiße 240)
= *Evelina, or, The History of a Young Lady's Entrance into the World* (1778)

[7] Burney, Fanny, *Cecilia oder Die Geschichte einer reichen Waise*, 3 vols (Weidmanns Erben und Reich, 1783–84)
(Lehmstedt I, 187: vols 1 & 2 1783 and vol. 3 1784; Lindner I, 73; Price/Price 147; Weiße 240)
= *Cecilia, or Memoirs of an Heiress* (1782)

[8] Burton, John, *Vorlesungen über die weibliche Erziehung und Sitten*, 2 vols (Gräff, 1795; 2nd, rev. edn 1798)
(Lindner I, 90; Weiße 241)
= *Lectures on Female Education and Manners* (1793)

[9] Cartwright, Mrs, *Briefe über die weibliche Erziehung an ein verheurathetes Frauenzimmer*, see [41]

[10] Chapone, Hester, *Brief an ein neu verheurathetes Frauenzimmer*, see [41]

[11] Coffey, Charles, *Die verwandelten Weiber oder Der Teufel ist los* (first stage production 6 October 1752 in Leipzig)
Revised and enlarged printings in C. F. Weiße and J. A. Hiller, *Komische Opern*, II (Leipzig: Dyck, 1768; 2nd edn 1772; 3rd edn 1777)
Printed separately (Junius, 1770; rev. edn Dyck 1776)
(Price/Price 191; Lindner I, 25)
An adaptation
= *The Devil to Pay; or, The Wives Metamorphos'd* (1731)

[12] Coffey, Charles, *Der lustige Schuster oder Der zweite Theil vom Teufel ist los* (first stage production 18 January 1759 in Leipzig)
Revised printings in C. F. Weiße and J. A. Hiller, *Komische Opern*, II (Leipzig: Dyck, 1768, 2nd edn 1772; 3rd edn 1777)
Printed separately (Junius, 1771; 2nd edn Dyck, 1772; rev. edn Dyck, 1776)
(Price/Price 192; Lindner I, 25)
An adaptation
= *The Merry Cobler, or The Second Part of the Devil to pay* (1735)

[13] Congreve, William, 'Ode auf die Harmonie', in C. F. Weiße, *Scherzhafte Lieder*, 3rd edn (Weidmanns Erben und Reich, 1763), pp. 242–54
Revised translation in C. F. Weiße, *Kleine lyrische Gedichte* (Weidmanns Erben und Reich, 1772), III, 187–202

= 'A Hymn to Harmony, Written in Honour of St Cecilia's Day' (1701)

[14] Cradock, Joseph, *Dorfmemoiren, in einer Reihe von Briefen zwischen einem Geistlichen und seiner Familie auf dem Lande und seinem Sohn in der Stadt* (Weidmanns Erben und Reich, 1775)
(Lehmstedt I, 97)
= *Village Memoirs* (1774)

[15] Cumberland, Richard, *Lehrreiche und unterhaltende Aufsätze aus dem Beobachter des Herrn Cumberland,* 2 vols (Weidmann, 1793)
(Lindner I, 87; Price/Price 251; Weiße 241)
= *The Observer* (1785)

[16] Day, Thomas, *Der kleine Jack, eine Volksgeschichte,* Weihnachtsgeschenk für die Jugend, 2 (Gräff, 1793)
(Lindner I, 85; Price/Price, 261; Weiße, 241)
= *The History of Little Jack, a Foundling* (1787)

[17] Dryden, John, 'Alexanders-Fest, oder Die Gewalt der Musik', in C. F. Weiße, *Scherzhafte Lieder*, 3rd edn (Weidmanns Erben und Reich, 1763), pp. 219–31
Revised translation in C. F. Weiße, *Kleine lyrische Gedichte* (Weidmanns Erben und Reich, 1772), III, 157–72
= 'Alexander's Feast, or the Power of Music' (1697)

[18] Fordyce, James, *Predigten für junge Frauenzimmer*, 2 vols (Weidmanns Erben und Reich, 1767)
(Lehmstedt I, 47; Lindner I, 23; Weiße, 239)
= *Sermons to Young Women* (1765)

[19] Fordyce, James, *Reden an Jünglinge,* 2 vols (Weidmanns Erben und Reich, 1778) (Lindner I, 62; Weiße, 240)
= *Addresses to Young Men* (1777)

[20] Gibbes, Phebe, *Hartlyhaus, oder Schilderungen des häuslichen und gesellschaftlichen Lebens der Europäer in Ostindien* (Weidmann, 1791)

(Lindner I, 82; Price/Price, 429; Weiße, 241)
= *Hartly House, Calcutta* (1789)

[21] Goldsmith, Oliver, 'Gemälde eines Landpredigers', in C. F. Weiße, review of Oliver Goldsmith, *The Deserted Village*, *NBSWFK*, 11.1 (1770), 165–68
(Price/Price, 431; a prose translation of an extended passage from Goldsmith's poem *The Deserted Village*)
= *The Deserted Village* (1770)

[22] Gray, Thomas, 'Der Barde, eine Pindarische Ode', see [38]

[23] Gray, Thomas, 'Die Höllenfahrt des Odin', see [38]

[24] Gray, Thomas, 'Die Schwestern des Todes', see [38]

[25] Gray, Thomas, 'Die Triumphe Owens, ein Fragment', see [38]

[26] Gregory, John, *Unterredung und Vermächtniß eines Vaters für seine Töchter* (Kave, 1793)
(Lindner I, 86; Price/Price, 448; Weiße, 241)
= *A Father's Legacy to his Daughters* (1774)

[27] Hawke, Cassandra, *Julie de Gramont, eine rührende Geschichte* (Weidmann, 1790)
(Lindner I, 79; Price/Price 468; Weiße 241)
= *Julia de Gramont* (1788)

[28] Haley, William, 'Gedichte über die Malerey. An Herrn George Romney', in *NBSWFK*, 29.1 (1783), 5–60; contd. 29.2 (1784), 187–225[1]
= *A poetical Epistle to an Eminent Painter* (1778)

[29] Hayley, William, *Ein philosophischer, historischer, und moralischer Versuch über die alten Jungfern, von einem*

1 Weiße is identified as the translator in the database *Neue Bibliothek der schönen Wissenschaften und der freyen Künste* (Potsdam: Forschungszentrum Europäische Aufklärung Potsdam, 2004) <http://141.89.36.83/digbib/start> [accessed 20 November 2019].

Freunde der Schwesterschaft, 3 vols (Weidmanns Erben und Reich, 1786)

(Lehmstedt I, 198; Lindner I, 74; Price/Price 472; Weiße 240)

A footnote added by Weiße in vol. II, 91–99 contains the translation of a lengthy passage from the *Tatler*, no. 32.

= *A Philosophical, Historical, and Moral Essay on Old Maids, by a Friend to the Sisterhood* (1785)

[30] Helme, Elizabeth, *Clare und Emmeline oder Der mütterliche Segen, von der Verfasserin der Louise* (Weidmann, 1789)

(Lindner I, 78; Price/Price 485; Weiße 241)

= *Clara and Emmeline or The Maternal Benediction* (1788)

[31] Keate, George, *Interessante und rührende Geschichte des Prinzen Li-Bu, eines Eingeborenen der Pelew-Inseln*, Weihnachtsgeschenk für die Jugend, 1 (Gräff, [1792])

(Lindner I, 83; Price/Price 572; Weiße 241)

The English original cited below is based on an episode in Keate's *Account of the Pelew Islands* (1788) and Weiße uses the German translation of this work as the basis for his own:

George Keate, *Nachrichten von den Pelew-Inseln in der Westgegend des Stillen Oceans*, trans. by Georg Forster (Hamburg: Hoffmann, 1789)

= *The Interesting and Affecting History of Prince Lee Boo, a Native of the Pelew Islands* (1789)

[32] Keate, George, *Skizzen aus der Natur, auf einer Reise nach Margate entworfen und ausgemalt* (Weidmanns Erben und Reich, 1780)

(Lindner I, 64)

= *Sketches from Nature Taken and Coloured in a Journey to Margate* (1779)

[33] *Landbibliothek zum angenehmen und lehrreichen Zeitvertreib aus verschiedenen Sprachen* (Weidmanns Erben & Reich, 1762–78)

(Lindner II, 3; Price/Price 594; Weiße 240: translated 'several novels' in this series)

[34] Law, William, *Eine ernsthafte Ermunterung an alle Christen zu einem frommen und heiligen Leben* (Weidmann, 1756)
(Lindner I, 6 and Weiße, 239: translation begun by Lessing; Lehmstedt I, 9: print sheets 6 and following translated by Weiße)
= *A Serious Call to a Devout and Holy Life* (1729)

[35] *Lesekabinet zum Nutzen und Vergnügen* (Weidmanns Erben und Reich, 1779–85) (Lindner II, 6; Price/Price 618; Weiße 240: translated 'several novels' in this series, the successor to the *Landbibliothek*)

[36] Mackenzie, Henry (ed.), *Der Spiegel, ein periodisches Blatt*, 3 vols (Crusius, 1782–83)
(Lindner I, 69; Price/Price 687; Weiße 240)
= *The Mirror: A Periodical Paper* (1779–80)

[37] Mackenzie, Henry (ed.), *Der beobachtende Müßiggänger, eine periodische Schrift*, 3 vols (Bern: Hortin, 1788–89)
(Lindner I, 77; Price/Price 554; Weiße 240)
= *The Lounger: A Periodical Paper* (1785–87)

[38] Macpherson, John, *Von den Barden, nebst etlichen Bardenliedern* (Dyck, 1770): a translation of Macpherson's 'Dissertation XIV, Of the Bards' in the collection cited below, joined with an apparently unrelated selection of poems by Thomas Gray (see [22]–[25])
(Lindner I, 35; Price/Price 741)
= *Critical Dissertations on [...] the Ancient Caledonians* (1768)
= 'The Bard, a Pindaric Ode' (*Poems by Mr. Gray*, 1768)
= 'The Descent of Odin, an Ode' (*Poems by Mr. Gray*, 1768)
= 'The Fatal Sisters, an Ode' (*Poems by Mr. Gray*, 1768)
= 'The Triumphs of Owen, a Fragment' (*Poems by Mr. Gray*, 1768)

[39] Mason, William, *Der englische Garten, ein Gedicht*, 4 vols (Schwickert, 1773–83)
(Lindner I, 53; Price/Price 667; Weiße 239)
= *The English Garden* (1772–82)

— Melmoth, Courtney, *Freymüthige Gedanken*, see [49]

[40] Moore, Edward, *Fabeln für das schöne Geschlecht* (Weidmanns Erben und Reich, 1762)
(Lehmstedt I, 20; Price/Price 692; Lindner I, 13; Weiße 239)
= *Fables for the Female Sex* (1744)

[41] More, Hannah, *Versuche mancherley Inhalts für junge Frauenzimmer* (Weidmanns Erben und Reich, 1778); includes Mrs Cartwright, *Briefe über die weibliche Erziehung an ein verheurathetes Frauenzimmer* and Hester Chapone, *Brief an ein neu verheurathetes Frauenzimmer* (see [9] and [10])
(Lehmstedt I, 142)
= *Essays on Various Subjects, Principally Designed for Young Ladies* (1777)
= *Letters on Female Education, Addressed to a Married Lady* (1777)
= *A Letter to a New-Married Lady* (1777)

[42] Peacock, Lucy, *Der Besuch von einer Woche oder Winke zum nützlichen Gebrauch der Zeit*, 2 vols (Gräff, 1798–99)
(Lindner I, 92; Price/Price 769; Weiße 241)
also as Weihnachtsgeschenk für die Jugend, 7–8
also as *Das geöffnete Schreibepult*, IV and V (see [3])
= *The Visit for a Week; or, Hints for the Improvement of Time* (1794)

[43] Pennyless, Peter [pseud.], *Empfindsame Gedanken bey verschiedenen Vorfällen* (Weidmanns Erben und Reich, 1770)[2]
= *Sentimental Lucubrations* (1770)

[44] Percival, Thomas, '[Die Empfindsamkeit für Schönheit]' in C. F. Weiße, 'Vorbericht des Uebersetzers', in John Aikin, *Naturkalender zum Unterrichte und Vergnügen junger Leute*

2 Weiße is identified as the translator in Christian Gottlob Kayser, *Vollständiges Bücherlexicon*, 6 vols (Leipzig: Schumann, 1834–36), IV, 316.

(Weidmanns Erben und Reich, 1787), pp. 3–26 (pp. 9–26) (cf. [2])

= *On the Advantages of a Taste for the General Beauties of Nature, and of Art; Section I: On the Beauties of Nature* (1784)

[45] Pinchard, Elizabeth [?], *Dramen zur Belehrung junger Frauenzimmer*, 2 vols (Weidmanns Erben und Reich, 1787)

(Price/Price, 707, with wrong author and original; Lehmstedt I, 203; Lindner I, 76; Weiße 240; cf. Price/Price 780 for the attribution to Pinchard, which could not be verified)

= *Dramatic Pieces, Calculated to Exemplify the Mode of Conduct* (1784)

[46] Pinchard, Elizabeth, *Das blinde Kind, eine kleine Familiengeschichte* (Gräff, [1793])

(Lindner I, 88; Price/Price 778; Weiße 241)

also as Weihnachtsgeschenk für die Jugend, 3 (Gräff, 1794)

= *The Blind Child; or Anecdotes of the Wyndham Family* (1791)

[47] Pinchard, Elizabeth, *Dramatische Unterhaltungen zur Belehrung und zum Vergnüngen junger Personen* (Gräff, 1794)

(Lindner I, 89; Price/Price 779; Weiße 241)

= *Dramatic Dialogues, for the Use of Young Persons* (1792)

[48] Pope, Alexander, 'Ode auf die Musik, am Tage der H[eiligen] Cecilia', in C. F. Weiße, *Scherzhafte Lieder*, 3rd edn (Weidmanns Erben und Reich, 1763), pp. 232–41

Revised translation in C. F. Weiße, *Kleine lyrische Gedichte* (Weidmanns Erben und Reich, 1772), III, 173–86

= *Ode for Musick on St. Cecilia's Day* (1708)

[49] Pratt, Samuel, *Courtney Melmoths freymüthige Gedanken über die Thiere, den Menschen und die Fürsehung in der Geschichte eines sonderbaren Mannes*, 3 vols (Weidmanns Erben und Reich, 1777–78)

(Lehmstedt I, 132: I publ. 1777, II and III publ. 1778)

= *Liberal Opinions, upon Animals, Man, and Providence* (1775–77)

[50] Reynolds, Joshua, *Reden* (trans. together with Adam Friedrich Oeser)[3]

Translations of Reynold's annual lectures at the Royal Academy, published consecutively in the *NBSWFK*:

'Rede an die Schüler, 11 December 1769 / Rede über das Studium der Malerey', *NBSWFK*, 14.2 (1773), 193–214

'Rede an die Schüler, 14 December 1770 / Von der zu genauen Nachahmung der Natur', *NBSWFK*, 16.1 (1774), 5–24

'Rede an die Schüler, 10 December 1771 / Rede von dem großen Styl', *NBSWFK*, 17.1 (1775), 5–33

'Rede an die Lehrlinge, 1772 / Rede über den verschiedenen Styl in der Malerey', *NBSWFK*, 17.1 (1775), 191–214

'Rede an die Schüler, 10 December 1774 / Rede von der malerischen Nachahmung', *NBSWFK*, 21.1 (1778), 5–39

'Rede an die Schüler, 10 December 1776 / Rede vom Geschmack in der Malerey', *NBSWFK*, 23.2 (1779), 195–217; continued in *NBSWFK*, 24.1 (1780), 1–25

'Rede an die Schüler, 10 December 1782 / Rede über das Genie der mechanischen Ausführung', *NBSWFK*, 31.1 (1785), 5–29

'Rede an die Schüler, 11 December 1786', *NBSWFK*, 35.1 (1788), 1–28

= *Discourses*

[51] Richardson, Samuel, *Gemeinnützige Lehren der Tugend, und der guten Sitten* (Weidmann, 1757)

(translated together with Lessing; Lindner I, 3, Price/ Price 828a and Weiße 239: 1752; Lehmstedt I, 14: '1752 wohl Druck- oder Erinnerungsfehler für 1757', citing the catalogue of the Easter Fair 1757; see also publication date of the English original)[4]

= *A Collection of the Moral and Instructive Sentiments* (1755)

[52] Rowe, Elizabeth, *Geheiligte Andachts-Uebungen in Betrachtung, Gebet, Lobpreisung und Herzens-Gesprächen [...] nebst [...]*

3 Cf. Minor, *Christian Felix Weiße*, p. 305.

4 Cf. also *Verzeichniß der Bibliothek*, 1758.

Anhang poetischer Stücke von Milton, Dryden, Prior, Addison, Pope, Watts, Young, und andern (Erfurt: Nonne, 1754) (translated together with Lessing; Lindner I, 5; Price/Price 856)

pp. 246–304 contain poetic selections from Addison, Dryden, Milton, Pope, Prior, Young and numerous other Early Modern poets

= *Devout Exercises of the Heart* (1737)

[53] Shenstone, William, 'In den Moosbewachsnen Zellen [...]', *Briefwechsel der Familie des Kinderfreundes*, 6 (1786), 164–65

An adaptation

= 'Here in Cool Grot'

[54] Smith, Charlotte, *Emmeline oder Die Waise des Schloßes*, 4 vols (Wien: Stahel [Schaumburg], 1790)

(Lindner I, 80; Price/Price 984; Weiße 241)

= *Emmeline, The Orphan of the Castle* (1788)

[55] Smith, Charlotte, *Ländliche Spaziergänge in Gesprächen*, 4 vols (Gräff: 1800–03) (Lindner I, 93; Weiße 241; Price/Price 994)

Also as Weihnachtsgeschenk für die Jugend, 9–12

Also as *Das geöffnete Schreibepult*, VI–IX (see [3])

= *Rural Walks: In Dialogues, Intended for the Use of Young Persons* (1795)

[56] Smith, John, *Gallische Alterthümer oder Eine Sammlung alter Gedichte aus dem Gallischen des Ulin, Ossian, Orran usw., ins Engländische und aus diesem ins Deutsche übersetzt*, 2 vols (Weidmanns Erben und Reich, 1781)

(Lehmstedt I, 175; Lindner I, 68; Price/Price 742 with false attribution of original author and title; Weiße 240)

= *Galic Antiquities; Consisting of a History of the Druids, [...] a Dissertation on the Authenticity of the Poems of Ossian; and a Collection of Ancient Poems* (1780)[5]

[57] Sterne, Laurence, *Briefe an seine vertrautesten Freunde, nebst einem Fragment im Geschmacke des Rabelais und einer von*

5 Cf. Tombo, *Ossian in Germany*, p. 20.

ihm selbst verfaßten Nachricht von seinem Leben und seiner Familie (Weidmanns Erben und Reich, 1776) (Lehmstedt I, 107; Lindner I, 58; Price/Price 1019; Weiße 240)
= *Letters of the Late Rev. Mr. Laurence Sterne, to his Most Intimate Friends* (1775)

[58] Thomson, James, *Sophonisbe* (unpublished, *c.* 1748)
(Weiße 16)
= *Sophonisba* (1730)

[59] *Unterricht und Zeitvertreib für das schöne Geschlecht in gesammelten Briefen und Erzählungen aus verschiedenen Sprachen*, 30 vols (Weidmanns Erben und Reich, 1765–76)
(Lindner II, 5; Weiße 239: translated 'several novels' in this series)

[60] Warton, Thomas [?], 'Die Unsterblichkeit der Seele', in C. F. Weiße, *Kleine lyrische Gedichte* (Weidmanns Erben und Reich, 1772), III, 203–26
(Price/Price 1132)
[Source unknown]

— Weihnachtsgeschenk für die Jugend (series), see [3], [16], [31], [42], [46], [55]

[61] Williams, Helen Maria, *Julie, ein Roman*, 2 vols (Weidmann, 1791)
(Lindner I, 81; Price/Price 1147; Weiße 241), includes appendix: *Rührende Geschichte des Herrn und der Madame du F.* (listed separately as [62])
= *Julia, a Novel* (1790)
= *Memoirs of Mons. and Madame du F–* (1790)

[62] Williams, Helen Maria, *Rührende Geschichte des Herrn und der Madame du F.*, see [61]

[63] Wilkes, Wetenhall, *Erinnerungen an ein junges Frauenzimmer, für alle Auftritte des Lebens* (Weidmanns Erben und Reich, 1763)
(Lehmstedt I, 33; Lindner I, 16; Weiße 239)
= *A Letter of Genteel and Moral Advice to a Young Lady* (1740)

[64] Wither, George, 'Der entschloßne Schäfer, eine Romanze', in Rudolf Erich Raspe, review of *Reliques of Ancient English Poetry*, ed. by Thomas Percy, *NBSWFK*, 2 (1766), 54–89 (pp. 87–88).

Reprinted in *Anthologie der Deutschen*, ed. by Heinrich Christian Schmid (Frankfurt and Leipzig: Schwickert, 1771), II, 354 (translation misattributed to Raspe; cf. [1])

Reprinted in C. F. Weiße, *Kleine lyrische Gedichte* (Weidmanns Erben und Reich, 1772), II, 253–54

= *The Shepherd's Resolution* | *Shall I Wasting in Despair* (1615; included in *Reliques of Ancient English Poetry* (1765))

[65] Wither, George, 'Antiseladon', in *Lyrische Bluhmenlese*, ed. by Karl Wilhelm Ramler (Weidmanns Erben und Reich, 1774), 4, p. 277

A considerably revised version of [64], containing only the first two stanzas of the poem

= *The Shepherd's Resolution* | *Shall I Wasting in Despair* (1615; included in *Reliques of Ancient English Poetry* (1765))

Translations from the French and Italian

[66] Carmontelle, Louis, *Der Ball*, in *Komisches Theater der Franzosen*, ed. by J. G. Dyck, I (Dyck, 1777)

(Lindner III, 2)

An adaptation

= *Le bal de province* (1775)

[67] Carmontelle, Louis, *Die beiden Hüthe*, in *Komisches Theater der Franzosen*, ed. by J. G. Dyck, I (Dyck, 1777; printed separately by Dyck in 1778)

(Lindner I, 61)

An adaptation

= *Les deux chapeaux* (1768)

[68] Crébillon, Prosper Jolyot de, *Catilina* (Berlin, 1749)

(translated together with Lessing; HB I, 10290; Lindner I, 1)

= *Catilina* (1748)

[69] Genlis, Stéphanie-Félicité de, *Erziehungstheater für junge Frauenzimmer*, 4 vols (Crusius, 1780–82)
(Fromm 10669; Weiße 240)
= *Théâtre à l'usage des jeunes personnes* (1779–80)

[70] Genlis, Stéphanie-Félicité de, *Abendstunden auf dem Lande oder Moralische Erzählungen für die Jugend*, 4 vols (Crusius, 1784–86)
(Fromm 10672; Weiße 240)
= *Les veillées du château, Ou cours de morale à l'usage des enfans* (1784)

[71] Guys, Pierre-Augustin, *Litterarische Reise nach Griechenland oder Briefe über die alten und neuern Griechen nebst einer Vergleichung ihrer Sitten*, 2 vols (Schwickert, 1772)
(Weiße 239; Lindner I, 48 claims that Weiße translated the book together with Karl Wilhelm Daßdorf)
= *Voyage littéraire de la Grèce* (1771)

[72] Marivaux, Pierre de, *Hannibal* (*c.* 1750–55)
(translated together with Lessing; cf. Weiße, *Selbstbiographie*, 13)
= *Annibal* (1720)

[73] Marmontel, Jean-François, *Walder* (Dyck, 1770)
(Fromm 11656; Lindner I, 38)
An adaptation
= *Sylvain* (1770)

[74] Mercier, Louis-Sébastien, *Das Jahr zwey tausend vier hundert und vierzig. Ein Traum aller Träume* (London [Leipzig]: Schwickert, 1772)
(Fromm 17333; Weiße 239; Lindner I, 46 claims that Weiße translated the book together with Karl Wilhelm Daßdorf)
= *L'An 2440* (1771)

[75] Mercier, Louis-Sébastien, *Johann Hennuyer, Bischoff von Lisieux* (Schwickert, 1773)

(Fromm 17376; Lindner I, 54)
= *Jean Hennuyer, Évêque de Lizieux* (1772)

[76] Metastasio, Pietro, *Das Leiden Jesu Christi, ein Singstück Unterhaltungen*, 3.3 (1767), 187–205
Reprinted in *Anthologie der Deutschen*, ed. by Heinrich Christian Schmid (Frankfurt und Leipzig: Schwickert, 1771), II, 314–31
Complete translation of the libretto for an oratorio; apparently, Weiße's only substantial translation from the Italian; possibly translated together with Daniel Schiebeler
= *La passione di Gesù Cristo* (1730)

[77] Moissy, Alexandre Guillaume de, *Die neue Weiberschule* (Gotha: Mevius, 1761)
(Fromm 17857; Lindner I, 14; Weiße 239)
= *La nouvelle école des femmes* (1758)

[78] Regnard, Jean François, *Der Zerstreute* (Dresden, 1752)
(HB III, 11322; Lindner I, 2; Weiße 16)
An adaptation
= *Le distrait* (1697)

[79] Regnard, Jean François, *Der Spieler* (*c.* 1748–50)
(translated together with Lessing; cf. Weiße, *Selbstbiographie*, p. 13)
= *Le joueur* (1696)

[80] Rousseau, Jean-Baptiste, *Cephalus und Aurore, Cantate*, in C. F. Weiße, *Scherzhafte Lieder*, 3rd edn (Weidmanns Erben und Reich, 1763), pp. 255–58
= *Cephale* (1723?)

[81] Saint-Lambert, Jean-François de, *Jahreszeiten* (Dyck, 1771)
(Fromm 23133; Weiße 239)
= *Les saisons* (1769)

[82] Saint-Lambert, Jean-François de, *Orientalische Fabeln nebst drey Erzählungen* (Dyck 1772)

(Fromm 23130; Weiße 239)
= *Fables orientales* (1772)

[83] Sedaine, Michel-Jean, *Der Dorfbalbier* (Dyck, 1769)
Reprinted in C. F. Weiße, *Komische Opern*, II (Dyck, 1770)
(Fromm 24086; Lindner I, 25)
An adaptation
= *Blaise le savetier* (1759)

[84] Voltaire, *Marianne* (1752)
(cf. Weiße, *Selbstbiographie*, 16; Lindner I, 4)
= *Mariamne* (1724)

Translations from Classical Languages

[85] Anon., 'König Regner Lodbrogs Leichengesang', in C. F. Weiße, Review of James Macpherson, *The Works of Ossian* [3rd edn, 1765], *NBSWFK*, 2.2 (1766), 245–61 (pp. 250–52)
A translation of eight stanzas (22–29) from the Latin version
Reprinted in *Anthologie der Deutschen*, ed. by Heinrich Christian Schmid (Frankfurt und Leipzig: Schwickert, 1771), II, 355–58
Slightly revised version in C. F. Weiße, *Kleine lyrische Gedichte* (Weidmanns Erben und Reich, 1772), II, 177–88
= *Regis Regneri Lodbrog epicedium*, in Olaus Wormius, [*Runir*] *seu danica literatura antiquissima* (also referred to as 'de Literatura Runica', in Hugh Blair, *Critical Dissertation on the Poems of Ossian*, Weiße's immediate source)

[86] Homer, 'Romanze. Der Bestrafte Verächter des Weins', in C. F. Weiße, *Scherzhafte Lieder*, 3rd edn (Weidmanns Erben und Reich, 1763), pp. 214–18
An adaptation of a passage from Book 6 of the *Iliad*
= *Ἰλιάς*

[87] Horace, 'Nachahmungen und Uebersetzungen aus dem Horatz', in C. F. Weiße, *Scherzhafte Lieder*, 3rd edn (Weidmanns Erben und Reich, 1763), pp. 167–213

Free renderings of Horace's Odes

Reprinted with minor revisions in C. F. Weiße, *Kleine lyrische Gedichte* (Weidmanns Erben und Reich, 1772), ɪɪ, 193–243

= *Carmina*

[88] Martial, 'Aus dem Martial', in C. F. Weiße, *Scherzhafte Lieder*, 3rd edn (Weidmanns Erben und Reich, 1763), pp. 277–81

Two translations of no. 47 from Book 10 of Martial's Epigrams

Reprinted with minor revisions in C. F. Weiße, *Kleine lyrische Gedichte* (Weidmanns Erben und Reich, 1772), ɪɪɪ, 246–51

= *Vitam quae faciant beatiorem*

[89] Sappho, 'Fragment einer Ode', in C. F. Weiße, Review of *Versuche aus der Litteratur und Moral*, by Christian August Clodius, ɪ, *NBSWFK*, 5.1 (1767), 78–96 (pp. 85–86)

The review features two translations by Weiße of the fragment, one of which is reprinted in *Anthologie der Deutschen*, ed. by Heinrich Christian Schmid (Frankfurt und Leipzig: Schwickert, 1771), ɪɪ, 341

Both translations reprinted in C. F. Weiße, *Kleine lyrische Gedichte* (Weidmanns Erben und Reich, 1772), ɪɪ, 255–58

= *φαίνεταί μοι κῆνος ἴσος θέοισιν*

[90] Tyrtaeus, 'Kriegslieder', in C. F. Weiße, *Amazonen-Lieder*, 2nd, enlarged edn (Weidmanns Erben und Reich, 1762), pp. 153–80

Reprinted in *Tyrtaei Quae Supersunt Omnia*, ed. by Christian Adolf Klotz (Altenburg: Richter, 1767), pp. 245–60

Reprinted in different order in C. F. Weiße, *Kleine lyrische Gedichte* (Weidmanns Erben und Reich, 1772), ɪɪ, 123–75

(HB ɪv, 6148; Lindner I, 15)

= *Πόλεμιστηρια*

Contested Attributions

Anon., *Der wegen besonderer Schönheit und seltener Tugenden liebenswürdigen Mariana merkwürdige Begebenheiten und Reisebeschreibung* (Frankfurt/Leipzig: n. pub., 1752)

(HB I, 4301 has Weiße as the translator (from the French); however, HB VII, 1170 contradicts this explicitly)

Somewhat unlikely given the date, style and subject matter

[Source unknown]

Anon., *Bibliothek für Jünglinge [...], nach der vierten englischen Ausgabe* (Weidmanns Erben und Reich, 1763; 2nd edn Böhme, 1773)

(Lehmstedt I, 22; Lindner 50; Price/Price 95b; Weiße 239)

Weiße seems to have brought the second edition to publication, but the translation itself is most probably by Johann Gottfried Gellius

[Source unknown]

Genlis, Stéphanie-Félicité de, *Adelheid und Theodor oder Briefe über die Erziehung*, 3 vols (Gera: Bekmann, 1783–84)

(According to the title page this book was translated by Peter Adolph Winkopp; Lindner II, 7 believes that Weiße had a share in the translation and Weiße 240 lists the book among his own translations)

= *Adèle et Théodore, Ou lettres sur l'education* (1782)

Le Blanc de Guillet, Antoine, *Albert der Erste oder Adeline* (Schwickert, 1775)

(Weiße as the translator in Lindner I, 56 and Weiße 239; HB I, 1056 has Johann Christoph Kaffka)

= *Albert Premier, ou Adeline* (1775)

Percival, Thomas, *Unterricht für seine Kinder, in Erzählungen, Fabeln, und Betrachtungen*, 2 vols (Weidmanns Erben und Reich, 1776–77)

In a letter to Werkmeister dated 30 April 1776 Weiße mentions that he has 'edited' ('herausgegeben') this translation, a term that in the period could encompass the act of translation[6]

= *A Father's Instructions to his Children; Consisting of Tales, Fables, and Reflections* (1775–77)

Riccoboni, Marie-Jeanne, *Briefe der Miss Fanni Butlerd an Milord Alfred von Caitombridge* (Weidmann, 1758; 2nd, revised edn 1761)

(Fromm 21935; Lindner 8; Weiße 239 all have Weiße as the translator; Lehmstedt II, 8, however, points to Johann Gottfried Gellius's assertion in his *Anmerkungen zum Gebrauche deutscher Kunstrichter* (Leipzig: n. pub., 1762), that he himself translated the work (p. 171). Given the date, Gellius seems to have the better claim, but Weiße probably contributed in some way)

= *Lettres de Mistriss Fanni Butlerd à Milord Charles Alfred, Duc de Caitombridge* (1757)

6 Weiße, 'Briefe an Werkmeister', p. 281.

Bibliography

Major Archival Resources

Briefe von Christian Felix Weiße an Friedrich Justin Bertuch, GSA 06/2093

Briefe von Christian Felix Weiße an Christian Ludwig Hagedorn, UBL Ms.0670u

Briefe von Christian Felix Weiße an Karl Wilhelm Ramler, GSA 75/229,1–4

Primary Sources

These exclude Weiße's translations listed in the Bibliography of Translations as well as his prefaces to these translations; because of their great number, the anonymous publications are listed chronologically.

Works by Christian Felix Weiße

Amazonen-Lieder (Leipzig: Weidmanns Erben & Reich, 1762)

Amazonen-Lieder, 2nd, enlarged edn (Leipzig: Weidmanns Erben & Reich, 1762)

'Auszug aus Briefen Christian Felix Weißes an Christian Ludwig von Hagedorn', ed. by C. Kirchner, *Euphorion*, 11 (1904), 420–32

Beytrag zum deutschen Theater [1], 2nd edn (Leipzig: Dyck, 1765 [1763])

Beytrag zum deutschen Theater, 2 (Leipzig: Dyck, 1763)

Briefwechsel der Familie des Kinderfreundes, 12 vols (Leipzig: Crusius, 1784–92)

'Briefe von Ch. F. Weisse an K. W. Ramler, im Auszuge mitgeteilt (I)', ed. by Karl Schüddekopf, *Archiv für das Studium der neueren Sprachen und Litteraturen*, 77 (1887), 1–46

'Briefe von Ch. F. Weisse an K. W. Ramler, im Auszuge mitgeteilt (Fortsetzung)', ed. by Karl Schüddekopf, *Archiv für das Studium der neueren Sprachen und Litteraturen*, 79 (1887), 149–216
'Briefe von Ch. F. Weisse an K. W. Ramler, im Auszuge mitgeteilt (Schluss)', ed. by Karl Schüddekopf, *Archiv für das Studium der neueren Sprachen und Litteraturen*, 82 (1889), 241–90
'Briefe des Herrn Kreissteuer-Einnehmers Christian Felix Weisse in Leipzig an Benedict Maria von Werkmeister', *Jahrschrift für Theologie und Kirchenrecht der Katholiken*, 6 (1824), 276–303
'Briefe von Christian Felix Weiße und Friedrich Jacobi an Lorenz Westenrieder aus den Jahren 1781–1783', ed. by A. Kluckhohn, *Sitzungsberichte der philosophisch-philologischen und historischen Classe der K.B. Akademie der Wissenschaften zu München* (1889), 2 vols, I, 237–70
'Christian Felix Weisses Briefe an F. J. Bertuch', ed. by Ludwig Geiger, *Zeitschrift für vergleichende Litteraturgeschichte*, 9th ser., 10 (1896), 235–51
'Felix Christian Weisse an Johann Peter Uz', *Morgenblatt für gebildete Leser*, 282 (1840), 1125–26
'Felix Christian Weisse an Johann Peter Uz', *Morgenblatt für gebildete Leser*, 284 (1840), 1134–35
'Felix Christian Weisse an Johann Peter Uz', *Morgenblatt für gebildete Leser*, 286 (1840), 1142–43
Kleine lyrische Gedichte (Leipzig: Weidmanns Erben & Reich, 1772)
Komische Opern, 3 vols (Leipzig: Dyck, 1768–71)
Lieder für Kinder (Leipzig: Weidmanns Erben und Reich, 1767)
[Review of Ossian [James Macpherson], *Temora, an Ancient Epic Poem*, *BSWFK*, 9 (1763), 315–16]
Review of [James Macpherson], *The Works of Ossian* [3rd edn, 1765], *NBSWFK*, 2.2 (1766), 245–61; cont. in 3.1 (1766), 13–38
Scherzhafte Lieder (Leipzig: Weidmanns Erben & Reich, 1758)
Scherzhafte Lieder, 3rd edn (Leipzig: Weidmanns Erben & Reich, 1763)
Selbstbiographie, ed. by Christian Ernst Weiße and Samuel Gottlob Frisch (Leipzig: Voß, 1806)

Other Primary Sources

Anon., *Nachricht von der erneuerten Deutschen Gesellschafft in Leipzig und ihrer ietzigen Verfassung* (Leipzig: Breitkopf, 1727)
Anon., review of Ossian [James Macpherson], *Fingal, an Ancient Epic Poem*, *BSWFK*, 8 (1762), 349

Anon., review of William Shakespeare, *Theatralische Werke*, I, trans. by Christoph Martin Wieland, *BSWFK*, 9 (1763), 257–70

Anon., review of Ossian [James Macpherson], *Temora, an Ancient Epic Poem*, *BSWFK*, 9 (1763), 315–16

Anon., review of Wetenhall Wilkes, *Erinnerungen an ein junges Frauenzimmer* [trans. by Christian Felix Weiße], *Göttingische Anzeigen von gelehrten Sachen*, 1.8 (1764), 64

Anon., review of *Anthologie der Deutschen*, II, ed. by Heinrich Christian Schmid, *Deutsche Bibliothek der schönen Wissenschaften*, 5.19 (1770), 509–26

Anon., review of John Macpherson, *Von den Barden* [trans. by C. F. Weiße], *Deutsche Bibliothek der schönen Wissenschaften*, 4 (1770), 726–27

Anon., review of J. F. de Saint-Lambert, *Jahreszeiten* [trans. by C. F. Weiße], *Allgemeine deutsche Bibliothek*, Anh. 13–24. Bd. 1 (1777), 431–32

Anon., *Allgemeines Verzeichniß derer Bücher, welche in der Frankfurter und Leipziger Michaelmesse des 1778 Jahres entweder ganz neu gedruckt, oder sonst verbessert, wieder aufgeleget worden sind, auch inskünftige noch herauskommen sollen* (Leipzig: Weidmanns Erben und Reich, 1778)

Anon., review of Stéphanie-Félicité Ducrest de Saint-Aubin, Comtesse de Genlis, *Erziehungstheater für junge Frauenzimmer* [1780] [trans. by C. F. Weiße], *Allgemeine deutsche Bibliothek*, 46.2 (1781), 579–81

Anon., review of John Smith, *Gallische Alterthümer* [trans. by C. F. Weiße], *Zugabe zu den Göttingischen Anzeigen von gelehrten Sachen*, 1.28 (1781), 442–47

Anon., review of John Smith, *Gallische Alterthümer* [trans. by C. F. Weiße], *Wöchentliche Nachrichten von neuen Landcharten, geographischen, statistischen und historischen Büchern und Sachen*, 9 (1781), 243

Anon., review of William Hayley, *Ein philosophischer, moralischer und historischer Versuch über die alten Jungfern* [trans. by C. F. Weiße], *Allgemeine deutsche Bibliothek*, 75 (1787), 305–10

Anon., review of Elisabeth Pinchard, *Dramen zur Belehrung junger Frauenzimmer nach ihrer ersten Erziehung, von einer englischen Dame* [trans. by C. F. Weiße], I and II, *Allgemeine deutsche Bibliothek*, 81 (1788), 245–47

Anon., review of John Aikin, *Naturkalender zum Unterrichte und Vergnügen junger Leute* [1787] [trans. by C. F. Weiße], *Allgemeine Literatur-Zeitung*, 3.221 (1789), 223–24

Anon., review of Frances Burney, *Cecilie Beverly*, I [1789], trans. by Wilhelm Heinrich Brömel, *Allgemeine Literatur-Zeitung*, 1.52 (1790), 415

Anon., review of Cassandra Hawke, *Julie de Grammont, eine rührende Geschichte* [trans. by C. F. Weiße], *Allgemeine Literatur-Zeitung*, 3.219 (1790), 295–96

Anon., review of Elizabeth Helme, *Clare und Emmeline, oder, der mütterliche Seegen* [1789] [trans. by C. F. Weiße], *Allgemeine Literatur-Zeitung*, 1.52 (1790), 414–15

Anon., review of Charlotte Smith, *Emmeline, oder, Die Wayse des Schlosses* [trans. by C. F. Weiße], *Allgemeine Literatur-Zeitung*, 4.364 (1790), 619–20

Anon., review of Anna Letitia Barbauld, *Das geöffnete Schreibepult zum Unterrichte und Vergnügen junger Personen*, I and II [trans. by C. F. Weiße], *Allgemeine Literatur-Zeitung*, 4.314 (1795), 400

Anon., review of C. F. Weiße, *A' Jelesebb Rendeken Lévö Nevendék Gyermekek*, trans. by K. Seelmann, *Siebenbürgische Quartalschrift*, 4 (1795), 291–93

Anon., review of John Burton, *Lectures on Female Education and Manners*, 2nd edn [1793] and *Vorlesungen über weibliche Erziehung und Sitten*, I [1794] [trans. by C. F. Weiße], *Allgemeine Literatur-Zeitung*, 1.49 (1795), 391–92

Anon., review of Letitia Barbauld, *Das geöffnete Schreibepult zum Unterrichte und Vergnügen junger Personen* [trans. by C. F. Weiße], *Neue allgemeine deutsche Bibliothek*, 60 (1801), 257–58

Anon., review of Anna Letitia Barbauld, *Das geöffnete Schreibepult zum Unterrichte und Vergnügen junger Personen*, IV–IX [1798–1803] [trans. by C. F. Weiße], *Allgemeine Literatur-Zeitung*, 2.84 (1805), 8

Anon., *Verzeichniß der Bibliothek Hrn. Christian Felix Weiße* (Leipzig: n. pub., 1806)

Akenside, Mark, *Die Vergnügungen der Einbildungskraft* [anon. trans.] (Greifswald/Leipzig: Weitbrecht, 1757)

Batteux, Charles, *Einleitung in die schönen Wissenschaften*, 4 vols, trans. by Karl Wilhelm Ramler, 4th, revised edn (Leipzig: Weidmanns Erben und Reich, 1774)

Beaumont, Francis and John Fletcher, *Die Braut: eine Tragödie; nebst kritischen und biographischen Abhandlungen über die 4 größten Dichter des ältern brittischen Theaters und einem Schreiben an den Kreis-Steuer-Einnehmer Weiße in Leipzig*, trans. and ed. by Heinrich Wilhelm von Gerstenberg (Kopenhagen/Leipzig: Rothens Wittwe & Profft, 1765)

Bertuch, Friedrich Justin, 'Versuch über Don Estevan Manuel de Villegas, einen lyrischen Dichter der Spanier', *Der teutsche Merkur*, 5 (1774), 237–58

Blainville, Joseph de [?], *Reisebeschreibung durch Holland, Oberdeutschland und die Schweiz besonders aber durch Italien*, trans. and ed. by Johann Tobias Köhler, 5 vols (Lemgo: Meyer, 1764–67)

Blair, Hugh, *A Critical Dissertation on the Poems of Ossian, the Son of Fingal* (London: Becket and De Hondt, 1763)

— 'Kritische Abhandlung über die Gedichte Ossians', in James Macpherson, *Ossians und Sineds Lieder*, trans. by Michael Denis, 6 vols (Vienna: Alberti, 1791–92), III (1791), unpag.

Blankenburg, Christian Friedrich von, review of Friedrich Nicolai, *Das Leben und die Meinungen des Herrn Magister Sebaldus Nothanker*, I (1773), *NBSWFK*, 17.2 (1775), 257–84

Bodmer, Johann Jakob, and Johann Jakob Breitinger, *Der Mahler der Sitten*, 2 vols (Zürich: Orell, 1746)

Bond, Donald F. (ed.), *The Spectator*, 5 vols (Oxford: Clarendon, 1965)

Breitinger, Johann Jakob, *Fortsetzung der critischen Dichtkunst*, intro. by J. J. Bodemer (Zürich: Orell; Leipzig: Gleditsch, 1740)

Burney, Frances, *Evelina, or, a Young Lady's Entrance into the World*, 3 vols (London: Lowndes, 1778)

— *Evelina, or the History of a Young Lady's Entrance into the World*, ed. by Edward A. Bloom (London: Oxford University Press, 1968)

Burton, John, *Lectures on Female Education and Manners*, 4th edn (Dublin: Milliken, 1796)

Casanova, Giovanni, 'Abhandlung über verschiedene alte Denkmäler der Kunst, besonders aus der churfürstl. Antiquitätensammlung zu Dresden', *NBSWFK*, 11.1 (1770), 1–42; contd. 11.2 (1771), 205–54

— *Discorso sopra gl'antichi e varj monumenti loro per uso degl'alunni dell'Elettoral' Accademia delle bell' arti di Dresda* (Leipzig: Dyck, 1770)

— *Abhandlung über verschiedene alte Denkmäler der Kunst, besonders aus der churfürstl. Antiquitätensammlung zu Dreßden* (Leipzig: Dyck, 1771)

Cesarotti, Melchiorre, 'Abhandlung über den Ursprung und Fortgang der Poesie', trans. by Johann Nicolaus Meinhard, *NBSWFK*, 2.1 (1766), 1–54

— *Saggio sulla filosofia delle lingue* (Naples: Bonis, 1818)

Cicero, Marcus Tullius, *De inventione; De optimo genere oratorum; Topica*, with an English translation by H. M. Hubbell, Loeb Classical Library, 386 (Cambridge, MA: Harvard University Press, 2014)

Congreve, William, 'A Hymn to Harmony, Written in Honour of St Cecilia's Day', in *Poems Upon Several Occasions* (Glasgow: Foulis, 1752), pp. 51–56
Couturier-Heinrich, Clémence (ed.), *Übersetzen bei Johann Gottfried Herder. Theorie und Praxis* (Heidelberg: Synchron, 2012)
Denis, Michael, *Die Lieder Sineds des Barden* (Vienna: Trattner, 1772)
Eck, Johann Georg, *Elegie auf Christian Felix Weisse* (Leipzig: Gräff, 1805)
Eschenburg, Johann Joachim, review of Jean-François Marmontel, *Walder, ein Lustspiel in einem Aufzuge* [1770], trans. by C. F. Weiße, *Allgemeine deutsche Bibliothek*, 18.1 (1772), 218–19
— *Ueber W. Shakspeare* (Zürich: Orell/Geßner/Füßli, 1787)
Fielding, Sarah, *Die Hofmeisterinn, oder Die kleine Akademie für das Frauenzimmer* [anon. trans.] (Leipzig: Weidmann, 1761)
Fritsch, Thomas, *Zufällige Betrachtungen in der Einsamkeit*, 2nd edn (Leipzig: n. pub., 1762)
— *Zufällige Betrachtungen in der Einsamkeit. Zwote Sammlung* (Leipzig: n. pub., 1762)
Garve, Christian, *Briefe an Christian Felix Weiße und einige andere Freunde*, 2 vols (Breslau: Korn, 1802–03)
Gellius, Johann Gottfried, *Anmerkungen zum Gebrauche deutscher Kunstrichter* (Leipzig: n. pub., 1762)
Gerber, Douglas E. (ed. and trans.), *Greek Elegiac Poetry*, Loeb Classical Library, 258 (Cambridge, MA: Harvard University Press, 1999)
Gibbes, Phebe, *Hartly House, Calcutta*, ed. by Michael J. Franklin (Manchester: Manchester University Press, 2019)
Góngora y Argote, Luis de, *Romanzen*, trans. by J. G. Jacobi (Halle: Gebauer, 1767)
Gottsched, Johann Christoph, *Versuch einer critischen Dichtkunst vor die Deutschen* (Leipzig: Breitkopf, 1730)
— *Versuch einer critischen Dichtkunst vor die Deutschen*, 4th edn (Leipzig: Breitkopf, 1751)
— *Ausführliche Redekunst*, 5th edn (Leipzig: Breitkopf, 1759 [1728])
— *Handlexicon oder kurzgefaßtes Wörterbuch der schönen Wissenschaften und freyen Künste* (Leipzig: Fritsch, 1760)
Gray, Thomas, *Poems* (London: Dodsley, 1768)
Gruner, Johann Ernst von, *Leben M. A. von Thümmels* (Leipzig: Göschen, 1819)
Helmer, Elizabeth, *Clara and Emmeline*, 2 vols (London: Kearsley, 1788)
Herder, Johann Gottfried, review of *Die Gedichte Ossians*, I, trans. by Michael Denis, *Allgemeine deutsche Bibliothek*, 10.1 (1769), 63–69

Homer, *Iliade*, trans. by Karl August Kütner (Leipzig: Dyck, 1771)

Horace, *Odes and Epodes*, ed. and trans. by Niall Rudd, Loeb Classical Library, 33 (Cambridge, MA: Harvard University Press, 2004)

Isla, José Francisco de, *Geschichte des berühmten Predigers Bruder Gerundio von Campazas*, trans. by Friedrich Justin Bertuch, 2 vols (Leipzig: Schwickert, 1773)

Kästner, Abraham Gotthelf, review of Luis José Velázquez, *Geschichte der spanischen Dichtkunst*, trans. by Johann Andreas Dieze, *NBSWFK*, 8.2 (1769), 240–60

Keate, George, *Sketches from Nature; Taken, and Coloured, in a Journey to Margate*, 2nd edn (London: Dodsley, 1779)

— *Nachrichten von den Pelew-Inseln in der Westgegend des Stillen Oceans*, trans. by Georg Forster (Hamburg: Hoffmann, 1789)

Lessing, Gotthold Ephraim, *Rettungen des Horaz*, in *Sämmtliche Schriften*, ed. by Karl Lachmann, 13 vols (Berlin: Voß, 1838–40), IV (1838), 5–43

Linguet, Simon Nicolas Henri, *Spanisches Theater*, trans. by Karl Christian Gärtner, 3 vols (Braunschweig: Waisenhaus, 1770–71)

Luther, Martin, *Ein Sendbrief vom Dolmetschen*, in Martin Luther, *Werke*, 127 vols (Weimar: Böhlau, 1883–2009), XXX (1909), 632–46

— *Ein Sendbrief vom Dolmetschen / An Open Letter on Translating*, trans. by Howard Jones, Treasures of the Taylorian: Reformation Pamphlets (Oxford: Taylor Institution Library, 2017) <https://ora.ox.ac.uk/objects/uuid:61dd3bfe-bd7d-48a2-adca-79e28d5cc63d/download_file?file_format=pdf&safe_filename=Reformation%2BPamphlets_Martin%2BLuther.pdf&type_of_work=Book> [accessed 14 December 2020]

Mackenzie, Henry (ed.), *The Mirror, A Periodical Paper*, 2 vols, 9th edn (London/Edinburgh: Strahan, Cadell and Creech, 1792–93)

Macpherson, James, *Die Gedichte Ossians, eines alten celtischen Dichters*, trans. by Michael Denis, I (Vienna: Trattner, 1768)

Mendelssohn, Moses, review of Mark Akenside, *The Pleasures of Imagination / Die Vergnügungen der Einbildungskraft*, *BSWFK*, 2.1 (1757), 91–124

Metastasio, Pietro, *La Passione di Gesù Christo* (Florence: Viviani, 1736)

Müller, J. v., review of Pierre Augustin Guys, *Litterarische Reise nach Griechenland* [1772] [trans. by Christian Felix Weiße], I and II, *Allgemeine deutsche Bibliothek*, 21 (1774), 605–07

Nicolai, Friedrich, review of *Amazonen-Lieder*, 2nd edn [1762], *Briefe, die neueste Litteratur betreffend*, 17 (1764), 3–16

— *Das Leben und die Meinungen des Herrn Magister Sebaldus Nothanker*, 3 vols (Berlin/Stettin: Nicolai, 1773–76)

Percival, Thomas, *Moral and Literary Dissertations* (Dublin: Graisberry, 1786)
Percy, Thomas (ed.), *Reliques of Ancient English Poetry [...] Together with some Few of Later Date*, 3 vols (London: Dodsley, 1765)
— *Balladen und Lieder altenglischer und altschottischer Dichtart*, ed. by August Friedrich Ursinus (Berlin: Himburg, 1777)
Prior, Matthew, *Heinrich und Emma, ein Gedicht nach dem Modell des Nußbraunen Mädchens*, trans. by Friedrich Justin Bertuch (Altenburg: Richter, 1772)
Ramler, Karl Wilhelm, *Kleine lyrische Gedichte* (Berlin: Voss, 1772)
Raspe, Rudolf Erich, 'Beschreibung der Armonica des Hrn. Franklins', *NBSWFK*, 4.1 (1767), 116–27
Rémond de Sainte-Albine, Pierre, *Der Schauspieler. Ein dogmatisches Werk für das Theater*, trans. by Friedrich Justin Bertuch (Altenburg: Richter, 1772)
Richardson, Samuel, *Clarissa. Die Geschichte eines vornehmen Frauenzimmers*, 8 vols (Göttingen: Vandenhoeck, 1748–53), II (1748)
Robertson, William, *Geschichte von Amerika*, trans. by Johann Friedrich Schiller, I and II (Leipzig: Weidmanns Erben und Reich, 1777)
Rozier, François, *Sammlung brauchbarer Abhandlungen aus des Herrn Abt Rozier Beobachtungen über die Natur und Kunst*, trans. by Christian Ernst Wünsch, 2 vols (Leipzig: Weidmanns Erben und Reich, 1775–76)
Saint-Lambert, Jean-François de, *Les Saisons* (Amsterdam: n. pub., 1769)
Schönaich, Christoph Otto von, *Die ganze Aesthetik in einer Nuß, oder neologisches Wörterbuch* ([Breslau: Hebold], 1754)
Schulz, Hans, 'Leipziger Stimmen von 1793 über Deutschland und die Revolution', *Euphorion*, 17 (1910), 48–55
Smith, Adam, *Untersuchung über die Natur und die Ursachen des Nationalreichthums*, trans. by Christian Garve and August Dörrien, 4 vols (Breslau: Korn, 1794–96)
Smollett, Tobias, *Begebenheiten des Peregrine Pickels*, 4 vols (Leipzig: Gleditsch, 1753)
Steele, Richard (ed.), *The Tatler* [1709] (Philadelphia: Woodward, 1831)
Unger, Friederike Helene, *Naturkalender zur Unterhaltung der heranwachsenden Jugend* (Berlin: Unger, 1789)
Wilkes, Wetenhall, *A Letter of Genteel and Moral Advice to a Young Lady*, 2nd edn (Dublin: Nelson, 1741 [1740])

Wolff, Odin, *Nyttige Kundskaber for Ungdommen i et morende, fatteligt Foredrag* (Copenhagen: Poulsen, 1791)

Wright, Edward, *Some Observations Made in Travelling through France, Italy, etc. in the Years 1720, 1721, and 1722*, 2 vols (London: Ward & Wickseed, 1730)

— *Beobachtungen, die er auf seinen Reisen durch Frankreich und Italien in den Jahren 1720. 1721. 1722. gemacht*, trans. by Johann Tobias Köhler, 2 vols (Lemgo: Meyer, 1767)

Young, Edward, *Klagen, oder Nachtgedanken über Leben, Tod, und Unsterblichkeit*, trans. by Johann Arnold Ebert, Uebersetzungen einiger poetischen und prosaischen Werke der besten englischen Schriftsteller, 1 (Brunswick: Schröder, 1751–52)

Zachariae, Justus Friedrich Wilhelm, *Die Tageszeiten. Ein Gedicht in vier Büchern* (Rostock/Leipzig: Koppe, 1756)

Secondary Literature

Ammon, Frieder von, 'Tereng! Tereng! teng! teng! Was der Postillion auf Münchhausens Posthorn geblasen hat', in *Das Phänomen Münchhausen*, ed. by Stefan Howald and Bernhard Wiebel (Kassel: Kassel University Press, 2020), pp. 110–23

Apel, Friedmar, and Annette Kopetzki, *Literarische Übersetzung*, 2nd edn (Stuttgart: Metzler, 2003)

Ashworth, E. J., 'Language, Renaissance Philosophy of', in *Routledge Encyclopedia of Philosophy*, ed. by Tim Crane (London/New York: Routledge, 2001–) <https://www.rep.routledge.com> [accessed 22 September 2020]

Baár, Monika, 'From General History to National History: The Transformations of William Guthrie's and John Gray's *A General History of the World* (1736–1765) in Continental Europe', in *Cultural Transfer through Translation: The Circulation of Enlightened Thought in Europe by Means of Translation*, ed. by Stefanie Stockhorst (Amsterdam/New York: Rodopi, 2010), pp. 61–82

Bachleitner, Norbert, 'Die Rezeption von Henry Homes "Elements of Criticism" in Deutschland 1763–1793', *Arcadia*, 20 (1985), 113–33

Bähring, Helmut, and Kurt Rüddiger, *Lexikon Buchstadt Leipzig. Von den Anfängen bis zum Jahr 1990* (Taucha: Tauchaer Verlag, 2008)

Baker, Mona, and Gabriela Saldanha (eds), *Routledge Encyclopedia of Translation Studies*, 3rd edn (Abingdon/New York: Routledge, 2020 [1997])

Bastin, Georges L., 'Adaptation', in *Routledge Encyclopedia of Translation Studies*, ed. by Mona Baker and Gabriela Saldanha, 3rd edn (Abingdon/New York: Routledge, 2020 [1997]), pp. 10–14

Beiser, Frederick C., *Diotima's Children: German Aesthetic Rationalism from Leibniz to Lessing* (Oxford: Oxford University Press, 2009)

Bell Price, Mary, and Lawrence Marsden Price, *The Publication of English Literature in Germany in the Eighteenth Century*, University of California Publications in Modern Philology, 17 (Berkeley, CA: University of California Press, 1934)

— *The Publication of English Humaniora in Germany in the Eighteenth Century*, University of California Publications in Modern Philology, 44 (Berkeley, CA/Los Angeles, CA: University of California Press, 1955)

Blackall, Eric. A., *The Emergence of German as a Literary Language, 1700–1775* (Cambridge: Cambridge University Press, 1959)

Blassneck, Marce, *Frankreich als Vermittler englisch>deutscher Einflüsse im 17. und 18. Jahrhundert*, Kölner Anglistische Arbeiten, 20 (Leipzig: Tauchnitz, 1934)

Bremer, Thomas, and Christine Haug, with Helga Meise, *Verlegerische Geschäftskorrespondenz im 18. Jahrhundert: Das Kommunikationsfeld zwischen Autor, Herausgeber und Verleger in der deutschsprachigen Aufklärung*, Buchwissenschaftliche Beiträge, 96 (Wiesbaden: Harrassowitz, 2018)

Briesemeister, Dietrich, *Spanien aus deutscher Sicht. Deutsch-spanische Kulturbeziehungen gestern und heute*, ed. by Harald Wentzlaff-Eggebert, Beihefte zur Iberomania, 20 (Tübingen: Niemeyer, 2004)

Brown, Hilary, *Luise Gottsched the Translator* (Rochester, NY: Camden House, 2012)

Buchner, Karl, *Aus dem Verkehr einer deutschen Buchhandlung mit ihren Schriftstellern* (Berlin: Weidmann, 1873)

Buruma, Ian, *Voltaire's Coconuts; or, Anglomania in Europe* (London: Weidenfeld & Nicolson, 1999)

Cantarutti, Giulia, '"La biblioteca di belle lettere del Sig. Weisse". Eine neue Quelle für den italienisch-deutschen Kulturtransfer', in *Sächsische Aufklärung*, ed. by Anneliese Klingenberg and others, Leipziger Studien zur Erforschung von regionenbezogenen Identifikationsprozessen, 7 (Leipzig: Leipziger Universitätsverlag, 2001), pp. 251–66

Cardi, Carola, *Das Kinderschauspiel der Aufklärungszeit*, Europäische Hochschulschriften I/693 (Frankfurt am Main: Lang, 1983)

Clayton, Timothy, 'Reviews of English Art in the Neue Bibliothek', in *Sächsische Aufklärung*, ed. by Anneliese Klingenberg and others, Leipziger Studien zur Erforschung von regionenbezogenen Identifikationsprozessen, 7 (Leipzig: Leipziger Universitätsverlag, 2001), pp. 231–37

Dettmar, Ute, 'Aufgeklärte Kindheit. Christian Felix Weiße als Autor für Kinder', in *Christian Felix Weiße und die Leipziger Aufklärung*, ed. by Katrin Löffler and Ludwig Stockinger (Hildesheim: Olms, 2006), pp. 71–93

Dittrich, Andreas, 'Traduire la pensée utopique: le transfert des paradigmes de L'An 2440', in *Cultural Transfer through Translation: The Circulation of Enlightened Thought in Europe by Means of Translation*, ed. by Stefanie Stockhorst and others (Amsterdam/New York: Rodopi, 2010), pp. 121–39

Dommes, Grit, 'Klopstock, Friedrich Gottlieb', in *Handbuch Sturm und Drang*, ed. by Matthias Luserke-Jaqui (Berlin/Boston, MA: de Gruyter, 2017), pp. 130–34

Döring, Detlef, 'Der Literaturstreit zwischen Leipzig und Zürich in der Mitte des 18. Jahrhunderts. Neue Untersuchungen zu einem alten Thema', in *Bodmer und Breitinger im Netzwerk der Europäischen Aufklärung*, ed. by Anett Lütteken and Barbara Mahlmann-Bauer (Göttingen: Wallstein, 2009), pp. 60–104

Durchholz, Sabine, 'Im "Lebenden Labyrinth der Literatur": Shakespeares "Richard der Dritte" in Versionen von Christian Felix Weiße und Carl Steinberg; mit einem Blick auf Lessings Weiße-Rezeption', *Lessing Yearbook*, 38 (2008/2009), 169–91

Eggers, Hans, *Deutsche Sprachgeschichte*, 2 vols (Reinbek: Rowohlt, 1986 [1963–77]), II, *Das Frühneuhochdeutsche und Neuhochdeutsche*

Espagne, Michel, *Les transferts culturels franco-allemands* (Paris: Presses Universitaires de France, 1999)

— 'Christian Felix Weiße und Paris – Literarische Aufklärung und Kunstgeschichte', in *Sächsische Aufklärung*, ed. by Anneliese Klingenberg and others, Leipziger Studien zur Erforschung von regionenbezogenen Identifikationsprozessen, 7 (Leipzig: Leipziger Universitätsverlag, 2001), pp. 161–72

Espagne, Michel, and Werner Greiling (eds), *Frankreichfreunde. Mittler des französisch-deutschen Kulturtransfers (1750–1850)* (Leipzig: Leipziger Universitätsverlag, 1996)

Espagne, Michel, and Matthias Middell (eds), *Von der Elbe bis an die Seine. Kulturtransfer zwischen Sachsen und Frankreich im 18. und 19. Jahrhundert* (Leipzig: Leipziger Universitätsverlag, 1993)

Fabian, Bernhard, *Die Meßkataloge des achtzehnten Jahrhunderts: eine Microfiche-Edition* (Hildesheim: Olms, 1977–79)

— *The English Book in Eighteenth-Century Germany*, The Panizzi Lectures 1991 (London: British Library, 1992)

— *Selecta Anglicana. Buchgeschichtliche Studien zur Aufnahme der englischen Literatur in Deutschland im achtzehnten Jahrhundert*, Schriften und Zeugnisse zur Buchgeschichte, 6 (Wiesbaden: Harrassowitz, 1994)

— 'Englisch-Deutsche Kulturbeziehungen im achtzehnten Jahrhundert', in *Europäischer Kulturtransfer im 18. Jahrhundert. Literaturen in Europa – europäische Literatur?*, ed. by Barbara Schmidt-Haberkamp, Uwe Steiner and Brunhilde Wehinger (Berlin: BWV, 2003), pp. 13–30

Fankhauser, Gertrud, '"Der Kinderfreund" (1775–84): die Kinderzeitschrift von Christian Felix Weiße als Spiegelbild der Erziehungs- und Gesellschaftsideale des Deutschen Bürgertums am Ende des Aufklärungszeitalters' (unpublished doctoral thesis, New York University, 1975; abstract in *Dissertation Abstracts*, 36 (1975–76), 11, 7451-A)

Ferguson, Frances, 'The Novel Comes of Age: When Literature Started Talking with Children', *Differences*, 28.1 (2017), 37–63

Fischer, Hannes, and Erika Thomalla, 'Literaturwissenschaftliche Netzwerkforschung zum 18. Jahrhundert', *Zeitschrift für Germanistik*, n.s., 26 (2016), 110–17

Flood, John L., and William A. Kelly (eds), *The German Book 1450–1750. Studies Presented to David L. Paisey* (London: British Library, 1995)

Fränzel, Walter, *Geschichte des Übersetzens im 18. Jahrhundert* (Leipzig: Voigtländer, 1913)

Frank, Christoph, and Sylvaine Hänsel (eds), *Spanien und Portugal im Zeitalter der Aufklärung*, Ars Iberica et Americana, 8 (Frankfurt am Main: Vervuert, 2002)

Fromm, Hans, *Bibliographie deutscher Übersetzungen aus dem Französischen 1700–1948*, 6 vols (Baden-Baden: Verlag für Kunst und Wissenschaft, 1950–53)

Füssel, Stephan (ed.), *Georg Joachim Göschen. Ein Verleger der Spätaufklärung und der Deutschen Klassik.* Studien zur Verlagsgeschichte und zur Verlegertypologie der Goethe-Zeit, 1 (Berlin: de Gruyter, 1999)

Gambier, Yves, Miriam Shlesinger and Radegundis Stolze (eds), *Doubts and Directions in Translation Studies: Selected Contributions from the EST Congress, Lisbon 2004* (Amsterdam: Benjamins, 2007)

Ganz, Peter F., *Der Einfluss des Englischen auf den deutschen Wortschatz 1640–1815* (Berlin: Schmidt, 1957)

Gaskill, Howard (ed.), *The Reception of Ossian in Europe* (London: Thoemmes Continuum, 2004)

Gendler Szabo, Zoltan, 'Language, Early Modern Philosophy of', in *Routledge Encyclopedia of Philosophy*, ed. by Tim Crane (London and New York: Routledge, 2001–) <https://www.rep.routledge.com> [accessed 22 September 2020]

Genton, François, 'Christian Felix Weiße et Arnaud Berquin ou l'influence de la littérature d'enfance et de jeunesse allemande en France au XVIIIe siècle et au-delà', in *Révolution, Restauration et les jeunes*, ed. by Gilbert Van de Louw and Elisabeth Genton (Paris: Didier Erudition, 1989), pp. 47–73

Ghanbari, Nacim, 'Netzwerktheorie und Aufklärungsforschung', *Internationales Archiv für Sozialgeschichte der Deutschen Literatur*, 38 (2013), 315–35

Giessing, Charles Paul, 'The Plagiarized Book Reviews of C. F. Weisse in the "Bibliothek der schönen Wissenschaften"', *Modern Philology*, 16 (1918), 77–88

Göpferich, Susanne, 'Translation Studies and Transfer Studies', in *Doubts and Directions in Translation Studies: Selected Contributions from the EST Congress, Lisbon 2004*, ed. by Yves Gambier, Miriam Shlesinger and Radegundis Stolze (Amsterdam: Benjamins, 2007), pp. 27–39

Graeber, Wilhelm, and Geneviève Roche, *Englische Literatur des 17. und 18. Jahrhunderts in französischer Übersetzung und deutscher Weiterübersetzung. Eine kommentierte Bibliographie*, ed. by Jürgen von Stackelberg (Tübingen: Niemeyer, 1988)

Häseler, Jens, 'Spanische Literatur in der Neuen Bibliothek der schönen Wissenschaften und der freyen Künste', in *Spanien und Portugal im Zeitalter der Aufklärung*, ed. by Christoph Frank and Sylvaine Hänsel, Ars Iberica et Americana, 8 (Frankfurt am Main: Vervuert, 2002), pp. 137–46

Heidenreich, Marianne, *Christian Gottlob Heyne und die alte Geschichte*, Beiträge zur Altertumskunde, 229 (München/Leipzig: Saur, 2006)

Heine, Carl, *Der Roman in Deutschland von 1774 bis 1778* (Halle: Niemeyer, 1892)

Herder, Emil Gottfried von (ed.), *Johann Gottfried von Herder's Lebensbild*, 3 vols (Erlangen: Bläsing, 1846–47)

Historische Commission bei der Bayerischen Akademie der Wissenschaften (eds), *Allgemeine deutsche Biographie*, 56 vols (Leipzig: Duncker & Humblot, 1875–1912)

— *Neue deutsche Biographie*, 28 vols (Berlin: Duncker & Humblot, 1953–2020)

Holzmann, Michael, and Hanns Bohatta, *Deutsches Anonymen-Lexikon 1501–1850*, 7 vols (Weimar: Gesellschaft der Bibliophilen, 1902–26)

Hönsch, Ulrike, 'Das deutsche Spanienbild in literarhistorischen Abhandlungen des 18. Jahrhunderts: Christian Heinrich Schmids *Theorie der Poesie* (1767) und Johann Friedrich Butenschoens *Versuch über die spanische schöne Litteratur* (1789)', in *Spanien und Portugal im Zeitalter der Aufklärung*, ed. by Christoph Frank and Sylvaine Hänsel, Ars Iberica et Americana, 8 (Frankfurt am Main: Vervuert, 2002), pp. 147–162

Howald, Stefan, and Bernhard Wiebel (eds), *Das Phänomen Münchhausen. Neue Perspektiven* (Kassel: Kassel University Press, 2020)

Huber, Thomas, *Studien zur Theorie des Übersetzens im Zeitalter der Deutschen Aufklärung 1730–1770*, Deutsche Studien, 7 (Meisenheim am Glan: Hain, 1968)

Hurrelmann, Bettina, *Jugendliteratur und Bürgerlichkeit. Soziale Erziehung in der Jugendliteratur der Aufklärung am Beispiel von Christian Felix Weißes 'Kinderfreund' 1776–1782*, Informationen zur Sprach- und Literaturdidaktik, 5 (Paderborn: Schöningh, 1974)

Hüttemann, Walter, *Christian Felix Weisse und seine Zeit in ihrem Verhältnis zu Shakespeare* (Duisburg: Buschmann / Doctoral Dissertation, University of Bonn, 1912)

Iphofen, Heinrich Curt, *Lebensgeschichte Christian Felix Weißens*, ed. by G. F. Döhner (Freiberg: Craz & Gerlach, 1826)

Jaubert, Elsa, '"Richard III" et "Roméo et Juliette" de Christian Felix Weiße: une voie médiane entre la barbarie anglaise et la superficialité française?', *Revue germanique internationale*, 5 (2007), 23–35

Jördens, Karl Heindrich (ed.), *Lexikon deutscher Dichter und Prosaisten*, 6 vols. (Leipzig: Weidmann, 1805–11)

Jost, Erdmut, 'Einführung: Das 18. Jahrhundert als Formierungsphase der Netzwerkgesellschaft', in *Briefwechsel. Zur Netzwerkbildung in der Aufklärung*, ed. by Erdmut Jost and Daniel Fulda, IZEA – Kleine Schriften, 4/2012 (Halle/Saale: Mitteldeutscher Verlag, 2012), pp. 7–14

Kahn, Robert L., 'Three Franklin-Raspe Letters', *Proceedings of the American Philosophical Society*, 99 (1955), 397–400

Kaiser, Gerhard R., and Siegfried Seifert (eds), *Friedrich Justin Bertuch (1747–1822). Verleger, Schriftsteller und Unternehmer im klassischen Weimar* (Tübingen: Niemeyer, 2000)

Kanz, Roland, *Giovanni Battista Casanova (1730–1795). Eine Künstlerkarriere in Rom und Dresden*, Phantasos, 7 (Paderborn: Fink, 2007)

Kayser, Christian Gottlob, *Vollständiges Bücherlexicon*, 6 vols (Leipzig: Schumann, 1834–36)

Killy, Walther, 'Über den deutschen Horaz', in *Geschichte des Textverständnisses am Beispiel von Pindar und Horaz. Vorträge gehalten anläßlich des 6. Wolfenbütteler Symposions vom 18. bis 22. September 1978 in der Herzog-August-Bibliothek*, ed. by Walther Killy, Wolfenbütteler Forschungen, 12 (München: Kraus, 1981), pp. 243–59

Klingberg, Göte, *Das deutsche Kinder- und Jugendbuch im schwedischen Raum. Ein Beitrag zum Studium der Verbreitungswege der Kinder- und Jugendliteratur*, Internationale Untersuchungen zur Kinder- und Jugendliteratur, 3 (Weinheim/Basel: Beltz, 1973)

Klingenberg, Anneliese, 'Die "Neue Bibliothek der schönen Wissenschaften und der freyen Künste" – Programm für eine europäische Républiqe des Lettres', in *Sächsische Aufklärung*, ed. by Anneliese Klingenberg and others, Leipziger Studien zur Erforschung von regionenbezogenen Identifikationsprozessen, 7 (Leipzig: Leipziger Universitätsverlag, 2001) pp. 173–96

— 'Sächsische Aufklärung und europäische "République des lettres" – die "Neue Bibliothek der schönen Wissenschaften und der freyen Künste"', in *Christian Felix Weiße und die Leipziger Aufklärung*, ed. by Katrin Löffler and Ludwig Stockinger (Hildesheim: Olms, 2006), pp. 9–30

Klingenberg, Anneliese, and others (eds), *Sächsische Aufklärung*, Leipziger Studien zur Erforschung von regionenbezogenen Identifikationsprozessen, 7 (Leipzig: Leipziger Universitätsverlag, 2001)

Knapp, Lore, and Eike Kronshage (eds), *Britisch-Deutscher Literaturtransfer 1756–1832*, Weltliteraturen, 11 (Berlin/Boston, MA: de Gruyter, 2016)

Knufmann, Helmut, 'Das deutsche Übersetzungswesen des 18. Jahrhunderts im Spiegel von Übersetzer- und Herausgebervorreden', *Börsenblatt für den deutschen Buchhandel*, 91 (1967), 2676–2716

Košenina, Alexander, 'Ein deutscher Horaz? Karl Wilhelm Ramler in der zeitgenössischen Rezeption', in *Urbanität als Aufklärung. Karl Wilhelm Ramler und die Kultur des 18. Jahrhunderts*, ed. by Laurenz Lütteken, Ute Pott and Carsten Zelle (Göttingen: Wallstein, 2003), pp. 129–52

Krämer, Jörg, *Deutschsprachiges Musiktheater im späten 18. Jahrhundert*, Studien zur deutschen Literatur, 149 (Tübingen: Niemeyer, 1998), pp. 130–201

Krätzer, Jürgen, 'Christian Felix Weiße in der deutschen Germanistik. Ein Forschungsbericht', in *Sächsische Aufklärung*, ed. by Anneliese Klingenberg and others, Leipziger Studien zur Erforschung von regionenbezogenen Identifikationsprozessen, 7 (Leipzig: Leipziger Universitätsverlag, 2001), pp. 147–60

Lamport, Francis, '"Des Menschen Herz, o Gott! Welch Elend kann es stiften!": The Tragedies of Christian Felix Weisse', *Publications of the English Goethe Society*, 82 (2013), 1–15

Lee, J. Patrick, 'The Unexamined Premise: Voltaire, John Lockman and the Myth of the English Letters', in *From Letter to Publication*, ed. by Robert V. McNamee, Studies on Voltaire and the Eighteenth Century, 2001:10 (Oxford: Voltaire Foundation, 2001), pp. 240–70

Lehmstedt, Mark, '"Uebersetzungsmanufactur" und "Proletarische Scribenten". Quellenstudie zur Sozialgeschichte der Deutschen Aufklärung' (unpublished diploma thesis, Humboldt University Berlin, 1987)

— *Philipp Erasmus Reich (1717–1787). Verleger der Aufklärung und Reformer des deutschen Buchhandels* (Leipzig: Karl-Marx-Universität, 1989)

— 'Ein Empfehlungsschreiben an "Herrn Jäschke" in Dessau', *Börsenblatt*, 157.9 (1990), 156–58

— 'Die erste Buchhandlungsgesellschaft in Deutschland', *Börsenblatt*, 157.19 (1990), Beiheft, 2–12

— 'Struktur und Arbeitsweise eines Verlages der Deutschen Aufklärung. Die Weidmannsche Buchhandlung in Leipzig unter der Leitung von Philipp Erasmus Reich zwischen 1745 und 1787' (unpublished doctoral thesis, Karl-Marx-University Leipzig, 1990)

— 'Die Geschichte einer Übersetzung. William Robertsons "Geschichte von Amerika" (1777)', *Leipziger Jahrbuch zur Buchgeschichte*, 1 (1991), 265–97

Lessing, Karl Gotthelf, *Gotthold Ephraim Lessings Leben*, 3 vols (Berlin: Voß, 1793–95), I (1793)

Lindner, Johann Wilhelm Sigismund, 'Vollständiges Verzeichnis der Schriften von und über Chr. F. Weiße', in Heinrich Curt Iphofen, *Lebensgeschichte Christian Felix Weißens*, ed. by G. F. Döhner (Freiberg: Craz & Gerlach, 1826), pp. 95–113

Linguet, Simon Nicolas Henri, *Spanisches Theater*, 3 vols (Braunschweig: Waisenhaus, 1770–71)

Löffler, Katrin, 'Aufklärung und Konfessionspolitik. Weißes Trauerspiel "Der Fanatismus, oder: Jean Calas"', in *Christian Felix Weiße und die Leipziger Aufklärung*, ed. by Katrin Löffler and Ludwig Stockinger (Hildesheim: Olms, 2006), pp. 95–127

Löffler, Katrin, and Ludwig Stockinger (eds), *Christian Felix Weiße und die Leipziger Aufklärung* (Hildesheim: Olms, 2006)

Louw, Gilbert Van de, and Elisabeth Genton (eds), *Révolution, Restauration et les jeunes* (Paris: Didier Erudition, 1989)

Luserke-Jaqui, Matthias (ed.), *Handbuch Sturm und Drang* (Berlin/ Boston, MA: de Gruyter, 2017)

Lütteken, Anett, and Barbara Mahlmann-Bauer (eds), *Bodmer und Breitinger im Netzwerk der Europäischen Aufklärung* (Göttingen: Wallstein, 2009)

Mai, Anne-Kristin, *Christian Felix Weiße, 1726–1804. Leipziger Literat zwischen Amtshaus, Bühne und Stötteritzer Idyll* (Beucha: Sax, 2003)

Marshall, Walter Henry, '"The Devil to Pay" and its Influence on Eighteenth-Century German Singspiel' (unpublished doctoral thesis, The Open University, 1985)

Martens, Wolfgang, 'Zur Einführung: Das Bild Leipzigs bei Zeitgenossen', in *Zentren der Aufklärung III. Leipzig*, Wolfenbütteler Studien zur Aufklärung, 17 (Heidelberg: Schneider, 1990), pp. 13–21

— (ed.), *Zentren der Aufklärung III. Leipzig. Aufklärung und Bürgerlichkeit*, Wolfenbütteler Studien zur Aufklärung, 17 (Heidelberg: Schneider, 1990)

Maurer, Michael, *Aufklärung und Anglophilie in Deutschland*, Veröffentlichungen des Deutschen Historischen Instituts London, 19 (Göttingen/Zurich: Vandenhoeck & Ruprecht, 1987)

Mayer, Christine, 'Female Education and the Cultural Transfer of Pedagogical Knowledge in the Eighteenth Century', *Paedagogica Historica*, 48 (2012), 511–26

Meek, Donald E., 'The Sublime Gael: The Impact of Macpherson's *Ossian* on Literary Creativity and Cultural Perception in Gaelic Scotland', in *The Reception of Ossian in Europe*, ed. by Howard Gaskill (London: Thoemmes Continuum, 2004), pp. 40–66

Meier, Uwe, 'Raspe, Rudolf Erich', in *Neue Deutsche Biographie*, ed. by Historische Commission bei der Bayerischen Akademie der Wissenschaften, 28 vols (Berlin: Duncker & Humblot, 1953–2020), XXI (2003), 164–66

Meisnest, F. W., 'Die Quellen zu Christian Felix Weißes Richard III.', *Euphorion*, 17 (1910), 538–56

— 'Wieland's Translation of Shakespeare', *Modern Language Review*, 9 (1914), 12–40

Mendelssohn, Harald, *Das Autorenhonorar. Seine Entwicklungsgeschichte vom 17. bis 19. Jahrhundert*, Buchwissenschaftliche Beiträge aus dem Deutschen Bucharchiv München, 59 (Wiesbaden: Harrassowitz, 1998)

Michelsen, Peter, *Laurence Sterne und der deutsche Roman des 18. Jahrhunderts*, 2nd edn, Palaestra, 232 (Göttingen: Vandenhoeck & Ruprecht, 1972 [1962])

Middell, Katharina, *'Die Bertuchs müssen doch in dieser Welt überall Glück haben'. Der Verleger Friedrich Justin Bertuch und sein Landes-Industrie-Comptoir um 1800* (Leipzig: Leipziger Universitätsverlag, 2002)

Middell, Matthias, 'Kulturtransfer und historische Komparatistik. Thesen zu ihrem Verhältnis', *Comparativ*, 10 (2000), 7–41

— 'Kulturtransfer, Transferts Culturels', *Docupedia-Zeitgeschichte*, 28 January 2016 <http://dx.doi.org/10.14765/zzf.dok.2.702.v1> [accessed 7 November 2020]

Minor, Jakob, *Christian Felix Weiße und seine Beziehungen zur deutschen Literatur des achtzehnten Jahrhunderts* (Innsbruck: Wagner, 1880)

— 'Einleitung', in *Lessings Jugendfreunde*, ed. by Jakob Minor, Deutsche National-Litteratur, 72 (Berlin/Stuttgart: Spemann, [1883]), pp. V–XXV

Mühlpfordt, Günter, 'Gelehrtenrepublik Leipzig', in *Zentren der Aufklärung III. Leipzig*, ed. by Wolfgang Martens, Wolfenbütteler Studien zur Aufklärung, 17 (Heidelberg: Schneider, 1990), pp. 39–101

Munke, Martin, 'Philipp Erasmus Reich und die Verbreitung britischer Literatur in Deutschland. Import und Übersetzung', in *Britisch-Deutscher Literaturtransfer 1756–1832*, ed. by Lore Knapp and Eike Kronshage (Berlin/Boston, MA: de Gruyter, 2016), pp. 21–38

Münzberg, Franziska, *Die Darstellungsfunktion der Übersetzung. Zur Rekonstruktion von Übersetzungsmodellen aus dem 18. Jahrhundert* (Frankfurt am Main: Lang, 2003)

Nebrig, Alexander, and Daniele Vecchiato, 'Einleitung: Translatorische Kreativität um 1800', in *Kreative Praktiken des literarischen Übersetzens um 1800. Übersetzungshistorische und literaturwissenschaftliche Studien*, ed. by Alexander Nebrig and Daniele Vecchiato, Untersuchungen zur deutschen Literaturgeschichte, 152 (Berlin/Boston, MA: de Gruyter, 2019), pp. 1–16

— (eds), *Kreative Praktiken des literarischen Übersetzens um 1800. Übersetzungshistorische und literaturwissenschaftliche Studien*, Untersuchungen zur deutschen Literaturgeschichte, 152 (Berlin/Boston, MA: de Gruyter, 2019)

Nover, Gerd, *Die deutschen Übersetzungen und Bearbeitungen englischer Komödien im 18. Jahrhundert*, Europäische Hochschulschriften, I/462 (Frankfurt am Main: Lang, 1981)

Ó Catháin, Diarmaid, 'An Irish Scholar Abroad: Bishop John O'Brien of Cloyne and the Macpherson Controversy', in *Cork. History and Society*, ed. by Patrick O'Flanagan and Cornelius G. Buttimer (Dublin: Geography Publications, 1993), pp. 499–533

O'Flanagan, Patrick, and Cornelius G. Buttimer (eds), *Cork. History and Society* (Dublin: Geography Publications, 1993)

Oergel, Maike, 'Die "Verurtümlichung" Homers – ein Beispiel transnationaler Antiketransformation: Die Rezeption des Homerischen Barden in Großbritannien und Deutschland im 18. Jh.', in *Topographien der Antike in der literarischen Aufklärung*, ed. by Annika Hildebrandt, Charlotte Kurbjuhn and Steffen Martus, Publikationen zur Zeitschrift für Germanistik, n.s., 30 (Berlin: Lang, 2017), pp. 181–200

Oppel, Horst, *Englisch-Deutsche Literaturbeziehungen*, 2 vols, Grundlagen der Anglistik und Amerikanistik, 1 & 2 (Berlin: Erich Schmidt, 1971), I, *Von den Anfängen bis zum Ausgang des 18. Jahrhunderts*

Overhoff, Jürgen, *Die Frühgeschichte des Philanthropismus 1715–1771. Konstitutionsbedingungen, Praxisfelder und Wirkung eines pädagogischen Reformprogramms im Zeitalter der Aufklärung* (Tübingen: Niemeyer, 2004)

Pape, Walter, *Das literarische Kinderbuch. Studien zur Entstehung und Typologie* (Berlin/New York: de Gruyter, 1981)

— '"Ein Billetdoux an die ganze Menschheit". Christian Felix Weiße und die Aufklärung', in *Zentren der Aufklärung III. Leipzig*, ed. by Wolfgang Martens, Wolfenbütteler Studien zur Aufklärung, 17 (Heidelberg: Schneider, 1990), pp. 267–95

Parisian, Catherine M., 'German Audiences for Frances Burney's *Evelina, Or a Young Lady's Entrance into the World*', *The Center and Clark Newsletter*, 49 (2009), 2–4

— *Frances Burney's 'Cecilia'. A Publishing History*, Ashgate Studies in Publishing History (London/New York: Routledge, 2016)

Paulin, Roger, *The Critical Reception of Shakespeare in Germany 1682–1914. Native Literature and Foreign Genius*, Anglistische und amerikanistische Texte und Studien, 11 (Hildesheim/Zurich/ New York: Olms, 2003)

Peitsch, Helmut, 'Englische Reisebeschreibungen in der Neuen Bibliothek der schönen Wissenschaften und der freyen Künste', *Internationales Archiv für Sozialgeschichte der deutschen Literatur*, 31 (2006), 1–50

Price, Lawrence Marsden, *English Literature in Germany*, University of California Publications in Modern Philology, 37 (Berkeley, CA/Los Angeles, CA: University of California Press, 1953)

Rau, Fritz, *Zur Verbreitung und Nachahmung des Tatler und Spectator*, Anglistische Forschungen, 145 (Heidelberg: Winter, 1980)

Rek, Klaus, 'Englandrezeption und Aufklärungskonzeption in der "Neuen Bibliothek der schönen Wissenschaften und der freyen Künste"', in *Sächsische Aufklärung*, ed. by Anneliese Klingenberg and others, Leipziger Studien zur Erforschung von regionenbezogenen Identifikationsprozessen, 7 (Leipzig: Leipziger Universitätsverlag, 2001), pp. 197–210

Richards, Alfred E., 'A literary Link between Thomas Shadwell and Christian Felix Weisse', *PMLA*, 21 (1906), 808–30

Riegler, Susanne, and Sebastian Schmideler (eds), *Kinder- und Jugendliteratur in Leipzig* (Leipzig: Leipziger Universitätsverlag, 2016)

Rosenstrauch, Hazel, 'Buchhandelsmanufaktur und Aufklärung; Die Reformen des Buchhändlers und Verlegers Ph. E. Reich (1717–1787). Sozialgeschichtliche Studie zur Entwicklung des literarischen Marktes', *Archiv für Geschichte des Buchwesens*, 26 (1986), 1–129

— 'Leipzig als "Centralplatz" des deutschen Buchhandels', in *Zentren der Aufklärung III. Leipzig*, ed. by Wolfgang Martens, Wolfenbütteler Studien zur Aufklärung, 17 (Heidelberg: Schneider, 1990), pp. 103–24

Schmideler, Sebastian, 'Christian Felix Weiße (1726–1804). Ein Kinderbuchautor und Jugendschriftsteller der Leipziger Spätaufklärung', in *Kinder- und Jugendliteratur in Leipzig*, ed. by Susanne Riegler and Sebastian Schmideler (Leipzig: Leipziger Universitätsverlag, 2016), pp. 221–52

Schmidt, Erich, 'Schiebeler, Daniel', in *Allgemeine deutsche Biographie*, ed. by Historische Commission bei der Bayerischen Akademie der Wissenschaften, 56 vols (Leipzig: Duncker & Humblot, 1875–1912), XXXI (1890), 176–78

Schmidt, Gerhard, 'Fritsch, Thomas', in *Neue deutsche Biographie*, ed. by Historische Kommission bei der Bayerischen Akademie der

Wissenschaften, 28 vols (Berlin: Duncker & Humblot, 1953–2020), v (1961), 624–25
Schmidt, Wolf Gerhard, *'Homer des Nordens' und 'Mutter der Romantik'. James Macphersons Ossian und seine Rezeption in der deutschsprachigen Literatur*, 4 vols (Berlin: de Gruyter, 2003–04)
— '"Abdruck der innern Empfindung" im "Abdruck des Äußern". Herders Ossianübersetzungen als Versuch kongenialer "Originalarbeit"', in *Übersetzen bei Johann Gottfried Herder. Theorie und Praxis*, ed. by Clémence Couturier-Heinrich (Heidelberg: Synchron, 2012), pp. 143–58
Schmidt-Haberkamp, Barbara, Uwe Steiner and Brunhilde Wehinger (eds), *Europäischer Kulturtransfer im 18. Jahrhundert. Literaturen in Europa – europäische Literatur?* (Berlin: BWV, 2003)
Schmitt, Albert R., 'Christian Felix Weißes *Jean Calas* – Dokumentarisches Theater im 18. Jahrhundert', in *Aufnahme – Weitergabe: Literarische Impulse um Lessing und Goethe*, ed. by John A. McCarthy and others (Hamburg: Buske, 1982), pp. 2–30
Scholler, Dietrich, 'Die Rezeption der romanischen Literaturen in der (*Neue*[n]) *Bibliothek* und im *Journal étranger*, dargestellt am Beispiel Algarotti', in *Sächsische Aufklärung*, ed. by Anneliese Klingenberg and others, Leipziger Studien zur Erforschung von regionenbezogenen Identifikationsprozessen, 7 (Leipzig: Leipziger Universitätsverlag, 2001), pp. 211–29
Schulz, Christiane, 'Eine nützliche und angenehme Lektüre. Christian Felix Weiße und die russische Literatur', in *Christian Felix Weiße und die Leipziger Aufklärung*, ed. by Katrin Löffler and Ludwig Stockinger (Hildesheim: Olms, 2006), pp. 31–70
Sdun, Winfried, *Probleme und Theorien des Übersetzens in Deutschland vom 18. bis zum 20. Jahrhundert* (München: Hueber, 1967)
Senger, Anneliese, *Deutsche Übersetzungstheorie im 18. Jahrhundert (1734–1746)*, Abhandlungen zur Kunst-, Musik- und Literaturwissenschaft, 97 (Bonn: Bouvier, 1971)
Stackelberg, Jürgen von, *Übersetzungen aus zweiter Hand. Rezeptionsvorgänge in der europäischen Literatur vom 14. bis zum 18. Jahrhundert* (Berlin/New York: de Gruyter, 1984)
Steiner, T. R., *English Translation Theory 1650–1800*, Approaches to Translation Studies, 2 (Assen: Van Gorcum, 1975)
Steiner, Walter, and Uta Kühn-Stillmark (eds), *Friedrich Justin Bertuch. Ein Leben im klassischen Weimar zwischen Kultur und Kommerz* (Cologne/Weimar/Vienna: Böhlau, 2001)
Stephen, Leslie, and Sidney Lee (eds), *Dictionary of National Biography*, 63 vols (London: Smith, Elder & Co., 1885–1900)

Stockhorst, Stefanie (ed.), *Cultural Transfer through Translation. The Circulation of Enlightened Thought in Europe by Means of Translation* (Amsterdam/New York: Rodopi, 2010)

Stockinger, Ludwig, 'Die Sächsische Aufklärung als Modell deutscher Aufklärungsvarianten', in *Sächsische Aufklärung*, ed. by Anneliese Klingenberg and others, Leipziger Studien zur Erforschung von regionenbezogenen Identifikationsprozessen, 7 (Leipzig: Leipziger Universitätsverlag, 2001), pp. 23–48

Strabone, Jeff, *Poetry and British Nationalisms in the Bardic Eighteenth Century: Imagined Antiquities*, Palgrave Studies in the Enlightenment, Romanticism and Cultures of Print (London: Palgrave Macmillan, 2018)

Teupser, Werner, 'Casanova, Giovanni Battista', in *Neue deutsche Biographie*, ed. by Historische Commission bei der Bayerischen Akademie der Wissenschaften, 28 vols (Berlin: Duncker & Humblot, 1953–2020), III (1957), 163–64

Tombo, Rudolf, *Ossian in Germany: Bibliography, General Survey, Ossian's Influence upon Klopstock and the Bards*, Columbia University Germanic Studies, 1 (New York: Columbia University Press, 1901)

Vail, Curtis C. D., *Lessing's Relation to the English Language and Literature*, Columbia University Germanic Studies, n.s., 3 (New York: Columbia University Press, 1936)

Venables, Edmund, 'Marsh, Herbert', in *Dictionary of National Biography*, ed. by Leslie Stephen and Sidney Lee, 63 vols (London: Smith, Elder & Co., 1885–1900), XXXVI (1893), 211–15

Waszek, Norbert, 'Übersetzungspraxis und Popularphilosophie am Beispiel Christian Garves', *Das achtzehnte Jahrhundert*, 31 (2007), 42–64

Wehinger, Brunhilde, and Hilary Brown (eds), *Übersetzungskultur im 18. Jahrhundert. Übersetzerinnen in Deutschland, Frankreich und der Schweiz*, Aufklärung und Moderne, 12 (Hanover: Wehrhahn, 2008)

Wilke, Jürgen, 'Der deutsch-schweizerische Literaturstreit', in *Formen und Formgeschichte des Streitens: Der Literaturstreit*, ed. by Franz Josef Worstbrock and Helmut Koopmann, Kontroversen, alte und neue, 2 (Tübingen: Niemeyer, 1986), pp. 140–51

Wilkie, Richard Francis, 'Christian Felix Weisze and his Relation to French and English Literature' (unpublished doctoral thesis, University of California, Berkeley, 1953)

— 'Weisse's Borrowings for the "Bibliothek der schönen Wissenschaften"', *Modern Philology*, 53 (1955), 1–7

Willenberg, Jennifer, *Distribution und Übersetzung englischen Schrifttums im Deutschland des 18. Jahrhunderts*, Archiv für Geschichte des Buchwesens – Studien, 6 (München: Saur, 2008)

Wölfel, Kurt, 'Garve, Christian', in *Neue deutsche Biographie*, ed. by Historische Commission bei der Bayerischen Akademie der Wissenschaften, 28 vols (Berlin: Duncker & Humblot, 1953–2020), vi (1964), 77–78

Zimmermann, Christian von, '"Fast fremder als Japan und manche entfernte Reiche ...". Die Aufklärung in Spanien und Portugal im Blick der deutschen Reisenden', in *Spanien und Portugal im Zeitalter der Aufklärung*, ed. by Christoph Frank and Sylvaine Hänsel, Ars Iberica et Americana, 8 (Frankfurt am Main: Vervuert, 2002), pp. 123–36

Index

www.ingramcontent.com/pod-product-compliance
Lightning Source LLC
LaVergne TN
LVHW052016300826
846742LV00019B/69